FRAGILITIES

Infrastructures Series

Edited by Paul N. Edwards and Janet Vertesi

A list of books in the series appears at the back of the book.

FRAGILITIES

ESSAYS ON THE POLITICS, ETHICS, AND AESTHETICS OF MAINTENANCE AND REPAIR

EDITED BY FERNANDO DOMÍNGUEZ RUBIO, JÉRÔME DENIS, AND DAVID PONTILLE

The MIT Press
Cambridge, Massachusetts
London, England

The MIT Press
Massachusetts Institute of Technology
77 Massachusetts Avenue, Cambridge, MA 02139
mitpress.mit.edu

The MIT Press would like to thank the anonymous peer reviewers who provided comments on drafts of this book. The generous work of academic experts is essential for establishing the authority and quality of our publications. We acknowledge with gratitude the contributions of these otherwise uncredited readers.

This book was set in Stone Serif and Stone Sans by Westchester Publishing Services. Printed and bound in the United States of America.

Library of Congress Cataloging-in-Publication Data

Names: Domínguez Rubio, Fernando, editor. | Denis, Jérôme, editor. | Pontille, David, editor.
Title: Fragilities : essays on the politics, ethics, and aesthetics of maintenance and repair / Edited by Fernando Domínguez Rubio, Jérôme Denis, and David Pontille.
Description: Cambridge, Massachusetts : The MIT Press, [2025] | Series: Infrastructures | Includes bibliographical references and index.
Identifiers: LCCN 2024022899 (print) | LCCN 2024022900 (ebook) | ISBN 9780262550758 (paperback) | ISBN 9780262381109 (epub) | ISBN 9780262381116 (pdf)
Subjects: LCSH: Human ecology. | Climatic changes—Effect of human beings on. | Infrastructure (Economics)—Environmental aspects. | Fragility (Psychology) | Geology, Stratigraphic—Anthropocene.
Classification: LCC GF41 .F685 2025 (print) | LCC GF41 (ebook) | DDC 304.2—dc23/eng/20240808
LC record available at https://lccn.loc.gov/2024022899
LC ebook record available at https://lccn.loc.gov/2024022900

10 9 8 7 6 5 4 3 2 1

EU product safety and compliance information contact is: mitp-eu-gpsr@mit.edu

CONTENTS

1 INTRODUCTION: AVOWING FRAGILITY

FERNANDO DOMÍNGUEZ RUBIO

Fragility has changed sides
—Michel Serres

. . . AND THEN THE EARTH HAPPENED

It is hard to believe it now, but there was a time, not that long ago, when the world was still a foregone conclusion—at least for some. This was a time when some philosophers could still dwell on the certainty that, as Husserl (1970, 142) once wrote, "the world is pregiven to us" as an "ontic certainty." The world was so unmistakably there, so evidently present, that it did not compel much thought. So much so that Wittgenstein (1972, §85) pondered why it was perfectly normal for his contemporaries to ask how long a house had been in its place, but the same question was rarely ever asked about a mountain—because mountains, like the world itself, seemed to belong to that realm of certainties that are evident to the point of invisibility.

Looking at the conversations that dominated Euro-American academia back then, one feels a distinctive sense of culmination, a sense of being on the verge of a new time. Some even proposed to give this new time a name. Terms such as "second modernity," "reflexive modernity," "high modernity," or even "postmodernity" were proposed to christen it. Amid the intense debates about its nomenclature and chronology—some located it around the post–World War II order, others around the 1960s, and still others around the 1970s—there was an element that was shared by virtually all the participants in these discussions. This was the tacit, but firm, belief in that hegemonic Western-centric narrative about how "We"—as in capital Humanity "We," although always clearly referring to the Global North section of it—had finally left behind that old unpredictable world that had instilled a cruel sense of fragility and powerlessness in the poets and thinkers of yore. Because "We" were now entering a time when it finally seemed possible to disavow this fragility, to eliminate it, not completely, but enough to quarantine it to proclaim, with Weberian confidence, that the world had been finally disenchanted and no longer inspired fear or awe. Such was the conviction that some, such as the sociologist Ulrich Beck (1992), claimed that the Moirai, the powerful goddesses of fate who had terrorized humanity with their inscrutable whims since times immemorial, had been tamed and reduced into calculable "risk." While others, such as Anthony Giddens (1991), celebrated how the great prowess of modern institutions had finally tilted the ancient balance of fate and had conquered, for the first time ever, a sense of "ontological security" for us—or, at any rate, for those of "us" living in the affluent sectors of the Global North.

For decades, these hegemonic discourses—along with their ecumenical "We" (Wynter 2015, 21–24)—were imposed on all of the world population presenting the progress and growth of the economies and democracies of the Global North as natural, and as inevitable, as gravity itself. It is not difficult to see why these optimistic narratives proliferated as they did and took root on the imaginations of many. The Green Revolution had lifted millions from hunger in what seemed to be the final rebuttal of the long-feared Malthusian prophecy. Medical advancements and new vaccines were providing a shield against illnesses that had razed humankind for millennia, resulting in an unprecedented growth of life expectancy across the globe. Meanwhile, massive improvements in the material conditions of life were creating expansive middle classes in the developed economies, providing a sense that fragility, insecurity, and uncertainty were now consigned to the past. Those for whom fragility, insecurity, and uncertainty were the inescapable realities of an overwhelming present—as it happens, the vast majority of the world—were told not to worry, since it was just a question of time until they could also enjoy the same type of ontological security as their northern neighbors. For them, economists and institutions prescribed "development plans," "big push" models, and "convergence theories" as the sure way to catch up with the prosperity of advanced economies. Fears about the contradictions and limits of capitalist growth, already made clear by the Club of Rome in 1972, were allayed by adding adjectives such as "sustainable," "resilient," "responsible," or "green." This was a time when politicians could dream about arcs of moral universes bending toward justice, or when the World War II "liberal consensus" could promise a new global order that would solve political contradictions and deliver peace, prosperity, and security across a world of falling iron curtains and walls. Such was the belief in this narrative among some Western intellectuals that it was even possible for some of them to wonder whether History might indeed had come to an end.

Propelling these narratives was the belief that science and technology were en route to sealing a final victory over the world—a victory that many believed to be so thorough, so complete, that it would confirm Le Corbusier's (1933, 42) iconoclastic proclamation about how the new "machine age" was going to shuffle the "old cards of the world," setting us on a course where human progress would be forever beyond the whims of Nature. Thanks to modern science and technologies, Nature could finally be tamed and reduced to playing harmless supportive roles, such as background scenery or material resource for our needs. "We" had grown powerful—too powerful. Such was "our" domination over the environment that some declared that Nature was dead or, at the very least, at risk of being killed by us. The once-feared and overwhelming Nature appeared now so fragile in comparison to the might of science and technology that it seemed to be in constant need of "our" protection, generously provided throughout the 1990s in the form of natural protected areas, biosphere reserves, or endangered species preservation acts (cf. Macnaghten and Urry 1998; Merchant 1990). The triumph over this fragile, and seemingly moribund, Nature was such that many social scientists did not even take it into account in their narratives and could devote their time to imagine the "social," the "cultural," and the "economic" as ever-elastic earthless forms unfolding unimpeded and according to their own internal dynamics. For a while, it truly seemed as though these internal dynamics were all that really mattered—hence the endless debates about structure versus agency, individual versus collective, medium versus message, signified versus signifier, simulacra versus reality. This was a time when Western academia enjoyed an overabundance of rhizomatic imaginations, self-propelling autopoietic systems, and ever-extending networks and assemblages hurtling into the future. A future that was every bit as indubitable as the world itself.

And perhaps most peculiarly, it was a time when time itself seemed to be the only relevant variable. Thanks to the transport and communication revolutions, capitalist globalization seemed to have vanquished age-old spatial barriers keeping people (and markets) apart. Digital technologies were moving us "from atoms to bits" (Negroponte 1995), thus emancipating us, once and for all, from the tyranny of space. This was a time of feverish secular faith. A time of magical thinking and technofixes, when politicians such as Ronald Reagan could proclaim that "the Goliath of totalitarianism will be brought down by the David of the microchip," ushering us into a new era that would bring "peace and freedom for all," while messianic tech gurus could unironically promise that the future could be conquered by simply "staying hungry and foolish" or that poverty could be erased with $100 laptops. Or when it was possible for well-fed charlatans at the centers of power to write bestsellers claiming that the world was now flat, and that capitalist prosperity had finally ushered us into a Kantian dreamland of perpetual peace (Friedman 2005).

This was, in sum, a time of disavowal and drunken hubris.

Looking back at that time, revisiting its conversations and narratives, one cannot help but wonder how those certainties and hopes that seemed so prescient and urgent just a couple of decades ago feel so unspeakably remote and disconnected now. What, exactly, happened in between?

The earth has happened.

The earth has gone from being a nonevent operating as the unheeded ontological foundation upon which to imagine ever-growing social, cultural, and economy forms, to a relentless event, short-circuiting, destabilizing, and interrupting those forms. The result of this transformation has been a massive gestalt inversion. The once-silent background has burst into the foreground, shattering the modern world, along with its narratives and certainties about progress and domination. All of a sudden, the world can no longer be taken for granted. It is no longer pre-given as a Husserlian "ontic certainty." Objects that once seemed timeless certainties, such as glaciers, lakes, forests, wetlands, and coral reefs, disappear before our eyes, revealing their earthly finitude. The result is that, paraphrasing Latour (2004), those old "matters of fact" that remained unthought in Wittgenstein's time have become unsettling "matters of concern." What once seemed exceptions have now become rules. Hitherto uncommon disasters have acquired an insidious seasonality, along with their sinister cohorts of death and devastation. Massive heat waves break decades-old, or even centuries-old, climate records on an almost yearly basis. We live on a planet where wildfires in Siberia can burn fifty-five million acres (almost the size of the United Kingdom), where glacier-fueled floods can submerge two thirds of a country such as Pakistan in the blink of eye, or where we are reminded that, despite our much-vaunted scientific prowess, a virus can still claim millions of lives in just a couple of years.

All the while, infrastructures and technologies that a few generations ago seemed to warrant narratives about "ontological security" are now revealed to be powerless to contain the excess of this relentless planet that can unilaterally upend decades of economic progress, bring global energy infrastructures to a halt, or sink Asian megacities, such as Jakarta, Ho Chi Minh, or Chittagong, under their own weight. It is no wonder that, aside from some irreducible pockets of increasingly delirious techno-utopianism fantasizing about planetary escapes, there is little left of the Promethean bravado that characterized modern dreams about controlling Nature while propelling ourselves into an endless future. Instead, there is a distinct, almost palpable, sense of collapse.

But what, exactly, is collapsing? It is not, as many seem to believe, the world. What is collapsing is a particular *narrative* about the world—that narrative of Western modernity that, as Achille Mbembe (2019, 64) has written, has "never properly thought through its own finitude," since it has always imagined, and imposed, itself as an unavoidable universal horizon. But we have now reached the earthly limits of the modern narrative and, with it, the realization that modernity and its dreams were never really fate or destiny but rather just an episode, with its beginning and its end, just like any other (Castro and Danowski 2016). That world-making project of modernity that self-expanded in the planet, trying to make it its own through ever-increasing domination and control, is now forced to confront its own collapse and come to terms with the fact that its narrative of progress, prosperity, and ontological security was just an irresponsible illusion fueled by blind arrogance. The scale of this realization is such that it exceeds our language to describe it. The word "unprecedented" is used, and abused, in newspapers and media to try to capture a time without language. Meanwhile, social scientists struggle to come up with names, such as Gaia (Stengers 2015), Chthulucene (Haraway 2016), Anthropocene, and Capitalocene (Moore 2016), to capture this new time when Nature can no longer be imagined as an external and constant variable; when growth and progress are no longer seen as inevitable as gravity; when "green," "sustainable," or "responsible" can no longer hide the fact that capitalism has run out of a planet to devour; or when neither "the West" nor "humans" can continue operating as the implicit center of the world.

It should come as no surprise, then, that the talk about "ontological security" is all but gone. There is, instead, a pervasive sense of ontological fragility. This, however, is a different fragility because, as Michel Serres (1995, 16) presciently put it, fragility has now changed sides. This is no longer a fragility belonging to an external "Nature" in need of "human" protection. This is a fragility that is felt as the inescapable condition of life on this planet. We can see how the very same "social," "cultural," and "economic" orders, which just a little while ago were imagined as ever-elastic forms endlessly projecting themselves into the future, are now rendered fragile and at risk of falling apart. As a result, those old conversations about growth and progress have given way to conversations about living in "catastrophic times" (Stengers 2015) on a "damaged planet" (Tsing et al. 2017); about the need to think about "de-growth," "tipping points," and "thresholds"; about the need to think about limits and ends (Tironi, González-Gálvez, and de la Cadena 2021); and about the need to recover that sense of fear and awe that was irresponsibly lost to modernist hubris (Chakrabarty 2021).

Amid all the confusion, one thing does seem clear: the fact that this is a world where fragility can no longer be disavowed, minimized, or wished away, with hopeful promises of better times, with capitalist dreamworlds and techno-fixes, or with uplifting poetics about moral arcs pointing to the inevitable triumph of good over evil. After modernity's midsummer night's dream, we find ourselves exactly *where we have always been*: in a world where fragility is not a variable that can be eliminated or domesticated but rather the unavoidable and insurmountable condition of life on this planet. In a world where fragility is not a problem to be solved but instead the condition that we need to face and live with.

This volume is an invitation to think *from* and *with* fragility and to dwell in the discomfort that it creates.

Fragility has been mostly absent in the vocabulary of the social sciences. As children of modernity, Western social sciences have tended to be more interested in studying how different social, cultural, and economic forms are produced and reproduced. As a result, most of their vocabularies have focused on disentangling the different forces propelling these processes such as agencies, interests, powers, structures, or capacities. Until very recently (e.g., Graham and Thrift 2007; Law 1992), moments of breakdown and collapse have not received much attention, as they have tended to be seen as secondary or peripheral, or they have been simply glossed over as exceptions, problems, or interruptions in this general process of creation, production, and growth. In this volume, we would like to argue otherwise. We would like to reclaim the importance of cultivating an attention to those moments when things, bodies, and worlds begin to fall apart and reveal their fragilities, and the need to reclaim those moments as critical places to think *with* and *from*.

At a time when it is easy to fall into defeatist melancholia, if not outright pessimism, our invitation to think *with* and *from* fragility may not seem to be particularly uplifting or hopeful. However, as we hope this volume makes it clear, this avowal of fragility needs not be a pessimistic, or defeatist, project—quite the opposite. Rather than using fragility to pile on collapsist narratives or nostalgic lamentations about some lost modern Eden or to dramatize catastrophic events further, we want to mobilize fragility as a generative space from which to assert the possibility to think, live, and build otherwise.

This volume is born out of the conviction that the collapse of the modern narrative is not a tragedy but rather an opportunity to reimagine life on this planet. Our central claim is that any such reimagining must be rooted in a radical avowal of fragility. This avowal, we argue, is a first and necessary step to bring a much-needed corrective to the modernist hubris and its arrogant refusal to think about limits and ends. By forcing us to reckon with these limits, and to think *from* them and *with* them, this avowal opens up not only the possibility to come to terms with, and hold us accountable for, those fragilities that have been consistently silenced, ignored, disavowed, and denied reality, but also the opportunity to re-ground our political vocabularies and ethical practices in a profound acknowledgment of the costs of nurturing and maintaining life on this planet.

But we do not simply want to offer fragility as a mere critique, or a counterfigure, to hubristic modern narratives by allowing us to acknowledge their limits and developing new forms of accountability and responsibility. We want to claim fragility as a positive space to think *with* and *from*. To do so, it is important to reclaim fragility as both an invitation to reckon with limits and an opportunity to think about what lies beyond them—or, put differently, to think from fragility is an opportunity to think about not only what is lost when something breaks but also what can be built with that which remains after breakage. This, we argue, is particularly urgent because ours is one of those times of monsters that, as Gramsci (2011, 32–33) once wrote, occur when a world dies but the new is yet to be born. Our interest here is to explore the kinds of worlds that can be born from a radical avowal of fragility—that is, from the recognition that fragility cannot be overcome on a planet that is always being un/made. What we want to argue is that this avowal of fragility does not need to be paralyzing—on the contrary. Our argument is that a radical avowal of fragility offers an opportunity for a different kind of world making—one that forces us to reckon with the precariousness and contingency of life and that uses this reckoning as a starting point to build, nurture, maintain, and repair life-affirming politics and ethics.

We should make clear from the start that our intention with this volume is not to use fragility as some sort of Borgian Aleph that enables us to see, much less solve, all the problems of our time at once. Our proposition is much more modest. The volume wants to offer fragility not as a response to solve all the ills of our time but rather as *one* possible place to think *from*. More specifically, we want to think *from* fragility as a way of slowing down thought, to make time to think. As Jérôme Denis and David Pontille write in the conclusion to this volume, we want to offer fragility as a *sensitizing concept* to shift our attention to places, practices, and agents that have been usually left outside modern narratives. This, we argue, is important because it offers the opportunity to cultivate modes of attention and responsibility for them that allow us to ask other relevant political and ethical questions and, hopefully, to imagine otherwise. But how do we think *from* or *with* fragility? What does fragility help us see? What kinds of questions does it allow us to pose? Why are those questions relevant? And, perhaps more importantly, what exactly do we mean by "fragility"?

WHAT IS FRAGILITY?

Fragility is typically defined as the quality of being breakable. This is precisely what the Latin *frangere* means: to break into pieces. This meaning of breakability is what separates fragility from its cousin vulnerability, with whom it is sometimes confused in ordinary parlance. This confusion is understandable, since both terms have a remarkable family resemblance. However, there is an important difference. While vulnerability refers to the condition of being liable to harm, fragility refers to that specific kind of harm that causes something to break down and become undone. Crucially, not everything that breaks down is necessarily fragile. The *Oxford English Dictionary* adds an important qualification when it defines fragility as the quality of "being *easily* broken." It is this "ease" that identifies the fragile. The fragile is that for which the distance between being and not being is the shortest, as it can become undone at the faintest of whims.

This concept of fragility has been typically used in three different, but complementary, ways: material, figurative, and moral. In its material sense, fragility has been employed to describe a physical property of things and bodies. It is often understood as what philosophers call "primary properties," which are those properties that are inherent to something (e.g., weight, density, molecular composition) and which are not dependent on any external observer (e.g., color, smell, or sound). According to this definition, whether something is fragile depends on its internal composition. Fragility thus defined is something that belongs to ontology, to the very being of things. As such, it is something fixed and given in advance in their nature and, consequently, cannot be helped. An obvious example would be a bubble, whose transient, almost liminal, existence epitomizes a limit case of fragility.

The second use of fragility has been figurative. When employed in this way, fragility is used to evoke a tragic sense of powerlessness in the face of fate, ephemerality, and death. One of the oldest, and most pervasive, figurative tropes has been that of "the fragility of life." This trope has been used in several ways. Some have used it to describe the radical exposure of life to being undone. In Ancient Greece, for example, fragility was seen as the inescapable price humans must pay for living in a world governed by capricious gods indifferent to our plans and desires (Nussbaum 2001). Others have used it to invoke the inherent finitude of human life, which makes fragility, like death, a great equalizer. As Seneca (1920 Ep. 91: 443) put it, "No man is more frail than another: no one more certain of his own life on the morrow." Still others have used the figurative sense of fragility to refer to a sense of precarity stemming from the inherent injurability of the human body. A recurrent example is that of the body of the newborn, whose radical exposure and powerlessness illustrates a life utterly at the mercy, and in need, of others. As happens with its physical use, these figurative uses define fragility as an ontological condition—that is, as a shared and universal quality inscribed deep into the grammar of our bodies. Hence, for example, the Buddhist notion of the body as a fragile clay pot (Radhakrishnan 1950, 72), or the Shakespearean notion of the body as "nature's fragile vessel" (Shakespeare 2009, 314). Fragility thus appears in a paradoxical position, being simultaneously considered an ineliminable and unsurmountable fact of life, but also as that which must be disavowed to make life possible—in other words, as something that cannot be disavowed but which must be disavowed. However, not everybody has the same capacity of disavowal, which leads to the third sense in which fragility has been used: the moral sense.

When employed in this moral sense, fragility has been typically deployed to denote a flaw, a weakness, or an affliction. This is, for example, how the writers in the Christian tradition have explained our (allegedly) congenial "moral weakness" stemming from the (allegedly) inherent quality of our imperfect and fallible human soul, which renders us forever fragile and corruptible (see Chrétien 2017). As in the previous cases, fragility is also understood here as a condition given in the nature of things or, in this case, souls. Crucially, while it may be true that we are all fragile, some have been understood as more fragile than others. This is the gist of Hamlet's famous line, "Fragility, thy name is woman," which is part of a long tradition that has weaponized fragility to explain and legitimize a position of moral superiority over those who are understood to be inherently fragile and, therefore, weaker and inferior, and who, *coincidentally*, tend to be those in subaltern positions such as women, the elderly, children, the disabled, racialized others, impoverished populations, refugees, immigrants, indigenous populations, and so forth.

This moral sense of fragility has been at the heart of the modern definition of politics as the struggle for autonomy. Ever since the days of Hobbes and Rousseau, the political has been imagined as a mechanism to overcome both the fragility of the individual human body and that of the collective body politic. In this tradition, fragility has normally appeared as an obstacle that needs to be overcome, or at least mitigated, in the quest to achieve collective and individual autonomy and self-governance. A recurrent argument has been to measure the progress of different political and social systems against how fragility has been overcome or minimized. This view, which was pervasive in social Darwinist and colonial discourses of the nineteenth century, is alive and kicking today in the "fragility indexes" produced by the likes of the World Bank, International Monetary Fund (IMF), or the Organisation for Economic Co-operation and Development, which rank countries according to the relative fragility of their institutions. It should not be surprising, then, that this notion of fragility has been used to justify interventions on those who are seen as fragile and, for that reason, always in need of help. One does not have to go far to remember, for example, how the notion of fragile states has been used to justify unjustifiable wars, or how notions such as fragile economies or fragile democracies are routinely invoked by organizations such as the World Bank or IMF to justify the imposition of their economic and political models.

This brief—and surely incomplete—survey of some of the material, figurative, and moral uses of fragility helps to reveal two tendencies about how fragility has been solidified in the Western common sense. The first is the tendency to see fragility as an ontological property—that is, as something that is given in the nature of things, bodies, and souls. Understood in this way, fragility emerges as fate or destiny: it is just the way *some* things are. The second is the tendency to see this ontological property as a negative and undesirable trait. Fragility is almost invariably presented in these narratives as a lack, an absence, or an insufficiency. It is something that subtracts, that diminishes, that weakens. The fragile is that which is not solid *enough*, not strong *enough*, not durable *enough*, not autonomous *enough*. No wonder, then, why fragility typically emerges in these narratives as something to be fixed, overcome, or, at a minimum, palliated.

Putting these tendencies together offers a vision of a world where identities are given in advance and positions are fixed—a world where there are, on the one hand, those things, bodies, and souls whose properties make them fragile and whose precarious existences make them perennially weak, dependent, and, for that reason, always in need of help and attention, and, on the other, those bodies and things whose properties make them solid, robust, and therefore autonomous.

What this understanding of fragility misses is that sometimes the sturdiest of rocks can crack like the softest of bubbles, just like a humble piece of paper can outlast the sturdiest of rocks. In other words, what this definition misses is that fragility is not something inscribed in the nature of things but rather a condition that is *rendered*, and that, consequently, when we talk about fragility, we are never talking about a fixed ontological property but rather about an *ecological form*.

ECOLOGIZING FRAGILITY

To illustrate what we mean when we say that fragility is an ecological form, let's take, for example, the aforementioned humble piece of paper. If you were to place it outdoors and leave it to its own devices, it will take just a few days for it to crumble and fade away. However, the very same note stored in a controlled environment at 35°C and 80 percent relative humidity (RH) would last for about three years. At 20°C and 50 percent RH, the same piece of paper would become a remarkably durable object that could last for about a century. And at 10°C and 40 percent RH, it could last 1,200 years, making our humble piece of paper as solid and reliable as iron or stone, if not more so. The change between fragility and solidity cannot be explained by simply looking at the piece of paper. Nothing has changed in it. It has not undergone any alchemic transmogrification that has made it acquire new properties. The only thing that has changed are the environmental conditions in and through which our paper note exists.

The example of the humble paper note reveals a simple fact: nothing is fragile by itself—because nothing *is* by itself. Everything is rendered fragile by something else or by reference to something else. This idea has four important corollaries.

The first is that fragility is an empty concept. Much like the concept of "near" or "tall," fragility only acquires meaning through the relations in and through which something exists. This is precisely what our piece of paper shows: paper is neither fragile nor solid. It becomes one or the other, depending on the relationships in which it is inserted or the purposes for which it is used. Fragility, it follows, is relational and deictic: the very same thing can be fragile under some conditions, or for a specific purpose, but exceedingly solid for others. A spiderweb may seem fragile to us, but it is a perfectly solid trap for the unknowing fly.

The second corollary, which follows directly from the first, is that there is no such thing as a single and pre-given fragility, only a plurality of fragilities rendered by different configurations. This is easily verifiable with a simple look at the appliances and technologies that organize our daily lives. As we all know (and suffer), it is just a question of a couple of years, if not months, before they stop working and break down. This fragility is not simply due to the natural propensity of things to break but also to the fact that we live immersed in a capitalist system whose solidity depends on the systematic production of fragility to perpetuate the consumption cycle and the extraction of profit (Domínguez Rubio and Wharton 2020; Jackson and Kang 2014).

The third corollary is that fragility is not a quality attached to a particular group of things. Everything, from a soap bubble to a star, can be rendered fragile, depending on the configurations in which it is inserted. Thus, when we describe something as fragile, we are describing not a property inherent to something but rather the *position* that it occupies in a certain correlation of forces at a given moment. This is precisely one of the fundamental lessons of critical disability studies when they remind us that what makes disabled bodies fragile and dependent is not a property inscribed in these bodies but rather the *position* these bodies occupy in particular socio-material configurations that subtract, inhibit, or prevent the realization of their capacities.

The fourth corollary is that describing something as fragile is never an innocent operation. Just like we cannot describe something as "far" without assuming a particular point of reference, we cannot describe something as fragile without simultaneously inscribing a particular framework of relations and assuming a position within it. To describe something as fragile, therefore, is to enact it in a particular way and to inscribe it (and ourselves) within a particular framework of relations. For example, when we describe a spiderweb as fragile, we are choosing to insert it into a human frame of reference, instead of an insectile frame from which it would probably never be so described, in much the same way as when we describe a disabled body as fragile, we do it assuming an ableist framework organized around a certain definition of what an able body is.

If we follow this ecological definition of fragility, we find ourselves in a very different world. A world where fragility is not a natural and fixed category but rather a relational and contingent condition. A world where things are not fragile, but where things are *rendered* fragile. A world where the question of fragility no longer refers us to the interior of things but instead to the asymmetric relationships in which they are placed. A world where the uneven geographies of fragility are explained not by reference to the uneven properties of things but rather by reference to asymmetries created by different systems of oppression and domination. A world where fragility is no longer part of the *explanans* but instead part of the *explanandum*. In other words, where fragility is not what does the explaining but what needs to be explained. A world, in short, where the question of fragility is always a question about an Other: Fragile compared to what? Fragile for what? Fragile for whom? What or who renders this fragile? How and why is it kept that way?

These questions put before us a very different task. Understanding fragility is no longer a matter of identifying what properties make such a thing or body fragile. Rather, it is about exploring the ethical and political frameworks that make it possible for some things, *and not others*, to become, or be described, as fragile. This is precisely what the chapters of this volume do by showing, for example, that we cannot understand why certain bodies are rendered (or described as) fragile without attending to the different relations, practices, and institutions in which those bodies are inserted (Mol Ch 2, Winance, Ch 3, and Cousins 9), just as it is not possible to understand the solidity of certain things, be it sovereign power (chapter 11), scientific knowledge (chapter 6), or biocapitalist meat production (chapter 5), without attending to the infrastructures and institutions in which these things are inserted.

The aim of this volume is not simply to ecologize fragility as a way of revealing that what seemed to be a natural and universal category is, in fact, a relational and contingent one. Rather, the purpose is to reclaim fragility as a central political and ethical problem. And this, we argue, requires exploring what it takes to render some things, *and not others*, fragile, and what kind of political and ethical consequences and possibilities such operation entails. To tackle these questions, we need to shift our attention to practices that have traditionally been left out of hegemonic modern narratives, such as those of care, maintenance, and repair.

MIMEOGRAPHIC LABORS

The practices of care, maintenance, and repair are part of what I have called elsewhere "mimeographic labor" (Domínguez Rubio 2020). Broadly defined, mimeographic labor can be described as those practices that (try to) prevent the worlds we inhabit from coming apart. Examples of this form of labor include the maintenance work required to sustain infrastructures and techno-scientific systems (Denis and Pontille 2015, 2023; Mattern 2018; Russell and Vinsel 2018; Callén and Criado 2016; Henke and Sims 2020); the constant work of care required to maintain the relations, bodies, and affects through which our lives take place (Bellacasa 2017; Martin, Myers, and Viseu 2015; Murphy 2015); and the work required to prevent the categories and symbolic orders through which we organize our lives from falling apart (Domínguez Rubio 2016, 2020; Yurchak 2015).

Despite its ubiquity, this mimeographic labor has not usually been a focus of the social sciences. This is not because this labor has been deemed unimportant. Almost everybody would readily agree that the work of care, maintenance, and repair is critical to weave and sustain the fabric of social life. Yet, while important, this labor has often been deemed ultimately inconsequential, since it has been associated with mechanical and dull, if not alienating and degrading, tasks that have a purely reproductive, reparative, or palliative role. As such, this mimeographic labor has been seen as playing a secondary or peripheral role aimed at simply "keep things the same" and, therefore, lacking any real political, aesthetic, or historical interest. As a result of this conception, mimeographic labor has been almost completely absent in most narratives, which have preferred to pay attention to those who are seen in charge of producing the new—for example, artists, politicians, philosophers, scientists, or architects—who have been considered the only ones capable of effecting real political, economic, or social change.

Over the last decade, a growing number of authors have contested this description of mimeographic labor (see Denis and Pontille 2022; Strebel, Bovet, and Sormani 2019; Jackson 2014). Building on 1970s feminist critiques against the neglect of reproductive labor, these scholars have invited us to flip the script around mimeographic labor. They have done so by arguing that, contrary to how they have tended to be described, these tasks of care, maintenance, and repair are not simply complementary or secondary but rather an essential part of the practices that define the continuity, or change, of the worlds we inhabit. To illustrate their importance, just imagine what the world around you would be like without these mimeographic labors of care, maintenance, and repair. Imagine, for example, what would happen in your house without the daily effort of housework that needs to be done day after day to keep it habitable. Or what would happen to the streets, buildings, and parks of your city without the routine work of maintenance workers, gardeners, garbage collectors, and so forth. Or what would happen to your computer, your car, or any of your appliances without the continuous work of taking care of them, repairing them, and updating them. What would happen is that, *pace* Marx, everything that seemed solid would melt into air.

This volume builds on this body of work to reclaim the importance of the mimeographic labor of care, maintenance, and repair. This, we will argue, requires cultivating a different economy of attention—one that shifts our attention away from the usual sites and heroes that adorn our narratives and that pays attention to those *other* "missing masses" (cf. Latour 1992) composed by those unheroic actors, mundane labors, and boring and banal places that do not usually feature in our narratives but without which our worlds would fall apart. One of the aims of this volume is to contribute to this effort by repopulating our narratives with some of those *other* missing masses, which, in our case, will include the technicians helping to produce scientific knowledge (Max Liboiron), the artisans that made possible to reimagine sovereign power (Chandra Mujerki), the volunteers and activists that help to sustain projects in the wake of their collapse (Tomás Sánchez Criado and Vincent Duclos), the plantation workers who resist capitalist extractivism (Thomas Cousins), the cows and farmers that organize capitalist meat production (Marisol de la Cadena and Santiago Martínez Medina), the parents and children redefining what is disability (Myriam Winance), or the farmers and bears that help to weave narratives and sensibilities around climate change (Cymene Howe).

But if we need to pay attention to these mimeographic labors of care, maintenance, and repair, it is not simply to fill a gap in our narratives but rather because they are essential to understand how orders are un/made. This requires breaking the fallacious equation that reduces mimeographic labor with reproduction. This equation is often invoked to describe the mimeographic labor of attendance and repair as purely reactive and inherently conservative, and to accuse these practices of constraining our ethical and political horizons within purely palliative and restorative frameworks. It is true that mimeographic labor has been often enlisted by different power regimes in their attempt to reproduce themselves and keep things the same (see Henke and Sims 2020). However, it is equally true that mimeographic labor never results in a return to the same, *even when it intends to*. Because, contrary to what it is often assumed, mimeographic work can never "return," "restore," "recover," or "reproduce" a lost identity. It cannot because, as Deleuze (1995) reminded us, there is no such as thing as repetition without difference, in the same way there is no reproduction without production. Mimeographic work is no exception to this, since it is a work that *always* operates through substitutions, additions, subtractions, and adjustments that leave scars, losses, and changes in its wake. That is why, when we look around us, we encounter not a world of pristine and undisturbed identities but instead a world of modified, mended, and retrofitted identities, continuously made and remade through patches, touch-ups, and changes. This is also why the work of care, repair, and maintenance is never a purely mechanical exercise of preserving the same but rather a work where the boundary between continuity and change, past and future, identity and difference, remembering and forgetting, and presence and absence is constantly generated and negotiated.

Paying attention to mimeographic labor reminds us that the orders we inhabit are never given in advance but instead have to be produced, and sustained, day by day. This is why, like Sisyphus, we are condemned to be incessantly engaged in this mimeographic work of maintenance and repair, constantly negotiating the boundary between continuity and change—a work that is, by definition, always unfinished and endless because no matter how mimeographic the work we invest in sustaining the orders, bodies, objects, and relations that organize our lives, they never stop being fragile. This, however, does not mean that they are less solid. What it means is that fragility and robustness are not mutually exclusive states. They are the obverse and reverse of the same coin, which is to say that everything is always simultaneously fragile and solid.

From the perspective of these mimeographic practices, fragility no longer appears as a lack to be fixed, eliminated, or overcome but instead as an inescapable *excess* that needs to be confronted. This excessive and unavoidable condition of fragility confronts us with a series of ethical and political dilemmas. Because while it may be true that, as Ricoeur (1995) wrote, fragility always calls for responsibility, this does not mean that every call needs to be heeded. Not everything that is fragile deserves to be cared for, repaired, or maintained. Whether that is the case depends on the ethical and political frameworks we use to define the fragile and how they allocate worth and responsibility. But even if we tried to respond to all of these calls, we would soon realize that our capacity to answer them is helplessly finite because the work of care, maintenance, and repair is a form of labor that is particularly onerous, costly, and time-consuming. We simply cannot afford to address every fragility. And not everything that is cared for, repaired, and maintained can be taken care of in the same way. Moreover, attending to one fragility always requires neglecting another. This is the situation that Cymene Howe (chapter 12) confronts us with when she explores how the melting glaciers in Iceland reveal a field of divergent, and often opposing, human, animal, and material fragilities. Each of these fragilities has different needs and temporalities, which call for different forms of care, repair, and maintenance. The question, then, is: How do we respond to the demands of these divergent fragilities? Which fragilities must be addressed, and which can be ignored? What are we willing to preserve, and what are we willing to discard—and at what cost? What or who deserves to be described as fragile?

UNCOMMON FRAGILITIES

These are difficult questions—questions whose answers lead into ethical binds. Each response implies giving preference to one fragility over another, resolving one fragility to create another, gaining something at the cost of losing something else. But it is precisely this difficulty that makes it important to insist on these questions, to sit with them, and to think from them, and to do it devoid of the temptation to solve them by appealing to a common good, or a universal ground, that can accommodate and respond to all of these fragilities. Because we live in a world not of common fragilities but rather of *uncommon fragilities*. This much became evident during the COVID-19 pandemic when governments around the world tried to instill a sense of solidarity and common action by invoking a common human fragility, which crystallized in the slogan "We are in this together." But if the pandemic revealed anything it is that we are *not* in this together. The virus did not travel through the equalized space of an abstractly defined human fragility but rather through the concrete furrows ploughed by racialized, gendered, class inequalities that have produced, and continue to reproduce, our uncommon fragilities and humanities.

Confronting the uncommonality of our fragilities should not lead us into paralysis. If anything, it is a call to cultivate political and ethical vocabularies and practices that come to terms with the fact that this uncommonality is not a problem to be solved (or a problem that *can* be solved) but rather the inherent and irresoluble condition of the world we inhabit. It is a call to creating vocabularies and practices that do not shy away from the frictions, divergences, and conflicts created by these uncommon fragilities but instead force us to attend to them, to confront them, and to respond to them—that, as Haraway (2016) would say, dare to be stuck in the trouble that fragility presents us.

This requires, first, coming to terms with the fact that there is never a self-evident definition of fragility. There are always competing definitions about what counts as fragile. Each of these definitions is consequential, since they define what kinds of political and ethical frameworks of responsibility and action are required to address fragility. For example, defining fragility by reference to a common human fragility, as often happened during the COVID-19 pandemic, leads to political and ethical frames of action premised upon a false sense of equality that elides, and fails to address, the uncommon fragilities created by unequal social, racial, and economic conditions.

It is not simply a question of coming to terms with fragility but also with the built-in asymmetries in the capacity to establish those definitions because not everybody is allowed to define what is fragile. There are always those who have the power to define what is fragile, and those for whom fragility is a condition imposed on them. It is the World Bank and the IMF who have the capacity to define countries as fragile, while the populations of those countries suffer the consequences of being described as fragile and in need of help. Acknowledging this asymmetry is as important as it is to acknowledge that defining something as fragile does not have the same political consequences in every case. In some contexts, calling something fragile can be a critical and emancipatory project. This is, for example, what Chandra Mukerji does in her contribution by showing how the seemingly solid and absolute power of Louis XIV was indeed a fragile and contingent achievement made possible by networks of artisans and their indefatigable work of care, maintenance, and repair. In contexts such as this, demonstrating that the seemingly solid, necessary, and natural is fragile, contingent, and historical allows us to demystify these orders and open the possibility of critique and political action. In other contexts, however, it is the *refusal* to describe something as fragile that can be an equally emancipatory and critical project. This is especially the case in contexts where fragility has been used to naturalize hierarchies that subtract agency from different groups, objects, and spaces. This is what Myriam Winance argues in her chapter when she discusses the importance of rejecting a description of disabled bodies as fragile to avoid robbing them of their agencies, or what Max Liboiron argues about the importance of resisting the use of the notion of fragility in those regions where this term has been routinely weaponized by governments to legitimate their interventions and perpetuate their hold on them.

Confronting the uncommonality of our fragilities also means coming to terms with the fact that these fragilities cannot be "solved" or "fixed" through the mimeographic work of care, maintenance, and repair. This is not just because this mimeographic work is never done but also because this work is never just about "keeping things the same," even when it tries to be just that. Each form of mimeographic labor is organized around a different regime of worth, which implies different ways of establishing the boundary between what needs to be erased and what needs to be kept, as well as different ways of acknowledging, forgetting, or ignoring what is lost or gained in the way. This is what Annemarie Mol argues in her contribution when she talks about the different "logics of good" that organize the work of care, maintenance, and repair and how they silently help to consolidate different ethical and political projects. And, needless to say, these ethical and political projects are not necessarily good. While practices of care, maintenance, and repair are typically associated with a positive ethical commitment toward those in need, this is not always the case. In fact, these practices are very often mobilized to secure the continuity of exclusionary, unjust, or exploitative systems. Think, for example, about the extreme care, and the immense work of maintenance and repair, that the US government invests to sustain its necropolitical project around its border (Chaar-López 2019; de Leon 2015). In this volume, Marisol de la Cadena and Santiago Martínez Medina illustrate the great care that is put toward maintaining and repairing the exploitative system of capitalist meat production, while Thomas Cousins shows how the work of repair is part of the logic of colonial violence and capital's exploitation that those in charge of South African timber plantations deploy to keep workers' bodies fragile and functional as parts of the extractive system that produces paper, pulp, and profit. And yet, as Cousins also shows, oppressive logics can be countered with other logics of care, maintenance, and repair that nurture spaces of resistance from within.

Confronting the uncommonality of fragilities should not be seen purely in negative terms as a reckoning with limits, ends, and impossibilities because limits are as much about ends as they are about beginnings. Thinking *from* them, rather than against them, is thus an opportunity to cultivate a different way of relating to fragility—one that does not see fragility as something to be prevented, avoided, or fixed but rather that reclaims it as a productive space from where to articulate alternative political and ethical vocabularies. Such vocabularies and practices help us recognize that, as Hartman (2019) argues, it is possible to affirm and generate life, even from the cruelest imposition of fragility, and to use this recognition productively to help us to emancipate ourselves from a nostalgic yearning to preserve, recover, restore, or fix lost identities. We need vocabularies and practices that do not see mimeographic works of care, repair, and maintenance as a mere promise to recover or return what was lost but instead as an opportunity to develop forms of attention for, and responsibility toward, what remains after breakdown—that reclaim those fragments that remain as starting points from where to build other ways of thinking, living, doing, and relating. This is precisely what Tomás

Sánchez Criado and Vincent Duclos argue in their contribution to this volume when they invite us to think about the afterlives of the fragments left after two government and activist projects broke down not as ruins of lost identities and relations but rather as the building blocks of new ones. When seen in this way, thinking from fragility is an opportunity not just to move away from Promethean modern politics and their promise of control and domination but also to embrace a more modest form of politics, a *fragile politics*, that confronts us with the discomfort of living in a world that is always falling apart, that needs to be continually repaired and maintained, but which, for that very reason, is also continually being reinvented, reconfigured, and reassembled—a world where the irresoluble uncommonality of our fragilities is always both tragedy and possibility.

BOOK PLAN

The volume is organized around four parts: Bodies, Environments, Labor, and Politics. Each part is composed of two empirical chapters followed by a conversation between an invited scholar and the editors of the volume, where we discuss the main ideas of the chapters and reflect more generally on the promises and limits of thinking about fragility. We have chosen this structure to emphasize the exploratory, partial, and open-ended nature of this volume. Our aim here is not to settle any conversation but rather to begin one by inviting others to think with us.

BODIES

The volume starts with bodies, since they provide us with one of the most proximate experiences of fragility. The aim of this section is to explore the role that different practices of care, maintenance, and repair play in attending different bodily fragilities and the kinds of ethical and political dilemmas that are created as a result.

Annemarie Mol gets us started with what is arguably the most basic and universal form of taking care of our bodies: eating. Mol zeroes in on a program developed by the Netherlands Nutrition Centre to promote healthy breakfasts for kids aged between four and thirteen. Mol uses this initiative, a seemingly uncontroversial and ethically laudable effort to take care of some of the more fragile among us, to invite us to think about the ethical and political frameworks that get silently reproduced in the name of care. Mol begins by confronting us with the fact that any project of care is necessarily built around an ethical choice that foregrounds the fragility of some elements while relegating others, and their fragilities, to the background. She does so by showing how nutrition programs such as the one under consideration are often built upon an unstated ethical choice that foregrounds the fragilities of children at the cost of sidelining the fragilities of all the others involved in the process, such as farmers, insects, or birds. These ethical choices, Mol argues, are related not simply to selecting which fragilities are attended but also to the different "logics of good" framing *how* those fragilities will be attended. Because, as Mol shows, the Dutch nutrition program advances a very particular understanding of "good"—one that erases the possibility of thinking about the fragilities of children as a collective problem by consolidating an understanding of childcare as an individual parental responsibility and by presenting the market as the proper mechanism to coordinate individual choices and ensuring the common good.

The attention to the political and ethical frameworks silently reproduced through the language of care is also at the heart of Myriam Winance's contribution. Like Mol, Winance focuses on a seemingly uncontroversial care practice: the care of multiply disabled children. Drawing on twenty-two interviews with parents of multiply disabled children in France, Winance shows how the fragility of these children should be understood not as a property inscribed in their bodies but rather as something that acquires its form and meaning through two contradictory logics of care. On the one hand, there is the logic of care developed by the parents, which, Winance argues, is not reduced to a purely palliative task of keeping children alive but instead organized as an ethical practice aimed at helping children flourish and become autonomous. On the other hand, there is the logic put forward by the children, who reclaim their autonomy by resisting parental care, even when it is at the cost of increasing their own bodily fragility. It is this fragility–resistance dynamic, Winance argues, that defines the unfinished, and unfinishable, struggle through which parents and children are constantly negotiating and transforming their identities and agencies, as well as the ethical and personal relations that hold them together.

As Lucy Suchman notes in the conversation at the end of this section, both chapters point at the question "What's our unit of analysis when thinking about care?" They reveal that there is no simple answer to this question. Both chapters illustrate that there is no such thing as a universal fragility that is common to us all, only uncommon fragilities stemming from the concrete needs of particular bodies. They also show how these uncommon fragilities are negotiated through different practices of maintenance and care. And more importantly, they show how these practices are never innocent interventions to care for or maintain a preexisting body but instead need to be understood as ethical and political projects that enact certain definitions of bodies and their fragilities while occluding others.

ENVIRONMENTS

This part explores the relations between humans with their environments and the role that different fragilities play in defining these relations. It opens with a chapter by Marisol de la Cadena and Santiago Martínez Medina on multispecies relations. Their chapter looks at the work of care, maintenance, and repair required to sustain the massive infrastructure of capitalist meat production. They focus on a particular point of this infrastructure: the Colombia farms where artificial insemination of genetically certified bull semen is used to impregnate cows, reproduce cattle, and improve the herd. De la Cadena and Martínez Medina contend that this process of artificial insemination is not merely an assisted reproductive technology, as it is usually described. Instead, they argue, it should be described as a "mutually assisted reproduction of cattle and capital" (MAR) organized around a series of material-semiotic activities whereby cattle and capital recursively become each other through the handling of life-producing substances (semen, ovulatory eggs, embryos) and lodging organs (uteri, penises, vaginas). De la Cadena and Martínez Medina argue that the robustness of MAR is organized around an "unachievable perfection" in human-cow/bull encounters. The quest for this unachievable perfection requires a massive effort to quarantine the fragility of these encounters through different tools, life substances, chemical mediums, infrastructures, and bacteria. However, de la Cadena and Martínez Medina note that despite this massive effort to quarantine fragility to assure the normal circulation of capital, this system never ceases to be fragile. Any small change, such as a bad encounter between the cow and farmers or an incorrect placing of the farmer's fingers inside the cow's vagina, can bring the system down. And yet, as de la Cadena and Martínez Medina note, this ever-present fragility does not mean that this system is not robust. Rather, they argue, it means that massive infrastructures such as the agro-food industry are always simultaneously robust and fragile. In other words, what it means is that robustness and fragility are not alternate, or mutually exclusive, states but rather two sides of the same coin.

De la Cadena and Martínez Medina's concern with the containment of fragility is at the heart of Max Liboiron's chapter, which focuses on the efforts of the Civic Laboratory for Environmental Action Research (CLEAR), a feminist marine plastics laboratory studying plastic pollution in the Inuit homelands of Nunatsiavut in the subarctic region of Labrador, Canada. Liboiron begins by highlighting the importance of resisting the use of the notion of fragility in a region where this term has been routinely weaponized by governments and international organizations to legitimate interventions over Indigenous populations and land territories. The chapter explores the possibility of enacting this resistance when producing scientific knowledge about the region. By presenting the chapter as a "choose your own lab adventure," Liboiron invites us to become a "sample slinger" looking for microplastics in animal gut samples collected by the CLEAR lab. This work is part of what Liboiron calls "purity chores," which are those practices of maintenance and repair required to contain the contamination of data samples. By placing the reader at the helm of the narrative, Liboiron forces us to face the ethical and political conundrums that emerge in these chores as they seek to contain fragility and produce "pure" scientific knowledge. The fact that this purity is unachievable, Liboiron argues, does not mean that these practices are to be disregarded as failures because, as they note, it is precisely the constitutive incompleteness of these purity chores that animates the recursive nature of the practices that render fragile data into solid scientific knowledge and also what makes it possible to orient these practices to future knowledge production.

These two chapters illustrate processes seeking to contain fragility to produce different effects: in one case, scientific knowledge; in the other, capital. They also show that this labor of care, maintenance, and repair is always unfinished and unfinishable, since there is no moment at which fragility is eliminated, fixed, or solved. As María Puig de la Bellacasa notes in her discussion of these chapters, they also reveal the ethical ambivalence of this work: the same care that is deployed in one setting to produce scientific knowledge is deployed in another to impose coercive reproductive practices on the cows. In so doing, both chapters help to remind us that the work of care, maintenance, and repair can be appropriated by different, even contradictory, political and ethical projects. The question, then, is: What kinds of possibilities do these practices of care, maintenance, and repair help to open up? This question is the focus of the next part of the book.

LABOR

This part explores different forms of mimeographic labor employed to attend diverse fragilities and the kind of politics and ethics they help to open up. In the first chapter, Tomás Sánchez Criado and Vincent Duclos explore the kinds of politics involved when care labor is organized *beyond* repair. To do so, they direct our attention to the fragments left after things have broken down and there is no possibility of repair. More specifically, they focus on the fragments left behind by two now defunct projects: the MOS@N, a mobile health initiative implemented in Nouna, rural Burkina Faso, as a network infrastructure using mobile communication to improve medical follow-up and care; and *En torno a la silla*, a Barcelona DIY-design activist coalition aimed at building and repairing technical aids for people with disabilities. Sánchez Criado and Duclos explore how the people working in the aftermath of these projects do not try to return to a lost unity or restore normality but rather seek to creatively appropriate the fragments left behind to open up new possibilities and relations. These practices, Sánchez Criado and Duclos argue, provide a model to move away from a form of care where fragility is understood in the negative form of a loss that needs to be repaired to a form of care that is attentive to the generative and divergent prospects of fragmentary afterlives.

If Tomás Sánchez Criado and Vincent Duclos invite us to think about politics *beyond* repair, Thomas Cousins explores the emancipatory potential of the mimeographic labor of repair. He does so by taking us to the timber plantations of South Africa—a context where labor has been profoundly shaped by the colonial, Apartheid, and post-Apartheid state. Cousins's focus is on the contradictory logics of repair that define the ethical and political life of the workers in these plantations. On the one hand, there is the logic of colonial violence and capital's exploitation that seeks to repair the bodies of these workers through nutritional programs aimed at preventing them from collapsing or falling ill and thus keeping them as functional parts of the extractive system that produces paper, pulp, and profit. On the other hand, there is the logic of repair deployed by these workers to cultivate *amandla*—defined as capacity or strength—to make the worlds around the plantations habitable against the violence of colonial extraction. Cousins invites to think how the work of repair involved in creating *amandla*, which ranges from building kinship networks to ingesting vernacular curatives, is not merely restorative or integrative but is also a form of creative resistance that seeks to nurture the fragile filaments of ethical and political life against the wounds of plantation capitalism.

As Geof Bowker notes in the conversation about these chapters, both chapters illustrate why maintenance, repair, and care are not necessarily just about making things whole but also about making things possible. In so doing, both chapters invite us to rethink the politics of maintenance and repair by moving beyond an understanding of these practices as merely restorative or palliative to one that attends to the potential of these practices to nurturing fragile spaces of resistance, hope, and possibility. This consideration of the kind of politics that can be imagined through different practices of care, maintenance, and repair is the focus of the last part of the book.

POLITICS

We finish our exploration by thinking about how attending to fragilities can help to unsettle received notions of the political and how it can help us to imagine politics otherwise. This part of the book begins with a chapter by Chandra Mukerji, exploring the material basis of power in seventeenth-century France. Building on Foucault, Mukerji begins by showing how modern power has always sought to legitimate itself using "prophetic truths." These prophetic truths, Mukerji argues, are "fragile fictions" made credible through the care work of modest social actors. Mukerji then dives into seventeenth-century France to explore the role that the regimes of care implemented by artisans played in sustaining these prophetic truths that transformed an otherwise weak king, like Louis XIV, into the powerful Sun King. These regimes of care, Mukerji argues, transformed France by materially weaving the imaginary of the Sun King in palaces, gardens, infrastructures, fortresses, weapons, and bodies. Crucially, Mukerji argues, they did so while remaining invisible because while "the mindful hands" of these artisans were crucial to flesh out the magnificence of the sovereign, they had to be removed from the cultural imaginary and narratives to sustain the illusion of inevitability, necessity, and destiny of his sovereign power. In so doing, Mukerji demonstrates how power, even absolute power, is not the absence of fragility but rather a fragile achievement on its own—one that needs to be constantly cared, maintained, and repaired.

Cymene Howe brings to our attention another powerful agent: glaciers. Based on several years of ethnographic research in Iceland, Howe explores how climate change is altering political boundaries by forcing us to care for elements, such as glaciers, which have been historically perceived as a threat to life. However, these once-massive bodies of ice are now fragile bodies in need of care and maintenance generating a field of divergent social and ecological fragilities. Howe explores how attending to these divergent fragilities calls for different practices of care, maintenance, and repair that generate political and ethical dilemmas about what needs to be saved, how it needs to be saved, and why it needs to be saved. Rather than seeing the dilemmas created by these divergent fragilities as a problem, Howe invites us to see them as an opportunity to develop a different ethical and political vocabulary—one that is rooted in recognizing the entanglements with one another and on reflection upon a world "that is not made by humans alone and whose fragilities need not be the end of the story."

As Steve Jackson notes in the conversation about these two chapters, they reveal how fragility is not just for the weak but also for the strong. They show how solidity is itself a fragile achievement that requires "forms of work that are typically occluded under the accomplished and reified form of things." And, in so doing, they provide a fitting way to conclude the volume with an invitation to develop theories of order and power that include fragility, care, maintenance, and repair at their core.

THINKING *WITH* FRAGILITY: AN INVITATION

I began this introduction by describing this volume as an invitation to come to terms with, and think from, the discomfort that fragility creates. I have argued that this requires cultivating a different way of relating to fragility—one that does not try to conquer it, solve it, or clarify it, but rather one that reclaims it as a productive space to think *from*. Let me now conclude by claiming that such effort will be moot if, in addition to cultivating forms of thinking *from* fragility, we do not also cultivate ways of thinking *with* fragility. By this, I mean forms of thinking that have the courage to reclaim their own fragility. At a moment when answers elude us, it is critical to develop forms of thinking and practice that rebel against the temptation of having the last word, that are willing to accept the fragility of their own certainties—forms of thinking and practice that see such fragility not as a weakness but rather as something to be embraced. In other words, we need to develop forms of thinking and practice that are willing to produce fragile knowledge because, as Édouard Glissant (2020, 9) wrote, "Fragile knowledge is not imperious science." It is a form of knowledge that is always willing to be rendered fragile, that is willing to accept that any interpretation, model, or idea it puts forward will always be partial, incomplete, and tentative. It is a form of knowledge that relates to cracks, hesitations, and doubts not as problems to be resolved but instead as ways of making room for the ephemeral, the precarious, to emerge and to challenge us. And, for that reason, it is a form of knowledge that sees its own fragility as an open invitation to think in the shared uneasiness of not having certainties in a world where our uncommon fragilities hold us together and apart. We would like this volume to be this kind of open invitation. We offer it as a fragile sharing, anchored in the conviction that, as the poet Naomi Shibab Nye (1986) wrote, "If we are not fragile, we do not deserve the world."

REFERENCES

Beck, Ulrich. 1992. *Risk Society: Towards a New Modernity*. 1st ed. London: SAGE.

Bellacasa, María Puig de la. 2017. *Matters of Care*. 3rd ed. Minneapolis: University of Minnesota Press.

Callén, Blanca, and Tomás Sánchez Criado. 2016. "Vulnerability Tests. Matters of 'Care for Matter' in E-Waste Practices." *Tecnoscienza: Italian Journal of Science & Technology Studies* 6 (2): 17–40.

Castro, Eduardo Viveiros de, and Déborah Danowski. 2016. *The Ends of the World*. Translated by Rodrigo Guimaraes Nunes. 1st ed. Malden, MA: Polity.

Chaar-López, Iván. 2019. "Sensing Intruders: Race and the Automation of Border Control." *American Quarterly* 71 (2): 495–518. https://doi.org/10.1353/aq.2019.0040.

Chakrabarty, Dipesh. 2021. *The Climate of History in a Planetary Age*. 1st ed. Chicago: University of Chicago Press.

Chrétien, Jean-Louis. 2017. *Fragilité*. Paris: Minuit.

de Leon, Jason. 2015. *The Land of Open Graves: Living and Dying on the Migrant Trail*. 1st ed. Oakland: University of California Press.

Denis, Jérôme, and David Pontille. 2015. "Material Ordering and the Care of Things." *Science, Technology, & Human Values* 40 (3): 338–367. https://doi.org/10.1177/0162243914553129.

Denis, Jérôme, and David Pontille. 2022. *Le soin des choses—Politiques de la maintenance*. Paris: La Decouverte.

Denis, Jérôme, and David Pontille. 2023. "Cultivating Attention to Fragility: The Sensible Encounters of Maintenance." In *Ecological Reparation: Repair, Remediation and Resurgence in Social and Environmental Conflict*, edited by Dimitris Papadopoulos, María Puig de la Bellacasa, and Maddalena Tacchetti, 1st ed., 344–361. Bristol, UK: Bristol University Press.

Domínguez Rubio, Fernando. 2016. "On the Discrepancy between Objects and Things: An Ecological Approach." *Journal of Material Culture* 21 (1): 59–86. https://doi.org/10.1177/1359183515624128.

Domínguez Rubio, Fernando. 2020. *Still Life: Ecologies of the Modern Imagination at the Art Museum*. 1st ed. Chicago: University of Chicago Press.

Domínguez Rubio, Fernando, and Glenn Wharton. 2020. "The Work of Art in the Age of Digital Fragility." *Public Culture* 32 (1): 215–245. https://doi.org/10.1215/08992363-7816365.

Friedman, Thomas L. 2005. *The World Is Flat: A Brief History of the Twenty-First Century*. New York: Farrar, Straus and Giroux.

Giddens, Anthony. 1991. *Modernity and Self-Identity: Self and Society in the Late Modern Age*. London, UK: John Wiley.

Glissant, Édouard. 2020. *Treatise on the Whole-World*. Liverpool, UK: Liverpool University Press.

Graham, Stephen, and Nigel Thrift. 2007. "Out of Order." *Theory, Culture & Society* 24 (3): 1–25. https://doi.org/10.1177/0263276407075954.

Gramsci, Antonio. 2011. *Prison Notebooks: Volume 2*. Translated by Joseph A. Buttigieg. New York: Columbia University Press.

Haraway, Donna J. 2016. *Staying with the Trouble: Making Kin in the Chthulucene*. 1st ed. Durham, NC: Duke University Press.

Hartman, Saidiya. 2019. *Wayward Lives, Beautiful Experiments: Intimate Histories of Social Upheaval*. 1st ed. New York: W. W. Norton.

Henke, Christopher R., and Benjamin Sims. 2020. *Repairing Infrastructures: The Maintenance of Materiality and Power*. Cambridge, MA: MIT Press.

Husserl, Edmund. 1970. *The Crisis of European Sciences and Transcendental Phenomenology: An Introduction to Phenomenological Philosophy*. Evanston, IL: Northwestern University Press.

Jackson, Steven. 2014. "Rethinking Repair." In *Media Technologies: Essays on Communication, Materiality and Society*, edited by Tarleton Gillespie, Pablo Boczkowski, and Kristen Foot, 221–240. Cambridge, MA: MIT Press.

Jackson, Steven, and Laewoo Kang. 2014. "Breakdown, Obsolescence and Reuse: HCI and the Art of Repair." In *CHI '14: Proceedings of the SIGCHI Conference on Human Factors in Computing Systems*, 449–458. New York: ACM. https://doi.org/10.1145/2556288.2557332.

Latour, Bruno. 1992. "Where Are the Missing Masses? The Sociology of a Few Mundane Artifacts." In *Shaping Technology/Building Society: Studies in Sociotechnical Change*, edited by Wiebe E. Bijker and John Law, 225–258. Cambridge, MA: MIT Press.

Latour, Bruno. 2004. "Why Has Critique Run Out of Steam? From Matters of Fact to Matters of Concern." *Critical Inquiry* 30 (2): 225.

Law, John. 1992. "Notes on the Theory of the Actor-Network: Ordering, Strategy, and Heterogeneity." *Systems Practice* 5 (4): 379–393. https://doi.org/10.1007/BF01059830.

Le Corbusier. 1933. *The Radiant City: Elements of a Doctrine of Urbanism to Be Used as the Basis of Our Machine-Age Civilization*. New York: Orion Press.

Macnaghten, Phil, and John Urry. 1998. *Contested Natures*. 1st ed. London: SAGE.

Martin, Aryn, Natasha Myers, and Ana Viseu. 2015. "The Politics of Care in Technoscience." *Social Studies of Science* 45 (5): 625–641. https://doi.org/10.1177/0306312715602073.

Mattern, Shannon. 2018. "Maintenance and Care." *Places Journal*, November. https://placesjournal.org/article/maintenance-and-care/

Mbembe, Achille. 2019. *Necropolitics*. Durham, NC: Duke University Press.

Merchant, Carolyn. 1990. *The Death of Nature: Women, Ecology, and the Scientific Revolution*. Reprint. New York: HarperOne.

Moore, Jason W., ed. 2016. *Anthropocene or Capitalocene?: Nature, History, and the Crisis of Capitalism*. 1st ed. Oakland, CA: PM Press.

Murphy, Michelle. 2015. "Unsettling Care: Troubling Transnational Itineraries of Care in Feminist Health Practices." *Social Studies of Science* 45 (5): 717–737. https://doi.org/10.1177/0306312715589136.

Negroponte, Nicholas. 1995. *Being Digital*. London: Hodder and Stoughton.

Nussbaum, Martha C. 2001. *The Fragility of Goodness: Luck and Ethics in Greek Tragedy and Philosophy*. 2nd ed. Cambridge: Cambridge University Press.

Nye, Naomi Shihab. 1986. *Yellow Glove: Poems*. Portland, OR: Far Corner Books.

Radhakrishnan, S. 1950. *The Dhammapada*. Oxford: Oxford University Press.

Ricoeur, Paul. 1995. "Fragility and Responsibility." *Philosophy & Social Criticism* 21 (5–6): 15–22. https://doi.org/10.1177/0191453795021005-603.

Russell, Andrew L., and Lee Vinsel. 2018. "After Innovation, Turn to Maintenance." *Technology and Culture* 59 (1): 1–25. https://doi.org/10.1353/tech.2018.0004.

Seneca. 1920. *Seneca: Epistles 66–92*. Translated by Richard M. Gummere. Latin/English Parallel ed. Cambridge, MA: Harvard University Press.

Serres, Michel. 1995. *The Natural Contract*. Illustrated edition. Ann Arbor: University of Michigan Press.

Shakespeare, William. 2009. *Timon of Athens: The Oxford Shakespeare*. Edited by John Jowett. Reissue edition. Oxford: Oxford University Press.

Stengers, Isabelle. 2015. *In Catastrophic Times: Resisting the Coming Barbarism*. London: Open Humanities Press. http://www.openhumanitiespress.org/books/titles/in-catastrophic-times/.

Strebel, Ignaz, Alain Bovet, and Philippe Sormani, eds. 2019. *Repair Work Ethnographies: Revisiting Breakdown, Relocating Materiality*. 1st ed. New York: Palgrave Macmillan.

Tironi, Manuel, Marcelo González-Gálvez, and Marisol de la Cadena. 2021. "Ends in Other Terms: An Introduction." *Tapuya: Latin American Science, Technology and Society* 4 (1): 2003051. https://doi.org/10.1080/25729861.2021.2003051.

Tsing, Anna Lowenhaupt, Nils Bubandt, Elaine Gan, and Heather Anne Swanson, eds. 2017. *Arts of Living on a Damaged Planet: Ghosts and Monsters of the Anthropocene*. 3rd ed. Minneapolis: University of Minnesota Press.

Wittgenstein, Ludwig. 1972. *On Certainty*. Edited by G. E. M. Anscombe and G. H. von Wright. Translated by Denis Paul. New York: Harper & Row.

Wynter, Sylvia. 2015. "Unparalleled Catastrophe for Our Species? Or, to Give Humanness a Different Future: Conversations." In *Sylvia Wynter: On Being Human as Praxis*, edited by Katherine McKittrick, 9–90. Durham, NC: Duke University Press.

Yurchak, Alexei. 2015. "Bodies of Lenin: The Hidden Science of Communist Sovereignty." *Representations* 129 (1): 116–157. https://doi.org/10.1525/rep.2015.129.1.116.

I BODIES

2 A HEALTHY BREAKFAST FOR YOUR CHILD: MAINTENANCE, CARE, AND THE PERSISTENCE OF FRAGILITY

ANNEMARIE MOL

In twentieth-century academia, "the new" was widely celebrated. Politics was praised for being creative and inventive. Craftmanship was just about respected, but activities such as peeling potatoes or washing the laundry were downgraded as menial, routine tasks that were repetitive and therefore boring. Those who took them on board stood low in the social hierarchy, and their emancipation was going to go together with their liberation from household chores.[1] Technology would help out here—human lives were bound to be improved by smart stuff, resulting from innovation, which, in its turn, was cast as a spin-off of scientific breakthroughs.[2] And if both politics and science were haunted by a celebration of the new, so, too, was art: it was praised when it stood out as surprising, groundbreaking, avant-garde.[3]

These days, in the wake of all but endless inventions, the world is crumbling. All kinds of fragilities that technoscience sought to surmount come to the fore in new guises and, in some cases, with a vengeance. As a part of this, the obsession with innovation wanes (at least somewhat), and maintenance is granted academic attention.[4] The present book is a case in point. In my contribution to this collective endeavor, I ask a few questions about how to direct this attention. First, I address the question of which *terms* we might want to use. Although "maintenance" is a fine term for talking about what it takes to keep material things going, where lively creatures are concerned, "care" might make more sense, and maybe elsewhere too. Because one case differs from the next, different terms deserve to be explored. Second, maintaining or caring for *this* particular entity (be it a thing or a body) has effects upon other entities too. This means that it makes sense not to focus too narrowly on one's pet object but rather always to ask *who else* is affected and how—for better or worse. Third, there are questions to ask about the particular *goods* that are strived after in practices of maintaining and caring. This means that in addition to asking *who* questions, we would do well to wonder *what* is being strived after and what, by contrast, is being avoided. Or, to put it differently, which *logics of the good* are relevant to the practices we study? These logics may pull and push in different directions, when what stands out as *good* in one of them turns out to be *bad* in another. And then, fourth, a particular way of orchestrating maintenance or caring practices may, by stealth, consolidate arrangements that do not necessarily deserve consolidation. Stabilizing and fostering are not invariably what is needed. How best to attend to that? To flesh out these four points, I use relatively simple materials that are not *new* so much as *illustrative*. They come from a Dutch website that stipulates what children might best eat for breakfast.

MAINTAINING, CARING, AND OTHER TERMS

To stay alive, children have to eat. The question of how much and what they might best eat is answered differently in different settings. As an example of a recommendation inspired by nutrition science, I turn to the website of the Netherlands Nutrition Centre, the Voedingscentrum. The page that I will be looking at here addresses adults in charge of feeding children between four and thirteen years old. They are called you. Here's breakfast: "Whole grain bread and brown bread are the healthiest choices. You can alternate with whole grain crispbread, oats or muesli. Healthy toppings are, for example, 100% peanut butter, 30+ cheese, vegetables and fruit. Think as well about semi-skimmed milk and fruit as accompaniments."[5] A bit further down on the same page, we learn that even if not ideal, it is okay sometimes to allow such toppings as honey, chocolate sprinkles, or halva jam, jam with half the traditional quantity of sugar. There are also pictures. These are meant to be inspiring and to give *you* an indication of the appropriate quantities. One of them shows a slice of bread topped with diary spread and then cut in two halves: carrots and raisins adorn one half, strawberries the other. Another half slice has been topped with peanut butter (without added salt and sugar!)

and cucumber, its accompanying half with 30+ cheese and tomato. There is a link to recipes for spreads made from fresh fruit and vegetables. And then *you* are told *why* children should eat in accordance with the "healthy choices" suggested. First, they need *energy* (calories), and if they are provided with a proper breakfast, they will not crave cookies and other sweet things halfway through the morning. Second, they are rapidly growing, and hence they need a diversity of *nutrients* (proteins, fats, carbohydrates), vitamins, and minerals.

The "healthy choices" that the Voedingscentrum suggests *you* should make do not match with what children in the Netherlands, in fact, eat for breakfast.[6] If they did, it would be superfluous to spell them out as *advice*. That children are growing, however, is not a recommendation but rather a fact. This fact is continuously established and reestablished by means of population research in which the growth of two categories of children, called "girls" and "boys," is meticulously registered. The result of such research is presented in charts in the form of growth graphs that make it possible for health-care professionals to compare the growth of any individual child in their consultation room with that of peers. These graphs say that at the age of four, the normal range for both girls and boys in the Netherlands is between 96 and 112 cm. By the time a girl is thirteen, her height is normal if it is between 148 and 174 cm, while for a boy of thirteen, the normal range is from 146 to 178 cm.[7]

These simple materials offer enough traction for a reflection upon the *words* we might use in the context of research into *maintenance*—but is it "maintenance"? For a start, that breakfasts help to keep children *alive* is something the Netherlands Nutrition Centre doesn't mention. *You* are not supposed to be so poor that your children risk starvation (this makes sense: there is significant welfare provision in the Netherlands). But if the Voedingscentrum keeps death threats out of its communication strategy, we, as analysts, may want to point out that globally, this is not self-evident and that breakfasts help to *maintain* something seriously fragile: human life. However, while sustenance helps to maintain a child's life, it *changes* that child's body.[8] Children who skip breakfast are listless and, as the website warns, will crave cookies and other sweet things halfway through the morning. Such edibles hold energy but lack the diverse nutrients needed for growth. Hence, if we go with the information the Netherlands Nutrition Centre provides, we may say that breakfasts do not simply *maintain* but also *transform* (the height of children) and *add* (energy and, along with that, the ability to learn and play). But then again, if on the growth chart a child's height stays "within the normal range," something is also being *maintained*: normality.

All of this illustrates that calibrating terms is not easy. In the case of childhood breakfasts, while some things are being maintained (life, normality), other things are added (energy) and yet other things are transformed (height). Hence, the term conventionally used in relation to what adults do for children—"caring"—might be helpful.[9] "Caring" doesn't have the resonance of constancy embedded in "maintaining." In other cases, other terms might be helpful. My point here is not to propagate the use of "care" or "caring" for every activity possible but rather to argue that we might want to keep our terms fluid and adapt them to our cases. Rather than looking for single solidified concepts to cluster around, we would do well to keep asking questions about the specificities of the cases we study and the terms that might best convey what is locally at stake.[10]

WHO ELSE IS AFFECTED?

If children are provided with the breakfasts recommended by the Netherlands Nutrition Centre, this may allow them to thrive. But *who else* is involved in this situation, and what about their fate? There is, for one, the you who is being tasked with making the "healthy choices." You make these choices as a particular kind of "consumer." This "consumer" is not an eater—after all, the child is tasked with eating the breakfast—but rather a buyer—an adult making choices in favor of whole grain or brown (but not white) bread and sugar-free peanut butter (and not, say, Nutella). If you were to make these choices at home from a cupboard full of goodies, this would not be ideal—as once the goodies are bought, it is better not to waste them.[11] So, going for sugar-free peanut butter (and so on) is first and foremost something better done in supermarket aisles or apps. That you have to somehow shoulder the task of carrying supplies to your house, or order them in, remains absent/present on the website, for while "choices" are evoked, the context where these have to be made (supermarket aisles and websites offering lots and lots of "unhealthy choices") is never mentioned. Nor does the Voedingscentrum pay attention to the painful fact that strawberries and tomatoes are considerably more expensive than jam, certainly jam with plenty of sugar. Hence, while *you* are called upon to be an ideal consumer, the *work* implied—both that of shopping and that of procuring money—is neglected.[12]

This is a classic concern in maintenance studies: the people who do the work are undervalued. In the case at hand, this applies not only to the you who is being addressed but also to the employees of the supermarket, the truck drivers who transport the different foods, the workers in the bakeries and peanut butter factories and so on, as well as to the farmers and farmhands. It is all taken for granted, which means that it remains invisible that if children's lives are being maintained, their energy supplemented, and their growth fostered, many others are putting in a lot of effort. As this effort remains hidden, no questions arise about the extent to which this is fine (it gives those involved a task, a sense of pride, an income) or not fine at all (in that, for instance, it may overburden some of those concerned, undermine their health or their ability to thrive). And if the Netherlands Nutrition Centre does not pay attention to the labor of the caring humans, neither does it wonder about the pleasure and pain of the creatures who serve as food. If *you* offer your child bread for breakfast, this affects the wheat from which that bread has been baked. If the child thrives, this is thanks to the wheat that has been harvested, milled, turned into dough, baked, sliced, and eaten. It is up for debate whether this is good or bad for wheat. After all, if some wheat kernels are being eaten, others are being saved and sowed again. A Darwinian line of reasoning, which has species struggling for survival, suggests that wheat might appreciate the enormous success that it owes to the bread coveted by humans.[13] In 2019, in the Netherlands alone, an area of 12,106,389 are (an "are" is 100 m^2) of land was planted with wheat.[14] Hence, *your* "healthy choice" of whole grain or brown bread for your child's breakfast comes *at the cost* of a few handfuls of grains of wheat, while at the same time, it helps to *maintain* wheat as a species.

The thriving of wheat as a species, in turn, affects other creatures. The website of the Netherlands Nutrition Centre, while it takes human labor for granted, has a background "encyclopedia" that pays attention to the ecological effects of growing diverse crops. "Grain cultivation may contribute to greenhouse gas emission, acidification and eutrophication. The more fertilizer is used, the more yield, but also the more environmental impact. Cultivating wheat and barley has a low impact if little fertilizer is being used and if there is no irrigation."[15] "Greenhouse gas emission," "acidification," and "eutrophication" sound bad, but wheat does comparatively well if contrasted with other edibles. "From all product groups, grains have the lowest environmental impact pro kilocalorie."[16] But then again, these "environmental impact" parameters do not include everything being impacted. What about the creatures that might have lived where wheat is now being grown? After all, if in the Netherlands an area of 12,106,389 are is reserved for wheat, in that entire area, all other plants are categorized as weeds. If they pop up at all, they are eliminated. This means that daisies, nettles, heather, birch trees, and so forth suffer when your child eats the slices of bread *you* so nicely adorned. This, in turn, is bad news for the insects that might have thrived on those plants and the birds predating those insects. None of this is new, and my point in raising it is not to offer you stunning facts. Instead, I wonder how best, as scholars, to deal with this complexity: that caring for one entity affects so many others. It is not as if this is a problem that can be solved—negotiated, yes; dealt with in different ways, that too; but solved, no.

Caring for one thing—here, a child—inevitably involves many other things—farmers and fields, insects and birds, water and eutrophication, fertilizer and noisy combine harvesters. And the complexity increases if we add in topics such as peanut butter (Where are the peanuts grown, and how does exporting them affect local food supplies?)[17] or fruit and vegetables (mind the water, transport, cooling and so on).[18] So, here is my question: How do we best to attend to the relations between those who are (that which is) being maintained or otherwise cared for and all the others involved in this, who are, for better or worse, tasked with a lot of work, turned into resources, made to disappear from the scene, or full out eliminated? Who is maintained, or allowed to transform, and whose fate is less favorable? And how, in this or that case, in this or that site, are such clashing interests negotiated?

WHAT STANDS OUT AS GOOD OR BAD?

The Netherlands Nutrition Centre asserts that a healthy breakfast provides children with energy and nutrients—the energy calling for a physics quantification expressed in (kilo-)calories; the nutrients specified by a biochemical allusion to substances. On the website, the fact that energy and nutrients abide with different logics is not explained in so many words, but they do.[19] After all, eating cookies and sweet things in the course of the morning would provide a child with ample energy. The problem that nutrition scientists have with these foods is that the nutrients they contain are not diverse enough. They are abundant in carbohydrates and, in the case of cookies, fats, but their protein, vitamin, and mineral contents fall short. Hence, the nutrient contents of these treats are not in accordance with what nutrition science suggests would be best for a child's growth. What is more, per portion, cookies and sweet things contain a lot of calories compared with the total amount of energy a child is likely to burn up in the course of a day. And while the website doesn't mention the threat of starvation, it displays an overriding concern with being overweight. This concern stretches from its reluctant tolerance of an occasional slice of bread with jam, if in a halva form, all the way through to advice on how best to handle grandparents who pamper your children with sugary stuff. Regarding such pampering, the website tries to reassure you that this is not necessarily disastrous: children can live with different rules. However, if you are really concerned, you may want to find a quiet moment to address the issue. "Frame your criticism in the I-form and do not throw accusations. You may for example say, 'I would appreciate it if you would give tea instead of Coca-Cola when the children return from school.'"[20]

The website doesn't squarely address the fact that there is a tension between two logics that stipulate what is *good* about food: an energy logic (which is about quantities of kilocalories) and a nutrient logic (which is about the building blocks that a growing body needs). The slices of bread with the recommended toppings are meant to assure both *goods* at the same time. They contain enough, but not too much, energy and diverse nutrients. There are more half-hidden logics in tension at play. Take the issue as to what makes a child eat this or that food. For one, this seems to hang on *rules*. You have rules, the grandparents have rules, and children are able to live with different rules: tea here, Coca-Cola there. If, as a parent, *you* cannot live with this discrepancy, *you* have to find a way to bridge the gap. (In the example given, *you* rule out Coca-Cola, which suggests that this is *your* rule—rather than the advice of the Netherlands Nutrition Centre). But is eating indeed a matter of following rules? If, at first, it suggests that children eat in accordance with parental rules, a little further along, the website sings another song, for it asserts that when a child has not eaten a proper breakfast, it will *crave* cookies or sweet things halfway through the morning. What emerges here, then, is that eating may not (or at least not only) be a matter of following externally imposed rules but also involves a body and its desires. This latter logic also speaks from the pictures in which bread is made appealing by adorning it with strawberries, carrots, tomato, or cucumber. These look attractive and offer interesting flavors, thus making what follows from advisory rules coincide with what will offer a child bodily *pleasure*.

The idea that *following rules* and *taking pleasure* are contrasting ways of handling life has a long tradition.[21] Once again, the website deftly hides the tensions involved and suggests that it is possible to hold on to rules while at the same time providing children with pleasure. However, to us as analysts, this example suggests that in other cases, too, we may want to wonder which diverse concerns are attended to in a particular practice. Which logic is foregrounded, which others are also taken into account or rather pushed into the background? Fostering one kind of *good* does not necessarily erode the others, but it may do. This clearly speaks from a further example: that of the tension between the immediate health of individual human eaters and the long-term sustainability of the environment. Take the skimmed milk that the food advice page suggests *you* may want to offer to your child as a breakfast drink. This suggestion is backed up by the information that may be found elsewhere on the site, on a page about drinks: "Milk is primarily important because of the calcium and the B2 and B12 vitamins it contains. Preferably choose semi-skimmed or skimmed milk. Buttermilk is also a good option."[22] That milk skimmed of (part of) its fat might be commendable is underscored by an impressive photo collage of small drink packages on offer in the supermarket. Beneath each of these packages, a row of sugar cubes makes visible how much sugar the package contains. These long rows of sugar cubes form a scary sight. By comparison, milk might stand out as *good*—that is, as less burdened with excessive amounts of nutrient-scarce calories.

But then again, if in comparison with sugary drinks milk comes out as healthy, other comparisons complicate the picture. Once again, all that is required is to click through to the "encyclopedia" pages of the website. These offer information about the effects of dairy cows on the environment. In the Netherlands, cows have for a long time been revered for their ability to thrive on the grass that grows in polders that are too wet to grow crops (grains, vegetables, fruit trees) from which humans are able to eat themselves. These days, this romance is falling apart. "Approximately half the emission of ammonia in the Netherlands comes from manure from dairy farms. Ammonia settles down as nitrogen. Nitrogen enriches the soil in naturally nutrient-poor nature reserves. Due to this, a lot of variation in flora disappears. That, in its turn, causes the disappearance of animal species."[23] There are also factoids on offer about greenhouse gases produced, water used, animal welfare measured, and so on. We are told that ecologically working dairy farms (certified in this or that way) are somewhat less detrimental than the (far more numerous) farms that work, as it is called, conventionally. But what should *you* do with all this information? Still hold on to the advice to give (skimmed or semi-skimmed) milk to the children in your care because it is healthy? Or skip the milk because dairy farms put such huge pressures on the environment? While earlier *you* were told *what* to "choose," this time round *you* are left alone with the task of balancing different goods in tension that, taken separately, make sense in themselves but do not add up because they fit in different logics. These logics make use of different units, quantify different things, and pull in different directions.

My point here is not to establish what you or I should offer any children in our care as their breakfast drink. The point of this text is not to give advice based on the use of some magic calculator that solves impossible sums. Instead, I seek to underscore that maintaining and caring may be torn between different logics. There are not just the interests of different entities, or different creatures, to negotiate. There are also different kinds of *good* and *bad*,—different ideals, different concerns—at stake. Sometimes, serving one of these may be reconciled with serving the other.[24] The website of the Netherlands Nutrition Centre contains examples of this: It recommends breakfasts that contain *both* the appropriate amounts of calories *and* varied nutrients. It suggests that *you* may abide by rules that secure the health of your children *and* afford them the pleasure of food that is tasty. But when it comes to the tension between health and environment, the advisors' propensity to smooth out tensions reaches its limits. Both *goods* are presented as commendable, each on its own page. But they are not made to relate. What, then, is a wise way of relating them? This is left to *you*, put in the impossible position of reckoning with different goods that irredeemably clash. Both health and the environment are fragile, and either one or the other will suffer. Good luck with negotiating that.

MAINTAINING BY STEALTH

As we analyze maintenance/care practices, we would do well to ask which entity (organism, thing) is being sustained and which others are being turned into laborers or resources. Likewise, there are questions to ask about the logics of worth brought into play: Which *goods* are being served, and which other *goods* are being undermined in the process? A further issue I would like to raise has to do with what, in any care/maintenance arrangement, is being consolidated by stealth by being left silently in the background. As scholars, we may want to point such side effects out and grant them attention. Take once again the website of the Netherlands Nutrition Centre. As it separates out advice about health and information about the environmental effects of farming practices, it also separates out two logics, two pertinent normative repertoires: your child's health here, the environment's sustainability there. And *you* are put in the middle of the tensions that ensue. This is not *you* in the ballot box, voting. Nor is it *you*, picking a bank where you deposit your savings, or *you*, pressuring your pension fund to make responsible investments. Neither is it *you* as a member of an ecologically minded nongovernmental organization or as an activist.[25] Rather, it is *you* as a consumerbuyer. It is as a buyer in the supermarket that you are tasked with settling the *trade-off* between this or that good, the health of your child, the sustainability of the environment. This impossible choice is made to weigh on your shoulders.[26]

Along the way, a few things are consolidated by stealth.[27] The first is an individualizing version of parenting. It is suggested that *you*—all by yourself—are responsible for feeding your children. That your child may have more than one parent is never mentioned. If the grandparents engage in childcare but then hand out Coca-Cola, *you* are the one who calmly has to put them right. There is no attention for what you might need to care well. The costs of food are not mentioned, and neither is the time required to adorn slices of bread in attractive ways in the morning while also somehow assuring that the kids in the house get out of bed, get dressed, take the appropriate bags to school (gymnastics today?) along with a well-filled lunch box, and still leave the house in time—or maybe you have to take them.[28] Life in the household is supposed to submit to *your* rules—and if your children resist those rules, crave after sweet things already at breakfast, or do not want to eat at all, somehow you have to find a solution. The tone of the website is suave. It all seems easy and obvious (Is filling that lunchbox a problem? Prepare it the evening before!). The implication, if never articulated, is that if things don't work out, *you* are the one to blame. This is moralism: a style of presenting the *good* in such a way that individuals are first made individually responsible and then readily shamed because all *bads* around are staged as their lamentable personal failings.

A second arrangement is consolidated as well: the market as a way of coordinating individual preferences and thus ensuring the common good. The Netherlands Nutrition Centre suggests that if *you* do the right thing, the market will add your wise choices together with those of other responsible consumers, and in this way, things will change for the better. This is even asserted in so many words on the page about what to eat and drink (in cafés and restaurants) on a day out: "As consumers you jointly determine what is on offer. If only the demand for, for example, water or fruit is high, then they will appear on the menu all by themselves. Therefore, you may want to inquire after healthy products if at your destination there are too few healthy products on offer."[29] In this way, the market appears to be a fine organizational format for the realization of a better world. This world is bound to follow from the sum total of lots of separate "good choices." What this cheerful take does not reckon with is that, in markets, there are precious few means for individual buyers to coordinate their "choices" with others. What to do if other buyers push and pull in other directions?[30] You may want to buy bread, as you are advised to do, but then what? Milk or no milk? While *you* are left to ponder how to negotiate between the health of your child and the sustainability of the environment, the supermarket goes on to sell stunningly cheap sugary concoctions and expensive fruit. Food industries make a profit by overruling well-meant, state-sponsored websites with shiny advertisements. And farmers, whatever *good* they might wish for, have to compete on price.[31]

Hence, along with the market, something else is maintained as well: the agricultural system that depends on it.,[32] The problem at this point is that if farmers try to reduce the detrimental effects of their cows on the environment, these cows are likely to produce less milk, which means that the farmers have to ask higher prices for that milk. *You* may, or may not, be offered the choice to pay that higher price (this depends on the supermarket you go to), but if you are, as a buyer, you are then faced with further trade-offs: expensive milk or strawberries? And if you have somehow found a way to balance different *goods*, a further problem kicks in, which is that in the market, you don't always know what you are doing. Take the wheat in your child's bread: "The amount of fertilizer being used in Germany and France is half that of the Netherlands, so that grain cultivation there leads to lower greenhouse gas emissions and lower emissions of ammonia."[33] That is interesting to know for a European regulator (who might want to tell the Dutch government to do something about it). It is also interesting for a Dutch voter (who might want to consider voting for a party that is going to support Dutch farmers to change how they ertilizes). But (and all the more so because bread is not adorned with information sheets that tell where the wheat it contains comes from) providing such facts to people in their guise as consumer- buyer is not going change present-day agricultural setups. Instead, it adds to the exasperation of everyone involved: the exasperation of the farmers, who stand accused but feel cornered by a market that sets them up as competing (and globally competing at that); and the exasperation of the buyers, who cannot tell where the wheat in the bread they buy for their children comes from and who have to somehow live with what is being offered to them in those shops that, practically speaking, they are able to buy from.

CONCLUSION

The new is overrated; innovation is an all too eagerly revered idol. However, that does not mean that everything deserves to be maintained as it is. Where to tweak with this or that and where to add, transform, improve, or change? This is a question that obviously lacks a one-size-fits-all answer. In this contribution to our collective attempt to explore forms and variants of maintenance and care, I have not even tried to give specific situated answers. Instead, I have left *you*—the reader this time, rather than the adult taking care of a child—with a few further questions to ponder. First, these are questions about which *terms* to use in which case, or rather which terms, more particularly, to use in the cases that you (for one reason or another) happen to study. Second, I raised *who* questions: who, in your case, is being cared for (maintained, transformed) and who else does the work, invisible or not—who figures as a resource and who is eliminated or never gets to live due to the care at the center of your analysis. Third, you may need to face questions to do with *what* is being fostered as a *good* (ideal, goal) in maintenance/caring practices, and which alternative *goods* are also served or instead suffer in the process. And then, fourth, there are questions to ask about what is consolidated along the way, while when it comes to it, it might deserve to be changed—even if it is often far from clear how this might be done—where to start, in which way.

All of which leaves us with a final question: Can the fragilities that mark life on earth be safely put to rest, all danger avoided, if not by offering to the gods, then at least, in modernist mode, by inventing deft technologies, designing clever policies, and astutely negotiating trade-offs? In fact, I have *not* left this particular question open for you to ponder. The analysis proposed in this text suggests an unequivocal answer: *no*. That is neither a reason for depression nor a call for cynicism. It is, instead, a revolt against suave tones and the false promise that all problems have solutions; that clashing logics can always, somehow, be accommodated; that there is a single, coherent "common good" that everyone would do well to serve. In all their modesty, the materials presented here illustrate the impossibility of maintaining without destroying, of caring without imposing costs. What is more, they remind us that not everything, fragile or tenacious, deserves to be strengthened and sustained. This firm conclusion, however, does not end up in the form of advice as to what *you*, reader, might best "choose" to do. Instead, it encourages the attempt to combine a vivacious, explorative activism with a heartfelt sense of tragedy. Try, in coordination with relevant others, to do whatever seems locally *good*. See where that goes awry. Invite comments. Adapt. Try again. This iterative tactic might hold whether it is your task to feed children, to do research, or to engage in something else again.

NOTES

1. For a more extensive analysis of, and attempt to escape from, the celebration of politics as creative and innovative and the downgrading of "menial" tasks as circular and boring, see Mol (2021).

2. For a classic historical analysis that brings out that the new technologies were not necessarily as helpful as advertised, if only because they came with an impressive increase in standards of, for example, cleanliness, see Cowan (1983).

3. The celebration of the new in art was entangled with that in both politics and technology. For the former, see, for example, Egbert (1967); for the latter, see, for example, Bishop and Phillips (2010).

4. The notion of "invisible work" has been around for a while, particularly in calls for more attention of (often unpaid) work done by (mainly) women. See, for example, Daniels (1987). For insights in how in/visibility is orchestrated, see Star and Strauss (1999).

5. My translation from the Dutch. See https://www.voedingscentrum.nl/nl/zwanger-en-kind/eten-4-13/wat-geef-ik-mijn-kind-bij-ontbijt-en-lunch-4-13-jaar-.aspx. 30+

cheese has a fat content between 30 percent and 40 percent and is therefore considered to be "low fat cheese."

6. The website gives *advice* and hence tells you what you *should* do, while at the same time it keeps talking about what you, or the children you care for, might eat as a "choice," that then may, or may not, be a "healthy choice." For the notion of "food choice," see also Vogel (2016).

7. I draw these numbers from charts published by the research organization TNO. See https://www.tno.nl/nl/aandachtsgebieden/gezond-leven/roadmaps/youth/groeidiagrammen-in-pdf-formaat/.

8. After their death, bodies go on changing, even if a lot of effort is put into maintaining them in a fixed state—as we may learn from the fascinating article by Yurchak (2015).

9. This term is more widely used in relation to living creatures. See, for example, the contributions to Mol et al. (2010), who seek to break out of the idea that "warm" care stands in contrast to "cold" technology, and Puig de la Bellacasa (2015), who highlights that soils, too, deserve care. "The logic of care" (Mol, 2008) does not stipulate *that* care is good but rather articulates how people in care practices differentiate between good and bad ways of caring differently from one site to the next (e.g., Pols, 2006).

10. This deserves to be stated in so many words, as many in academia take it that concepts should be solidified. For a text that shifts between using "maintenance" and "care," see Denis and Pontille (2015). For an example where the objects cared for are buildings, see Edensor (2011). For one that pursues the issue that what is called maintenance may entail crafting, see Jones and Yarrow (2013). For the arguments that analytic terms should be fluidly adapted to one's case, see Domínguez-Guzmán et al. (2021).

11. A lot is written about food waste. For an interesting, non-moralizing example, see Abrahamsson (2019).

12. For examples of the care involved in providing food to others or self, see Zivkovic et al. (2016).

13. In his *Botany of Desire*, Michael Pollan (2002) describes apple trees along these lines—as happily celebrating their having spread so widely over the globe, way beyond their region of origin in the Caucasus, by their having seduced humans into carrying their seeds and carefully growing and grafting them. For wheat, see, for example, Zabinski (2021).

14. This number is retrieved from the website of the CBS, the Dutch statistical bureau. https://www.cbs.nl/nl-nl/cijfers/detail/80780NED?dl=2E10F (accessed September 2021).

15. See https://www.voedingscentrum.nl/encyclopedie/granen-en-graanproducten.aspx#blokzijn-graanproducten-duurzaam?.

16. See https://www.voedingscentrum.nl/encyclopedie/granen-en-graanproducten.aspx#blokzijn-graanproducten-duurzaam?.

17. For an analysis of what exporting peanuts may amount to locally, see Tousignant (2020).

18. For a wonderful analysis of the various relationalities eating calls forth, or, as the authors call it, for the *togetherness* in which it is implicated, see Abrahamsson and Bertoni (2014).

19. For a more extensive analysis of the different logics implied in food advice, see Mol (2013).

20. See https://www.voedingscentrum.nl/nl/zwanger-en-kind/eten-4-13/eten-bij-andere-en-op-uitjes.aspx.

21. For a fine version of this history, in which the rules of nutrition science are cast as a continuation of those of Christian self-restraint, see Coveney (2006). For an analysis of the contrast between following the rule of counting calories or rather fostering one's food pleasure, see Vogel and Mol (2014).

22. See https://www.voedingscentrum.nl/nl/zwanger-en-kind/eten-4-13/wat-geef-ik-mijn-kind-te-drinken-4-13-jaar-.aspx.

23. See https://www.voedingscentrum.nl/encyclopedie/melk-en-melkproducten.aspx.

24. For an interesting example of the complexities that follow on from the large diversity of "goods" at stake, see Sexton et al. (2019). And what may be at stake in eating does not just include tradition, home, culture, monetary costs, pride in cooking, companionship, control, animal welfare, diversity, climate, and so on. For the issue that one may have to prove that one is a fine Japanese citizen by foregoing questions about the potential radioactivity of one's food, see Burch (2018).

25. There is an obvious resemblance here with the way in which surveys do not just produce a result in the form of opinions measured but also perform the people being surveyed as individuals who may answer questions in citizen mode, either in line with how they act as consumers or not. For that analysis, with the case of a survey on farm animal welfare, see Law (2009).

26. In the last decades of the twentieth century, governments have shifted (in different ways and to different degrees) from directly regulating food to providing people in their guise of "consumers" with "information." For the US version of this transition, see Frohlich (2017).

27. For an interesting example of how a variety of things/relations that are not ostensibly at stake may still be tinkered with by stealth, see de Wilde (2020).

28. In the Netherlands, schools (bar preciously few exceptions) do not offer school meals. They do not have the space or the kitchens due to a still-recent history in which mothers were meant to offer lunch at home.

29. See https://www.voedingscentrum.nl/nl/zwanger-en-kind/eten-4-13/eten-bij-andere-en-op-uitjes.aspx.

30. For an interesting analysis of the way these "choices" are orchestrated in a physical supermarket, see Cochoy (2007).

31. And so on. For a tragic example of how people are encouraged to make "healthy food choices" while pushed to grow vegetables and fruits for the international market using lots of unhealthy pesticides, see Yates-Doerr (2015).

32. A lot has been written about farming systems. For an interesting analysis of how in Aotearoa / New Zealand modernist agriculture came to overrule Māori attempts to live off the land and is now cracking, see Campbell (2020). For the Dutch case, see, for example, Bos et al. (2013).

33. See https://www.voedingscentrum.nl/encyclopedie/granen-en-graanproducten.aspx#blokzijn-graanproducten-duurzaam?.

REFERENCES

Abrahamsson, S. (2019). Food repair: An analysis of the tensions between preventing waste and assuring safety. *Ephemera: Theory and Politics in Organization, 19*(2), 283–301.

Abrahamsson, S., & Bertoni, F. (2014). Compost politics: Experimenting with togetherness in vermicomposting. *Environmental Humanities, 4*(1), 125–148.

Bishop, R., & Phillips, J. (2010). *Modernist avant-garde aesthetics and contemporary military technology: Technicities of perception*. Edinburgh University Press.

Bos, J. F., Smit, A. B. L., & Schröder, J. J. (2013). Is agricultural intensification in the Netherlands running up to its limits? *NJAS-Wageningen Journal of Life Sciences, 66*(1), 65–73.

Burch, K. A. (2018). *Eating a nuclear disaster: A vital institutional ethnography of everyday eating in the aftermath of Tokyo Electric Power Company's Fukushima Daiichi Nuclear Power Plant disaster* [Doctoral dissertation, University of Otago].

Campbell, H. (2020). *Farming inside invisible worlds: Modernist agriculture and its consequences*. Bloomsbury Academic.

Cochoy, F. (2007). A sociology of market-things: On tending the garden of choices in mass retailing. *The Sociological Review, 55*(2_suppl), 109–129.

Coveney, J. (2006). *Food, morals and meaning: The pleasure and anxiety of eating*. Routledge.

Cowan, R. S. (1983). *More work for mother: The ironies of household technology from the open hearth to the microwave*. Basic Books.

Daniels, A. K. (1987). Invisible work. *Social Problems, 34*(5), 403–415.

Denis, J., & Pontille, D. (2015). Material ordering and the care of things. *Science, Technology, & Human Values, 40*(3), 338–367.

de Wilde, M. (2020). "A heat pump needs a bit of care": On maintainability and repairing gender–technology relations. *Science, Technology, & Human Values, 46*(6), 1261–1285.

Domínguez-Guzmán, C., Verzijl, A., Zwarteveen, M., & Mol, A. (2021). Caring for water in Northern Peru: On fragile infrastructures and the diverse work involved in irrigation. *Environment and Planning E: Nature and Space, 5*(4), 2153–2171.

Edensor, T. (2011). Entangled agencies, material networks and repair in a building assemblage: The mutable stone of Saint Ann's Church, Manchester 1. *Transactions of the Institute of British Geographers, 36*(2), 238–252.

Egbert, D. D. (1967). The idea of "avant-garde" in art and politics. *American Historical Review, 73*(2), 339–366.

Frohlich, X. (2017). The informational turn in food politics: The US FDA's nutrition label as information infrastructure. *Social Studies of Science, 47*(2), 145–171.

Jones, S., & Yarrow, T. (2013). Crafting authenticity: An ethnography of conservation practice. *Journal of Material Culture, 18*(1), 3–26.

Law, J. (2009). Seeing like a survey. *Cultural Sociology, 3*(2), 239–256.

Mol, A. (2008). *The logic of care: Health and the problem of patient choice*. Routledge.

Mol, A. (2013). Mind your plate! The ontonorms of Dutch dieting. *Social Studies of Science, 43*(3), 379–396.

Mol, A. (2021). *Eating in theory*. Duke University Press.

Mol, A., Moser, I., & Pols, J. (Eds.). (2010). *Care in practice: On tinkering in clinics, homes and farms* (Vol. 8). transcript Verlag.

Pollan, M. (2002). *The botany of desire: A plant's-eye view of the world*. Random House.

Pols, J. (2006). Accounting and washing: Good care in long-term psychiatry. *Science, Technology, & Human Values, 31*(4), 409–430.

Puig De La Bellacasa, M. (2015). Making time for soil: Technoscientific futurity and the pace of care. *Social Studies of Science, 45*(5), 691–716.

Sexton, A. E., Garnett, T., & Lorimer, J. (2019). Framing the future of food: The contested promises of alternative proteins. *Environment and Planning E: Nature and Space, 2*(1), 47–72.

Star, S. L., & Strauss, A. (1999). Layers of silence, arenas of voice: The ecology of visible and invisible work. *Computer Supported Cooperative Work (CSCW), 8*(1), 9–30.

Tousignant, N. (2020). Toxic residues of Senegal's peanut economy. *Anthropology Today, 36*(6), 5–8.

Vogel, E. (2016). Clinical specificities in obesity care: The transformations and dissolution of "will" and "drives." *Health Care Analysis, 24*(4), 321–337.

Vogel, E., & Mol, A. (2014). Enjoy your food: On losing weight and taking pleasure. *Sociology of Health & Illness, 36*(2), 305–317.

Yates-Doerr, E. (2015). *The weight of obesity: Hunger and health in Postwar Guatemala*. University of California Press.

Yurchak, A. (2015). Bodies of Lenin: The hidden science of communist sovereignty. *Representations, 129*(1), 116–157.

Zabinski, C. (2021). *Amber waves: The extraordinary biography of wheat, from wild grass to world megacrop*. University of Chicago Press.

3 CARE AS ATTENTION TO FRAGILITY AND CONFRONTING RESISTANCE: PARENTS' NARRATIVES OF CARE PRACTICES WITH MULTIPLY DISABLED CHILDREN

MYRIAM WINANCE

> With what energy, what patience, what rage, what intransigence must we arm ourselves to face the multiple disabilities of our child?
>
> Multiple disabilities? "Significant multifaceted disability with severe or profound motor and mental impairments leading to major restrictions on autonomy and perceptual, expressive and social abilities." (Definition suggested in Annex XXIV (ter) of the statute of October 29, 1989).
>
> The definition intellectualizes the thing, makes it presentable and even ordinary, but are we aware of what a multiply disabled child is, what they go through on a daily basis, of the 'miracles' their family accomplishes at each moment to sustain a given or specific life (in French, "une vie donnée"[1]) that is unable to sustain itself? (Saby 2009, 7–8)

This citation is taken from the preface of the book by Annie Saby, mother of a multiply disabled little girl, Claire. From the outset, Colette Sapin, the author of the preface and a special education teacher, gets the reader's attention. In France, the term "polyhandicapped" is used to refer to children or adults with "profound intellectual and multiple disabilities."[2] It was defined in the regulatory text cited above.[3] It emphasizes the multiplicity of impairments and the restriction of autonomy. However, for the author, this definition says nothing "about the nature of a multiply disabled child." She then uses a compelling word—"miracle"—to describe the nature of support work carried out by the family, as though this work required superhuman effort, verging on the impossible. Finally, she evokes a "given or specific life" that is unable "to sustain itself." Here, the author joins thinking related to the ethics of care (Kittay 2011, 2019; Ruddick 1980; Tronto 1993). According to this approach, "we are all some mother's child" (Kittay 1999). In order to live, every child needs the care of a mother. This adage focuses attention on the essential vulnerability of each person. For philosophers of the ethics of care, this notion of vulnerability refers to the situation of dependency everyone experiences at one time or another during their lifetime and the resulting need for care. In this sense, vulnerability is a condition shared by all. In this chapter, I draw on the ethics of care to analyze the specific support work performed by parents of a multiply disabled child. However, I suggest carrying out a dual shift in relation to this current.

The first, suggested by this joint publication, is a shift toward the notion of fragility. The use of this term results from a pragmatist approach (Hennion 2019; Hennion and Monnin 2020) whose objective is to describe the concrete and wide-ranging variations of fragility. While this is a shared condition, it is not a common or essential characteristic. However, it gains meaning and form in the range of situations. In other words, while we are all some mother's child, we are not all equally vulnerable. Rather, we are fragile in specific ways. Multiply disabled children, like all children, depend for life on care given by someone else. Nevertheless, their dependency is special compared to that of other children. Kittay (1999, 2019), a philosopher of care, has studied certain aspects of this specificity. Drawing on her own experience as the mother of a multiply disabled child,[4] she has highlighted the temporal dimension of long-term dependency. For multiply disabled children, the dependency that defines every human being lasts a lifetime. Usually, their dependency does not develop into interdependent relationships with others or inverted roles. In addition, Kittay describes this dependency as inevitable to the extent that it is linked to biological limitations.[5] Finally, she suggests that each situation of dependency is unique, without, however, empirically analyzing this uniqueness. Continuing her line of thinking, the initial question addressed in this chapter will be to explore the way the fragility of multiply disabled children acquires a particular form in the care relationship. My hypothesis is that their specific fragility is due not solely to their unavoidable biological condition but also to different forms of resistance that emerge in the relationship and which characterize these children a posteriori. Analyzing their fragility requires analyzing their forms of resistance as well.

The second shift I will make concerns the concept of care. Increasingly, this is used in a broad sense to describe a variety of practices (Martin 2008). This broad use cancels out not only the actual diversity of practices but also the ambivalence of some of them (Duclos and Criado 2020). Therefore, the second issue addressed in this chapter will be the nature of support work done by parents. Why is this work described in terms of a "miracle" by Sapin? What are the various characteristics of this work? How is this work similar to or distinct from support work carried out by any parent? What are its objectives? Answering these questions leads me to explore the tensions—inherent in any support work—between maintaining and developing. Giving support to a particular life or experience "is not to render more fixed and ordinary a 'same' experience, but to enable it to transform itself, to make it live by giving it greater consistency, intensity and interest: in other words, it endures because, on the contrary, it is constantly renewed, it is never the same" (Hennion and Monnin 2020, 13). In the case of parental care, this tension is especially high, since, as noted by Sapin, it's a question of "supporting a given or specific life": the life of the child is both given and to be developed. Analyzing this tension amounts to analyzing the tension suggested above between fragility and resistance. I will show that the support work done by parents manifests itself as both the attention given to different forms taken by the child's fragility and as confrontation with different forms of resistance. In other words, fragility will not be considered as the reverse side of resistance but rather as inherent to it, and vice versa. Both of them create, and are created by, the relationship of dependency between the parent and the child. Furthermore, by manifesting itself through its attention to the fragilities and forms of resistance of the child, support work brings out and shapes the qualities of the child and those of the parent. It is in this fragility–resistance dynamic that the child and the parent become "what they are" and are "what they become": special parents and children, defined by specific qualities. I will use the concept of "qualification" to describe this process through which the parent and the child are correlatively endowed with unique qualities, including fragility, which at certain moments becomes a characteristic of the child and of the parent. My use of this concept draws on the observation by Macé (2013, 2016) relative to forms of life and to what she suggests calling "a qualified life." According to this author, a qualified life is both a life that is the object of a discourse (described)—a life taken into consideration (Macé 2017; which demands attention and is therefore vulnerable)—as well as a life endowed with qualities (which is worthwhile and has value). The process of qualification revolves around description and evaluation and is constantly being done and redone. In my chapter, I will show that the work of parents is part of such qualification work whose stakes are the existence of their child in all his or her singularity, as well as their own existence as singular parents.

USING NARRATIVES WRITTEN BY PARENTS

This chapter is based on the analysis of a body of twenty-two narratives published in French between 1997 and 2019 by parents of multiply disabled children. Most (seventeen) are written by the mother, with only three by the father and two by both parents. The socio-professional profiles of the authors are varied. However, the majority of the authors work in the social or medical sector or come from intellectual professions (publishing, journalism, etc.). These narratives resemble testimonies in style, describing a life experience as it happened. Generally speaking, the number of testimonies published increased considerably starting in the 1990s. This increase is related to the emergence of a new concept in French literature, whose function is "to do good" and "to repair the world" (Gefen 2017). Intended for the general public, the testimonies ensure this function by creating empathy between people from different backgrounds. The testimonies by parents of multiply disabled children were published primarily starting at the end of the 1990s.[6] They were a part of this literary movement. Marie Garnier (2011), for example, justifies her book by writing "To finally be able to see everyone's view change, for her [her multiply disabled daughter], for them [all multiply disabled children]. How satisfying it is to go to bed at night and say to yourself that you have just done a great thing for the wellbeing of a multitude of persons who were previously invisible, 'unregardable'"(Garnier, 2011, 10).

In writing out these narratives, parents have the common goal of making children with multiple disabilities known to society at large and transforming the way society views them. This objective takes different forms, depending on the parents. Some try to make other people understand their experience and share it. Others want to reflect on what it means for them and to attribute personal or social importance to it. Still others have the main goal of politically defending the cause of multiple disabilities. To meet these objectives, the parents describe in detail their experience and that of their children as they see it. They portray their day-to-day lives. They describe the ways they help and interact with their children. They explain the difficulties they face. The importance of these narratives is thus to provide access to this daily experience of parents with their child. They give us access to care practices and support work carried out by parents described from their perspective. Therefore, the analysis proposed in this chapter is done from the viewpoint of the parents.[7] The following text is composed of three parts. The first deals with keeping alive, the second with developing abilities, and the last with producing speech. These three themes do not encompass an exhaustive analysis of parents' support work, but they allow me to explore the particular fragility of these children as perceived by the parents. To do this, each section will start with an excerpt from one of the narratives, which will be analyzed in detail and put into perspective at times with other excerpts.

KEEPING ONE'S CHILD ALIVE

> She's hungry, I prepare the first bottle of my princess at home. . . . There, there my angel, drink my love! Anaïs starts shaking her head looking for her milk, energetically pushing the nipple of the bottle out of her mouth. She starts crying, she gets annoyed, upset by the bottle from which nothing seems to flow. I shake, I loosen, I increase the rate of flow of the milk, 1, 2, then 3, maximum rate, still nothing, I shake the bottle, a big drop of milk splashes on the back of my hand. It seems to be flowing though, so to make sure I even put the nipple in my mouth, the pungent milk fills my mouth.
>
> What should be done, what's happening?
>
> I begin to panic, as though I hadn't had enough training, the kind that makes it possible to become what I am supposed to be, a mother. . . .
>
> I start the operation over again, I take a new bottle, a different nipple but nothing works, she energetically refuses all my attempts.
>
> I fail miserably in the first face-to-face session, the first duty towards her: feeding her by myself. (Garnier 2011, 20–21)

Keeping a child alive is one of the first challenges of maternal care (Ruddick 1980). Feeding one's baby is part of this challenge; it is one of the basic acts of care that every parent owes a child. Garnier writes that, through this act, her responsibility as a mother is at stake. This act is guided by the usual way of doing things, specific to each society. When these usual ways of doing things are put into practice, they become subject to adjustments (Winance 2006) and tinkering (Mol, Moser, and Pols 2010; Winance 2010). Caring appears as a collective action shared between all members of the collective. It is an open-ended process that requires permanent adaptation and perseverance in order to improve life with disease or to keep this from deteriorating (Mol 2008). This process depends on permanent attention to the child and on a willingness to understand the child's needs, its discomfort, and the reasons it is unable to drink. In this excerpt, Garnier describes her attempts to adjust the way she does things to discover what suits Anaïs. But her narrative enables a deeper analysis of care by showing that tensions between the particular fragility and resistance of a child are inherent in care work.

Garnier's narrative draws attention to an initial form of resistance on the part of the child, which lies in the impossibility of Anaïs to act as she is expected to. At home, parents adjust the way they bottle-feed according to their child's particular condition, but this adjustment is often minimal, since drinking from a bottle is possible for most babies. This adjustment in the way bottle-feeding is done is discreet. It becomes invisible and implicit. It progressively slips into the parents' way of doing things because their baby does what is expected of it. However, Anaïs is unable to drink from her bottle despite adjustments that I would describe as ordinary. She cries, she gets upset, she is hungry, it doesn't work. Anaïs resists. This resistance lies ultimately in the impossibility for her to get the care initiated by her mother. This phase of receiving care is essential to being able to give care. Tronto (1993) analyzed the care process by distinguishing four phases: being concerned, taking charge, giving care, and receiving care. These four phases describe the timeline of the care process and the various dimensions of adequate care. The last phase is the recognition by the caregiver that the care receiver reacts to the care received. Tronto analyzes this phase from the caregiver's perspective. Garnier's narrative adopts this point of view in reproducing the active role of the care receiver. Here, this active part appears in the form of the impossibility of receiving care—what I have described as "resistance." It also enables exploring the consequences of this impossibility to receive care for the continuation of the relationship.

This impossibility causes distress in the parent—a feeling not of sovereign temptation (Blondel and Delzescaux 2018)[8] but rather of helplessness and anxiety because, without this care, the child cannot survive. Above all, this impossibility obliges the parent to abandon what I referred to above as ordinary adjustments and instead to invent a very specific way of doing things. Garnier then continues her narrative. Faced with Anaïs's resistance, she decides to call a doctor. The latter doesn't find a solution and suggests hospitalizing the child. The mother refuses, thinks about it, and then proposes trying *nourettes*. These are single-use disposable baby bottles that Anaïs drank from without difficulty during her stay in the maternity hospital. The doctor agrees to write a note for her to the maternity hospital so she can obtain several emergency *nourettes*. Finally, Anaïs drinks her milk from a *nourette*. "We're saved, she ate, she's had enough, it's over, the nightmare is over. Over? She's full, tired, she sleeps peacefully, everything's okay. Fortunately the hospital gave us several *nourettes*. But later, what are we going to do? We need a lot of them, too many! How can we reuse them? It's impossible to fill them" (Garnier 2011, 23).

The child's resistance transforms the usual process of adjustment and tinkering. The adjustment process becomes obvious, indiscreet, and fragile. The child's resistance forces the mother to explicitly adjust the usual ways of doing things, to transform them radically and permanently. This other way of doing things works; for the time being, Anaïs is saved. But her mother immediately sees the tenuousness of the care and the collective effort put in place and essential for carrying out this care. She immediately sees the work and energy necessary to organize this collective effort and the difficulties that may arise. Finding sufficient new *nourettes* by making the rounds of all the maternity hospitals is not possible. She then envisions a new adjustment. She tinkers with the single-use *nourettes* in order to reuse them, but this new solution is also fragile. Garnier tells us how one evening, because she was tired out, she forgot to turn off the gas at the end of the sterilization: "The result was that half the *nourettes* melted, it was a disaster, we'll have to go hunting around for *nourettes* again. We'll have to consider a more solid food, start using a spoon much sooner than normal. For the first time we'll be able to boast that Anaïs is ahead for something" (Garnier 2011, 25).

With experimentation and through a process of adjustment, Anaïs's mother envisions and invents a specific way of doing things, a way of caring for her child, but it's tenuous and subject to mishaps, forcing her mother to rethink it, to put in place other approaches, based on a new collective effort of humans and nonhumans that she must hold together. Through the child's resistance, it is fragility that is apparent and which becomes tangible as a "defining characteristic": fragility of the child, fragility of the parent, fragility of the care relationship. Resistance and fragility are both integral parts of this empirical relationship of care and affect the qualification of the child and the parent. This impossibility of receiving care transforms the process of care and then, correlatively, the parent and the child.

This resistance by the child—the impossibility for it to receive care—leads initially to the disqualification of the mother "who doesn't become what she is supposed to be, a mother," and "who fails miserably in her first duty towards her: to feed her unaided." On the other hand, the process of adjustment, which in the long run is a process of learning, qualifies Garnier as a mother. Through this process, she becomes a mother. However, this attribute remains fragile; it can be called into question at any time by the appearance of a new form of resistance by the child or, for example, by the judgments of friends or professionals:

> Today, for the first time, the mothers, the real ones, the professional child-raising specialists as I call them, will go into action. . . .
>
> She's being capricious.
>
> She'll eat when she's hungry. . . .
>
> A bottle is a bottle; poor you, she's playing with you. (Garnier 2011, 23–24)

Similarly, this resistance by the child during care and to care affects the qualification of the child. Further on in the text, Garnier explains that she understood why "Anaïs liked the *nourettes*, it flowed by itself, there was no effort to be made, the height of irony was that Anaïs didn't know how to suck" (23–24). In this case, she linked Anaïs's resistance to a physical inability[9] and qualifies this inability as "the first difference" associated with the different bottles ("small ones" or "normal ones"). In other situations, parents link this resistance to a child's pain, to a desire, a feeling, to the child's stubbornness, and so on and always in the context of relative uncertainty and vagueness. Sometimes, the child's resistance remains unexplained. Finally, it is interesting to observe that the interpretation by Anaïs's mother, in terms of inabilities, differs from the interpretations in terms of capriciousness suggested by those around her. An interpretation in terms of capriciousness would have given a very different direction to her actions. Anaïs's resistance led her mother not only to adjust to it but also to look for and identify an origin, a cause, a reason, and so forth to this resistance. By doing this, she identifies it; she gives it tangible form. This is one of the difficulties of parental support work, since this identification is always uncertain but gives direction to action.

Finally, parents describe how the resistance of the child to care, notably to basic care, forces them to be attentive to what this particular relationship contains and engenders, on the one hand, and to the qualities of the child, on the other. Having become sensitive to the richness of this relationship, as a care relationship, they discover a certain number of values such as attentiveness, patience, joy, and love, and in return, this relationship endows not only the child but also the parent with special qualities. It defines them in a certain way. Their descriptions are thus surprisingly close to reflections on the ethics of care, insisting on the ability of the child to "love and be loved" and situating the child and the parent in an "affective" register.

> The atmosphere in our life with Fiona is joyful and filled with sweetness. Over the years, we have become as dependent on her as she is on us. It's a fusion that is difficult to express and the key word is love. Fiona is the oxygen that keeps us alive, the presence that soothes us, the fighter that boosts us. Decisive, funny, seductive, cheerful, playful, and lively, she offers us her happiness in life, and in her constant contact, we learn the meaning of life. (Delmee 2015, 70)

The child's resistance forces the mother to be attentive to the particularities of the child and to become involved in a process of adjustment. Conversely, it is through this process that the qualities of the child and the parent are specified: that they become "parent" and "child," one for the other and each one by the other, without it being possible to determine who qualifies the other. If care is giving attention to the singular fragility of the child and a confrontation with its singular resistance, it is also, conversely and correlatively, what brings out and specifies the agency and the singular qualities of the child.

RAISING THE CHILD: DEVELOPING HIS OR HER ABILITIES

> I leave you the time to put your toothbrush under the stream of water. You look at the water flowing on your toothbrush, you are proud to do it by yourself. You accept to take it out so I can put a little toothpaste on it. . . . I start to brush; the left side isn't too difficult to do. . . . Above, on the right, your jaw suddenly refuses the intrusion. . . . So I dissemble like a Sioux. . . . Then comes the fun time: drink a little water from the cup and spit it back out if you can. You take in the water and you swallow it. I scold you and ask you to spit it out again: you start over, without results. Then, in the mirror, I show you what I want you to do. You laugh out loud and say: again! . . . You happily try it, you sputter into the lavatory, and I say: bravo! . . . And so every day, over the years. We nibble little bits of autonomy, obstinately, courageously. (Saby 2009, 18–19)

Caring for one's child is not only keeping them alive but also helping them grow. This means allowing their development; helping them gradually acquire certain physical, mental, and social abilities; and working toward their autonomy. This is true for any child, including the multiply disabled child. Every parent knows only too well that their baby is dependent on them but that their role is to make them into an autonomous adult. Autonomy, which is at the heart of demands by the disability movement (Barnes 2015; Morris 2004; Reindal 1999), exists as a normative ideal for all parents.[10] It's a goal to be achieved and a daily guide for their actions. Saby mentions this at the end of the excerpt. Education and care are thus interwoven. The education of all children begins during these moments of care, such as a meal, brushing teeth, and going to bed. It's during and through the care relationship that we teach the child to become autonomous. As philosophers of care ethics have argued, autonomy is relational (Davy 2019; Hennion et al. 2012; Mackenzie and Stoljar 2000)—that is, it is anchored in these care relationships in two ways. First, this anchoring happens on a daily basis, linked to the distribution/allocation of activities into a collective. Second, it is temporal, associated with some learning task. On each of these points, the narrative by Saby and those of other parents encourage us to continue our analysis of care, which we defined in the preceding section as paying attention to fragility and confronting the child's resistance.

In Saby's narrative, autonomy refers primarily to the ability to do things alone and, sometimes, the ability to decide. At the beginning and end of the session, Claire is the person doing things. Her mother watches and waits. She describes her support as discreet and Claire as the one who decides, directs the action, and acts. She explains to the reader the pride this gives Claire to thus be the one to take the initiative. But since Claire can't brush her teeth correctly, her mother describes how she takes over. She does things for her, hoping that progressively Claire goes a bit further in doing things alone. At the end of the session, her "bravo" of congratulations is a sign of recognition that Claire "did it," even though the presence of her mother and her help were necessary. In this way, the narrative makes apparent the dynamics of "distribution/attribution" of the action. The action is always distributed. It involves a collective composed of hybrid entities (Latour 1993; Law and Moser 1999). Autonomy, then, is a result of a process of attribution of the action to a subject, thanks to which he or she is recognized as being the initiator of the action, whether that is in terms of "choosing," "doing," or "deciding" (Pols 2006). Working on the child's autonomy means working on this attribution of the action by making its distribution disappear and making the relationships that support it inconspicuous. This attribution of the action to the child is done in practice on a daily basis and, in this particular instance, through the narrative. But Saby's narrative also enables us to see the laborious aspect this process has in Claire's case.

This process is difficult[11] because, at times, the child resists. Resistance by the child, in this case, happens differently from the example of Anaïs. More specifically, the mother describes this resistance differently by attributing their own agency to certain entities, such as Claire's jaw or to Claire herself. When she describes a distributed activity, she describes the work necessary for guiding the action toward teeth brushing at the same time. She says that this dynamic includes a part of "letting go" or "letting do" on both sides. The ability of the mother to turn what can be a disagreeable moment into a moment of pleasure thus resides in the attention she pays to various examples of resistance during the activity. It resides in her ability to transform the child's resistance into participation in the activity, into "an ability to brush her teeth," which she hopes will one day become "the ability to brush her teeth by herself." While action may result from a situation of indeterminacy, from an interweaving of relationships that make things happen without it being apparent who is acting and who is acted upon (Hennion 2017; Latour 1999), action is also gradually determined by the support work of parents (on a daily basis and in the narrative), according to the nature and abilities of the child or the mother. For Claire, as for most multiply disabled children, this process of qualification for the child and the parent is spread out over time: daily time, the extensive time of life, and the biographical time of the narrative. In addition, the process remains unfinished. It remains associated with the support work of the parents, hence the fragility of the abilities and correlative qualities of the child and the parent.

Indeed, for the multiply disabled child, the process of developing their abilities takes on a specific scope and temporal dimension. Julie's mother summarizes the process in this way:

> All of these steps [learning to move about, toilet training, communicating, behaving in a certain way, expressing and controlling one's feelings, etc.], so natural and obvious in other children, become real challenges with Julie. . . . We could talk for hours about this obligatory dance, one step forward, one step back. Julie's disability, associated with multiple and unpredictable medical complications, showed us, in

> its own way, the instability of life. Nothing is ever certain or taken for granted. Each day, it is necessary to question events, their meaning and what they can represent for the other person, the so-called deficient. (Auber and Auber 2013, 89–93)

Moving about, being toilet trained, behaving properly, expressing one's feelings, and so forth are abilities that the child acquires progressively with the help of its parents. For Julie, these abilities remain fragile. Each achievement may collapse at any moment, and the child can regress. The fragility of these abilities depends on the work of support, always necessary and repeated day after day. Each achievement is based on daily support that attempts to bring about enduring change. As the child grows, the parents are transformed at the same time.[12] But in Julie's case, and for multiply disabled children, the direction of this transformation is always uncertain[13]—hence the need, mentioned at the end of the quotation by Julie's mother, for the parents to question themselves constantly, to doubt themselves and their child as well, to ask questions about what is happening, about the way they have qualified the child. Again, the fragility of the child is the fragility of the parent. The act of writing a narrative emerges as an extension of the support work carried out daily and as an integral part of this work. The parents thus give shape to the specific fragility–resistance tension that characterizes their relationship with the child.

CONFERRING EXISTENCE THROUGH WORDS

> My name is Armelle. This is my book, I composed it from my life, but I didn't write it! Because I don't know how to write. . . . So it's my father who takes up the pen for me. Or rather, let's be clear, he writes from his own position; that of a father, with his vision of a father. . . . This book is a bit like a diary that reports on words I don't dare speak in real life. And who can really say what might be the thoughts of a young woman like me, not quite like the others. . . . It's a delicate task: guessing at the words I would speak if I had the ability; there is the risk of being wrong about my impressions, feelings or ideas that, by necessity, I leave unspoken. (Belluteau 2009, 7)

Most multiply disabled children, the focus here, are children who don't speak, who communicate primarily by means other than spoken language.[14] Faced with a child who speaks little or not at all, speaking, saying, and writing are both delicate and necessary tasks for their parents[15] and are part of support work owed to the child.[16] The difficulty of the task is related to the asymmetry of the situations between the parents and the children. Parents recognize this asymmetry as a potential source of error, of misunderstanding, even of abuse. If they speak in the name of their child, they do so from their position of parent. None claims to be speaking from the child's position, not even the father cited above who chose to write his narrative by making his daughter speak and using the "I" of his daughter. The concept of asymmetrical reciprocity (Young 1997) helps account for the ambivalent position of parents. According to Young, the ability of partners in a relationship to understand each other is rooted in the recognition of their differences and the irreversibility of their positions. According to her, moral respect flows from this asymmetrical reciprocity. The study of the parents' narratives shows as well that reciprocity and differences do not preexist the relationship but are accomplished by it—by the support work carried out daily by the parents and by their narrative.

Indeed, these parents create the necessity and the possibility of speaking for their child and making their child speak from their daily relationship of dependency. Supporting one's child is thus making him or her exist. Not only is this being attentive to their particularities, but it is also giving them a reality in the care relationship, and for others—the readers—through the narratives. Saby thus wrote:

> We put words to the emotions our child is unable to express rather than the vacuum, the void, the anguish. Speaking for you is to recognize you are alive. Not putting words to what dwells within you is to dismiss you. And yet, there is a great temptation to stop thinking for her, speaking for her. Thinking she is cold and asking her the question, thinking she is sad and suggesting it to her. . . . Until when these mental gymnastics? (Saby 2009, 13–14)

Getting Claire to speak is to bring out her words via a care relationship. Saby's narrative shows the work done daily and that is done again by the act of narrating it. The daily work of putting into words—and the putting into words of daily life—is necessary for Saby and for Belluteau because it has an existential significance. Every day, as in the narratives, the issue for these parents is to help the children develop, to help them exist "in their own realities." It is supporting them without taking their place. It is to let them be what they are (sad, cold, or hot), without imposing one's own definitions. What a child is, his or her personality, is defined by this tension between forms of resistance and forms of fragility found throughout the parents' support work and which the parents describe in their narrative.

TO END

Is the multiply disabled child fragile? This question at the end could have been the question to begin this chapter. I have attempted to show here that the fragility of a multiply disabled child cannot be defined in an a priori manner as though it were a fundamental characteristic of these children. Basically, these children are no more fragile than any other children. But they are fragile relatively—and therefore specifically—speaking. To indicate their fragility, I have tried to describe the daily support work carried out by the parents as depicted in their narrative accounts. I distinguished three purposes of this work: keeping the child alive, helping the child develop, and giving him or her an existence through relationships and in the eyes of others. I have shown that each one of these develops in the form of attention to the child's frailties and through confrontation with elements of his or her resistance.

As with any child, the fragility of multiply disabled children is related to the situation of dependency in which they find themselves. But for them, this is an enduring and unavoidable dependency, as shown by Kittay. As for me, I have emphasized a different aspect of this dependency. It can engender forms of resistance in the care relationship. In return, this resistance transforms the care relationship. This relationship itself becomes fragile, requiring a constantly repeated and renewed work of adjustment on the part of the parents. I have also shown that parents attempt to identify these examples of resistance in everyday life and through narrative. They try to link them to an incapacity or capacity of the child, a pain or another sensation, a desire, a wish, and so on, and in so doing, interpret and perform them as such. The child, through this support work, is then endowed with diverse qualities, which are also specific, and shape his or her personality. In this sense, support work has an existential significance. It makes the child exist as a particular child, without, however, determining what he or she becomes. I have used the notion of qualification to designate this work. Finally, I have shown that this support work involves the parents themselves, in what they are and in their own qualities.

This analysis thus follows a pragmatist approach. According to this position, people (and things) are never "done" but are always "to be done." They exist through support work and dependency relationships. This approach has shown that things and people are shaped through processes of transformation. But it has particularly emphasized the "transformation" dimension—the recurring and unfinished dimension of this work. While following this line of reasoning, in this chapter, I have also tried to emphasize the "formation" dimension. I have insisted on what this support work produces and which is, paradoxically, "a given life" (in the dual sense of granted and unique). In other words, to say that this work has an existential scope is also to say that it has an "essential" scope: it *defines a given state*. Of course, fragility and resistance are not fundamental characteristics of children with multiple disabilities or their parents. But they appear as relative, even correlative, as qualities that define a given state of people. In this sense, children with multiple disabilities and their parents *are* fragile. Or rather fragility characterizes them.

ACKNOWLEDGMENTS

I would like to thank the three coordinators of this book, J. Denis, Fernando Domínguez Rubio, D. Pontille, A. Mol, and S. Bateman for their careful rereading of my chapter. I also thank J. Cook for the translation.

NOTES

1. This expression has two meanings in French: given or specific. A decision based on the text as to which meaning the author gave to this cannot be made—hence the use of two English words to retain the ambiguity.

2. This is the expression most often used in English for designating these people. In place of this expression, I will use the term "multiply disabled." On the one hand, it is closer to the French term "polyhandicapé." On the other, it leaves open the question of the nature of the associated impairments.

3. "Polyhandicap" is a French political category linked to the history of the organization of care for disabled persons (Winance and Barral 2013). Its definition has evolved over time. The regulatory text cited by Sapin was revised in 2017, and the definition was reformulated. The new definition emphasizes the early origins in the brain of the dysfunction; the multiplicity, the severity, and the changing nature of impairments and incapacities; and their consequences for building relationships with the physical and human environments.

4. Today, her daughter is an adult. In her last book, *Learning from My Daughter* (Kittay 2019), she describes her personal history and her philosophical thinking. She recounts how raising a multiply disabled daughter has altered her views on what matters and gives meaning in life.

5. She distinguishes between this unavoidable dependency and a derivative or secondary dependency. This refers to the dependency of the carer, created by the necessity of caring for someone else.

6. Thus the choice of the 1997–2019 period. Before 1997, few narratives by parents of multiply disabled children were published. The end of the 1990s corresponds to a period of change in the representations of and policies concerning disability in France (Winance, Ville, and Ravaud 2007) and, more specifically, concerning multiple disability (Winance and Barral 2013). This dual evolution doubtless contributed to making the publication of this type of testimony possible.

7. We should note that this viewpoint was at one time delegitimized by the disability rights movement, which advocated the possibility for people to speak for themselves and not through the voice of their parents or professionals (Campbell and Oliver 1996; Charlton 1998; Scotch 1988). Some authors of disability studies then demonstrated the importance of reintegrating the voice of parents in the movement (in particular, Brett 2002; Vaughan and Super 2019). In the last section of the chapter, I will again discuss this particular position concerning parents. This position itself teaches us about the tensions relative to fragility–resistance that I want to understand.

8. These authors emphasize the total dependence of the multiply disabled person vis-à-vis others and the radical asymmetry of their positions. The situation of extreme dependency of the multiply disabled person, which they call a situation of "disaid," places the carer in the position of dominance compared to the multiply disabled person and gives them the possibility of deciding alone the norms to be used for defining the accompaniment of the multiply disabled person. Compared with these authors, my position is more nuanced. Like them, and I will come back to this point, I show the asymmetry of the positions between the multiply disabled child and that child's carers—in my case, the parents. This asymmetry leads to power relationships. Nonetheless, contrary to these authors, I defend the idea that the direction of these power relationships is neither predefined nor one way. If parents exercise power over children, the latter also exercise power over their parents. This is one of the forms of "resistance" that I wish to describe. Finally, I hypothesize that the power exercised by parents is not solely one of domination but also has a positive and performative potential: that of helping a child, then an adult, develop their possibilities.

9. This dimension corresponds to the inevitable dependency identified by Kittay.

10. This normative ideal is linked especially to the desire for normality found in all parents (Kittay 2006). This desire for normality is ambivalent. It's the desire that one's child be accepted as both normal and special. Kittay defends the importance of this desire and the possibility of transforming norms to make them more inclusive.

11. Kittay (2019) suggests that every acquisition by a multiply disabled child means the parents have to "move mountains" to achieve progress that is often infinitesimal or even invisible to others.

12. Ruddick (1980, 352) wrote on this subject in reference to maternal practices: "The 'holding,' preserving mother must, in response to change, be simultaneously a changing mother."

13. The same goes for the definition of the child's abilities and disabilities.

14. Through alternative techniques of communication, either based on defined methods or through ways of communicating and understanding proper to the child and those around the child. Often, the two are combined.

15. In her last book, Kittay (2019) again addresses the necessity and difficulty of "speaking for one's child who doesn't talk," referring to the slogan of the disability rights movement "Nothing about us without us." She describes herself as the advocate of her child: "As the mother of a daughter, now an adult, who is disabled in this fashion, I speak as an advocate. Otherwise, my daughter and those who share her disability will be doubly disabled and silenced. So, I am left in the awkward position of speaking of an individual with a disability—needing to speak not only *about* her but, contra the disability dictum, *for* her, and to speak for and about her in a way that captures who she is and does her justice" (Kittay 2019, 7). This citation summarizes the paradox that parents face: "to make the child speak is to speak for it." But the two actions are not the same.

16. According to Ruddick, the third purpose of a mother's care is to socialize her child to make it more acceptable to others. We can hypothesize that the writing by the parents of a narrative furthers this objective while reversing it: the purpose is to socialize society so that it accepts these singular children such as they are.

REFERENCES

Auber, Jeanne, and Tristan Auber. 2013. *Bonjour, jeune beauté*. Montrouge, France: Bayard.

Barnes, Colin. 2015. "Independent Living, Politics and Policy in the United Kingdom: A Social Model." *Review of Disability Studies: An International Journal* 1 (4).

Belluteau, Emmanuel. 2009. *Journal d'une princesse à roulettes*. Paris, France: Desclée de Brouwer.

Blondel, Frédéric, and Sabine Delzescaux. 2018. *Aux confins de la grande dépendance: le polyhandicap, entre reconnaissance et déni d'altérité*. Toulouse, France: Eres.

Brett, Jane. 2002. "The Experience of Disability from the Perspective of Parents of Children with Profound Impairment: Is It Time for an Alternative Model of Disability?" *Disability & Society* 17 (7): 825–843.

Campbell, Jane, and Mike Oliver. 1996. *Disability Politics. Understanding Our Past, Changing Our Future*. London: Routledge.

Charlton, James I. 1998. *Nothing About Us Without Us: Disability Oppression and Empowerment*. Berkeley: University of California Press.

Davy, Laura. 2019. "Between an Ethic of Care and an Ethic of Autonomy." *Angelaki* 24 (3): 101–114.

Delmee, Patricia. 2015. *Pluie de Joie. Hyères*. France: Sudaresnes.

Duclos, Vincent, and Tomás Sánchez Criado. 2020. "Care in Trouble: Ecologies of Support from Below and Beyond." *Medical Anthropology Quarterly* 34 (2): 153–173.

Garnier, Marie. 2011. *Le nid des papillons*. Lyon, France: Baudelaire.

Gefen, Alexandre. 2017. *Réparer le monde: la littérature française face au XXIe siècle*. Paris: José Corti.

Hennion, Antoine. 2017. "Attachments, You Say? . . . How a Concept Collectively Emerges in One Research Group." *Journal of Cultural Economy* 10 (1): 112–121

Hennion, Antoine. 2019. "'Maintenir/Soutenir: De la fragilité comme mode d'existence,' Séminaire de recherche du Centre de sociologie de l'innovation (CSI), 2017–2019." *Pragmata, Revue d'études pragmatistes* (2): 484–499.

Hennion, Antoine, and Alexandre Monnin. 2020. "Du pragmatisme au méliorisme radical: Enquêter dans un monde ouvert, prendre acte de ses fragilités, considérer la possibilité des catastrophes. Introduction au Dossier." *SociologieS*. https://journals.openedition.org/sociologies/13931

Hennion, Antoine, Pierre Vidal-Naquet, Franck Guichet, and Léonie Hénaut. 2012. "Une ethnographie de la relation d'aide: De la ruse à la fiction, ou comment concilier protection et autonomie, rapport de recherche pour la MiRe (DREES), " ENSMP, Paris, France. https://minesparis-psl.hal.science/hal-00722277.

Kittay, Eva Feder. 1999. *Love's Labor: Essays on Women, Equality, and Dependency*. New York: Routledge.

Kittay, Eva Feder. 2006. "Thoughts on the Desire for Normality." In *Surgically shaping children: Technology, ethics, and the pursuit of normality*, edited by Erik Parens, 90–110. Baltimore: Johns Hopkins University Press.

Kittay, Eva Feder. 2011. "The Ethics of Care, Dependence, and Disability." *Ratio Juris* 24 (1): 49–58.

Kittay, Eva Feder. 2019. *Learning from My Daughter: The Value and Care of Disabled Minds*. New York: Oxford University Press.

Latour, Bruno. 1993. *La clef de Berlin et autres leçons d'un amateur de sciences*. Paris: La Découverte.

Latour, Bruno. 1999. "Factures/Fractures From the Concept of Network to the Concept of Attachment." *Res* (36): 20–31

Law, John, and Ingunn Moser. 1999. "Managing, Subjectivities and Desires." *Concepts and Transformation* 4 (3): 249–279.

Macé, Marielle. 2013. "Ways of Reading, Modes of Being." *New Literary History* 44 (2): 213–229.

Macé, Marielle. 2016. *Styles. Critique de nos formes de vie*. Paris: Gallimard.

Macé, Marielle. 2017. *Sidérer, considérer: Migrants en France*. Paris: Verdier.

Mackenzie, Catriona, and Natalie Stoljar, eds. 2000. *Relational Autonomy: Feminist Perspectives on Autonomy, Agency, and the Social Self*. New York: Oxford University Press.

Martin, Claude, 2008. "Qu'est-ce que le social care? Une revue de questions." Revue française de socio-économie (2) : 27–42.

Mol, Annemarie. 2008. *The Logic of Care: Health and the Problem of Patient Choice*. London: Routledge.

Mol, Annemarie, Ingunn Moser, and Jeannette Pols, eds. 2010. *Care in Practice. On Tinkering in Clinics, Homes and Farms*. Bielefeld: transcript Verlag.

Morris, Jenny. 2004. "Independent Living and Community Care: A Disempowering Framework." *Disability & Society* 19 (5) :427–442.

Pols, Jeannette. 2006. "Washing the Citizen: Washing, Cleanliness and Citizenship in Mental Health Care." *Culture, Medicine and Psychiatry* 30 (1): 77–104.

Reindal, Solveig Magnus. 1999. "Independence, Dependence, Interdependence: Some Reflections on the Subject and Personal Autonomy." *Disability & Society* 14 (3): 353–367.

Ruddick, Sara. 1980. "Maternal Thinking." *Feminist Studies* 6 (2): 342–367.

Saby, Annie. 2009. *Le polyhandicap au fil des saisons*. Paris: L'harmattan.

Scotch, Richard K. 1988. "Disability as the Basis for a Social Movement: Advocacy and the Politics of Definition." *Journal of Social Issues* 44 (1): 159–172.

Tronto, Joan. 1993. *Moral Boundaries: A Political Argument for an Ethic of Care*. New York: Routledge.

Vaughan, Kelly P., and Gia Super. 2019. "Theory, Practice, and Perspectives: Disability Studies and Parenting Children with Disabilities." *Disability & Society* 34 (7–8): 1102–1124.

Winance, Myriam. 2006. "Trying out Wheelchair. The Mutual Shaping of People and Devices through Adjustment." *Science, Technology and Human Values* 31 (1): 52–72.

Winance, Myriam. 2010. "Care and Disability. Practices of Experimenting, Tinkering with, and Arranging People and Technical Aids." In *Care in practice. On Tinkering in Clinics, Homes and Farms*, edited by Annemarie Mol, Ingunn Moser, and Jeannette Pols, 93–117. Bielefeld: transcript Verlag.

Winance, Myriam, and Catherine Barral. 2013. "From 'Ineducability' to 'Rare Disabilities.' Evolution and Emergence of Political Categories Involved in Shaping the French Medico-Social Sector." *ALTER—European Journal of Disability Research / Revue Européenne de Recherche sur le Handicap* 7 (4): 244–259.

Winance, Myriam, Isabelle Ville, and Jean-François Ravaud. 2007. "Disability Policies in France: Changes and Tensions between the Category-Based, Universalist and Personalized Approaches." *Scandinavian Journal of Disability Research* 9 (3–4): 160–181.

Young, Iris Marion. 1997. *Intersecting Voices: Dilemmas of Gender, Political Philosophy, and Policy*. Princeton, NJ: Princeton University Press

4 CONVERSATION WITH LUCY SUCHMAN

FERNANDO DOMÍNGUEZ RUBIO (FDR): Can you tell us what you've learned from Annemarie Mol's and Myriam Winance's chapters and what you think the main points of connection and divergence are between them.

LUCY SUCHMAN (LS): I'm thinking about the way that you've framed the volume overall in terms of maintenance and repair and then its division into these parts: Bodies, Environments, Labors, and Politics. In a way, that's the whole point of this research—to talk about one of them, we find ourselves needing to talk about the others. But within that, my assignment is specifically to think through bodies, about fragility as an ineliminable lived condition, and the different forms of elemental care and maintenance and repair through which bodies are kept alive. I am haunted by the knowledge that at this moment when we're speaking, people in many places in the world are on the verge of starving. I'm reading these chapters with this contemporary moment very much in mind, and I know that's influencing my reading.

Annemarie's chapter opens by talking about the politics of the new and the idea of innovation. This is, of course, something that I've thought about, including the dissonance of a growing recognition that the valorization of the new and of technoscientific solutionism is really a politics of destruction. Annemarie questions how we think about the objects of care, in the sense of the subjects receiving care but also the objectifications that are involved, in circumstances where care is always and necessarily relational. Of course, Annemarie Mol has done a great deal, along with others in science and technology studies, to remind us about the relationality of things. Then the question becomes how do we delineate the unit of analysis in studies of care?

And what are the consequences of doing that? This, for me, connects very much with Karen Barad's argument that the constitution of entities is always an act. Entity boundaries are not intrinsic but rather are constituted through the relational practices that generate their delineation. There are times when we delineate the individual body, and it's important to do that, but it's also important to remember that the body is not a self-evidently bounded entity but rather something that we ourselves are engaged in making, with particular consequences. So, if we're thinking about care, both of these chapters are pointing to the question: What is our unit of analysis when thinking about care?

Annemarie is asking what the consequences are of drawing the boundaries in different ways and recognizing those consequences. She also asks what logics of the good inform and animate projects and practices of care. This chapter for me opens the question of who is addressed in calls for care. Whenever there's an address that's to an unspecified audience, I always want to ask who the "we" is, who the "you" is. It's hard for me not to be struck by how, in the cases that Annemarie is studying. the questions are not of access to food but rather of which foods you choose as a purchasing consumer. And the call is to remedy damage done by the commodification of food. The call is basically that you, who are being addressed, those who live in what I think of as the hyper-developed world, need to return to a kind of wholesomeness that's been lost through this commodification. Annemarie also takes us into the realm of the *statistical norm*: what should your height and weight be according to your age and sex. And that norm again presumes that food is available. It's measuring the growth of children for whom precarity is not an issue. The issue is a less than ideal level of nutrition.

What's being maintained is normality—a norm within a very specific, and in this case a relatively privileged, location. She writes: "So, here is my question: How best to attend to the relations between those who are (that which is) being maintained or otherwise cared for and all the others involved in this, who are, for better or worse, tasked with a lot of work, turned into resources, made to disappear from the scene, or full out eliminated?" This is the kind of question where we see how the unit of analysis works to bring some things into presence and render other things absent, which is a central theme for Annemarie.

Two further critical points about Annemarie's chapter. One is that it seems to me that not all goods that are relevant in this discussion are commensurable or reconcilable. There are some moral dilemmas in the prescriptions that Annemarie is reading that are framed as a choice between the well-being of the individual or that of the planet. And this is one of the things she's concerned about: how neoliberalism—I don't think she uses that term, but I would characterize it as neoliberalism—renders this as a matter of individual choice between incommensurable alternatives. We have a kind of trade-off: our security, our well-being, or theirs. Getting out of that kind of thinking is one of the challenges.

And the second point is that one of the things that is made absent—at least in the prescripts that Annemarie is reading—is inequality. Annemarie is suggesting that making inequality absent is how it is consolidated. But I wondered here about the collective. Something else that is being made absent here is a more collective way of thinking. And I don't feel that's being consolidated through its absence. I feel that it is being erased. I'm interested in the argument that things that are made absent are simultaneously consolidated, and I really see that in the case of inequality. If we don't talk about inequality, we are reproducing it. But, on the other hand, if we don't talk about thinking more collectively, we're not reproducing collectivity, we're reproducing individualism. I think there's an interesting tension or contradiction in the way that presence and absence work in different cases.

So, then, to talk about Myriam. I was struck by the fact that both chapters raise questions of how care and maintenance operate in relation to a presumed normal body. In Annemarie's case, it's a body assumed to have access to resources it needs to live and to exercise choice. In Myriam's case, the body is assumed to share ability with a kind of unmarked normal. So, the disabled body is read against the normal. In both cases, I'm struck by the presence of autonomy as an issue. The autonomous body figures particularly in Myriam's chapter. I think of it as a kind of trouble we need to stay with, as Donna Haraway would say. So much of our recent theorizing has been trying to undo autonomy as a good, as a kind of fiction, especially when we talk about maintenance and repair. And yet, in the case Myriam is writing about, there is a value, there's something good here about autonomy, that is hard to dismiss in relation to the ability of a child to brush her teeth or feed herself autonomously. There's an interesting tension then in terms of autonomy. Myriam's work challenges a too-easy deconstruction of autonomy. It's not that I think we need to recover autonomy in the received ways, but we need to recognize that while bodies are always relational and vulnerable, they are not all in the same way. The question, then, is: In what circumstances does the availability of life-sustaining care come to be experienced as extraordinary, as a kind of miracle? Things that are taken for granted in terms of self-care become an enormous project to be achieved.

Another thing that comes out of this chapter is the question of the temporalities of normal care, its expectations of reciprocity. Myriam cites Kittay on fragility with a quote that I really like: "The initial question addressed in this chapter will be to explore the way the fragility of multiply disabled children acquires a particular form in the care relationship. My hypothesis is that their specific fragility is due not solely to their unavoidable biological condition but also to different forms of resistance that emerge in the relationship and which characterize these children a posteriori. Analyzing their fragility requires analyzing their forms of resistance as well." I really like the way she works with this idea of resistance, and she gives us some powerful examples.

I also think it is important that this chapter by Myriam reminds us that against the connotation of maintenance as being about staying the same, sustainability requires continual renewal, inventiveness, and transformation. She writes: "I will show that the support work done by parents manifests itself as both the attention given to different forms taken by the child's fragility and as confrontation with different forms of resistance. In other words, fragility will not be considered as the reverse side of resistance but rather as inherent to it, and vice versa."

Myriam takes us out of the idea that fragility involves a kind of passivity and an absence of resistance. In the cases she's talking about, that's dramatically not true. It's so poignant in the story of Anais that resistance to drinking from a bottle actually threatens hospitalization. It threatens a kind of breakdown of home, of family, if they can't find a way to feed her at home. The structure and relations that constitute a family are under threat. I love what Myriam says about qualification: "a qualified life is both a life that is the object of a discourse (described)—a life taken into consideration (Macé 2017; which demands attention and is therefore vulnerable)—as well as a life endowed with qualities (which is worthwhile and has value)." And also the place of testimony in qualified lives. The narratives by parents that tell these stories and qualify the children's lives are about bringing these children into a kind of recognizable humanity: "the purpose is to socialize society so that it accepts these singular children such as they are."

FDR: How do you think these two chapters relate to your work?

LS: In many ways, these chapters are very far from work that I've been doing. Because they don't foreground technological systems, they really foreground these quite intimate relations, domestic relations. Moreover, my work has recently been about so-called foreign (opposed to domestic) relations. The points of connection are around questions of othering, of the addressee—who the addressee is of discourses that we're interested in, how often the addressee is unmarked, both the locations of the speaker and of the addressee are unmarked.

These considerations are important in the kinds of discourses that I've been looking at recently, which are about the revived promise of artificial intelligence as the technological solution to the problems of maintaining US hegemony, military hegemony. I've thought quite a bit about international humanitarian law and, in particular, the principle of distinction, which is the foundational principle that enables the idea that wars, that just wars could be fought, that killing can be legal. In the context of war, the principle of distinction turns completely on the possibility of distinguishing between those who are in and out of combat. It's a profoundly consequential sorting procedure, which should be enacted in moments of enormous conflict. I feel that we desperately need such legal structures, and at the same time, maintaining their coherence requires making absent a lot of the realities that characterize violent conflict. We've long passed the point of a fiction of a time when there were battlefields, where there were two sides that each wore uniforms, Where you could tell who was a combatant and who was not. That's the kind of narrative fiction that sustains these principles. So, you could also say that the fiction of just war has become increasingly clear.

In that context, we find bodies like the National Security Commission on Artificial Intelligence that promote AI as a machine for making the necessary discriminations. There's an imaginary in the US Department of Defense (DoD) of what they call sensor-to-shooter infrastructure—this fantasy of creating a comprehensive infrastructure of sensors, signal processing, data storage, and data analysis for warfighting. The DoD has built out the infrastructures of surveillance way beyond the point that they can meaningfully analyze the data that they collect. This is an enormous act of magical thinking.

FDR: This point connects the chapters with something that you said at the beginning when you were talking about how entities need to be constituted and that act of constituting an entity always implies making something visible at the expense of making something invisible. Both chapters show us that it is impossible to establish that boundary in a clear-cut way. The result is always messy, and that messiness engenders a tension that can only be resolved in moral terms. But this happens in systems that pretend that this is not happening—systems that pretend to disavow those consequences by translating that irresoluble moral dilemma into a resoluble technical or technological problem. This resonates with your case, where you have a system running on the fantasy that it can disaggregate bodies in a technical way, distinguishing them according to logics of good that do not create any moral issue. This is similar to the kinds of dilemmas that Annemarie talks about in her chapter—with one difference: in your case, it is not a person who has to deal with the tension and arrive at solution but rather an algorithm that "solves" it for us by establishing a firm distinction. But then you said something that was really interesting, which is that these are maybe necessary distinctions—between combatants and civilians—and yet, at the same time, they're impossible, since they are always fraught, imperfect, partial. And we end up caught up in between their necessity and their impossibility.

LS: This is where I think that holding together critique and trying to think generatively about how it could be otherwise is really important. Think of all the work that we've done to undo the autonomous body, to articulate the fiction of the autonomous individual. At the same time, as Myriam's chapter makes so clear, it is necessary to recognize that the world that we inhabit requires us to inhabit the world as if we were individuals—at least in some moments or in some modes—including as individuals who may be systematically excluded. The disability rights movement has been very much about pointing this out—that it's the design of the world that excludes the disabled body. This is the tension of undoing the autonomous individual and also respecting the ways in which the world is organized to require that one is able to enact one's body in an autonomous way, at some times, and similarly, that we need new institutions that enable collective bodies, even if those institutions are also flawed.

I'm thinking here about the United Nations and the laws of war, these normative prescriptions about something that is inevitably chaotic and totally ungovernable. And yet it's really important that we have those collective bodies and legal frameworks. It's incredibly frustrating in the case of the United Nations because, in many ways, it's structured to enable the obstruction of progress. Similarly, the Geneva Conventions and international humanitarian law, human rights law, they presuppose things that are fictions like just war. But, at the same time, they also provide a resource for appeals for accountability, for adjudication. There's an enormous amount of discussion now about the International Criminal Court. The United States generally just blows off the International Criminal Court and doesn't recognize it. We're living with all of these contradictions, and this forces us to stay with that trouble, recognizing that when we're working within those very flawed normative structures we're reinforcing their legitimacy. But also, that we can mobilize them in creative ways and engage in critique that tries to think in more radical ways about legal frameworks and collective bodies.

JÉRÔME DENIS (JD): I was wondering if these two chapters could also be understood as displaying, or facing, the costs of both universality and singularity. Because there is something like the fiction of the universal child that is in Annemarie's work, and the cost of that is what is silenced by this fiction. And there is also the work of recognizing and dealing with a very specific kind of singularity in a world made for this kind of universal child.

LS: Absolutely! This reminds me of Claudia Castañeda's book, *Figurations* (2002), about the figure of the child. The book is a discussion of figuration and how it works both as the historical accretion of significance and as the generative force in variously reproducing or transforming that which is figured. She takes the child as her case. The figure of the child is so central in the discourses of war that I've been looking at. The child is the quintessential innocent. That's why when we hear the statistics about who's dying, "women and children" is the phrase. And I always have mixed feelings about that because I know this is part of the premise that you can sort people into men or combatants, women and children or innocents. There are so many grounds on which we'd want to push back on that. And yet, we need those categories.

As you're saying, the figure of the child is universalized—the figure of the healthy child, the "normal" child. And in particular, I think the tendency for *us*—and when I say "us" here, I mean those of us who are academics within the relatively affluent, largely Euro/Anglo/American world—is to have as our figure of the child those with whom we are familiar. I think this is another important point—that the universal figure gets filled in with the specifics with which we are familiar, and those that are unfamiliar get othered, placed outside the frame. They become the exceptions. Annemarie's chapter is both staying within this normative discourse and critiquing it, whereas Myriam's chapter is bringing us, with the multiply disabled children that she's writing about, inescapably into that specificity. And in so doing, she discloses the achievement of that normativity, that it's not a default. It's an enormous achievement that is usually part of the invisible infrastructures that remain invisible so long as they work. So, the chapter discloses the enormous achievement of being a child who can brush their own teeth. And for that reason, it makes that taken-for-granted universalized figure much more problematic in ways that open it up to rethinking.

FDR: I have a follow-up to that. There is an explicit figure here, which is that of the child, which we are talking about, but there is also another implicit figure: that of the parent. Both chapters talk about parenting. This is interesting because if there's a place in which a simple critique of autonomy cannot fly, it is in parenting. Every parent knows that there is no way of establishing firm distinctions between a right way and a bad way: it is just messiness all the way. A never-ending tension and fragile equilibrium between autonomy and heteronomy. Parenting, in this sense, is a good place to see that fragility is not something that can ever be overcome. Whatever you do, you are enmeshed in this endless quest in which you are pulled between different tensions. There is a constant negotiation that will never be resolved or settled. There is no solution. It is fragile all the way. But this also brings the question of responsibility. Because parenting always implies framing a type of responsibility that can never be solved and will always be fragile, about to be broken.

LS: Yes, I think that's so interesting. While I haven't really thought about the connections between warfighting and parenting, in both cases, there are endless normative prescriptions for how it should be done, for what it should look like—idealizations. And in both cases, those who experience it directly are aware of the irremediable chaos and mess. But that chaos is suppressed in the discourse. What do we make of that? I guess that's a place where it's incredibly important to understand the work that the discourse is doing. What about the slippage between that normative discourse and the realities, the lived realities? What are the openings for challenging the fictions of the normative discourse? Or maybe we don't want to do that entirely. I don't know. It seems to me that anything that sustains the fiction of just war is helpful because so long as wars are being fought, these legal frameworks are incredibly important. But if we want to move away from militarism, then these legal frameworks and the premises of just war on which they rest are part of what sustains war's legitimacy. And I guess, if we think about parenting, well, I don't know, what would the analogy be?

FDR: What I was thinking is that what is interesting about the three cases—the two cases of parenting presented by the chapters and your case about war—is that someone is called to make an adjudication about something that cannot be adjudicated, or something that, whatever the adjudication is, will be fraught and fragile. And yet, someone (or something) is needed to make that call. One of the things that Annemarie mentions is there are these two logics of good, which are not commensurable, and then the parent is asked to make that call between the two, to somehow bridge the incommensurability. In the case of Myriam, the parents and the kids are thrown between all these tensions, but the parent is called to sort something out that is not sortable. And in the case of war, we call upon the UN or any of these bodies to make a decision, to make a call and adjudicate responsibility, to draw boundaries, into something where it is impossible to have any neat boundaries, where there is only the possibility of fragile and contested boundaries.

LS: That's right.—whether it's a technological solution, or it's the individual making a choice, or the international body making the decision. Those are all, in a sense, magical solutions. Where did the need for those adjudications come from? How does that arise? What is implied by making decisions? And how could we reconceptualize the relations in such a way that they would be distributed differently, that the responsibilities would be distributed differently? We'd have a different understanding of any kind of normative prescription and the messy realities of bringing it into relation with some actually existing situation. I think that relationship itself is fragile, the relationship between any kind of prescription and its consequences—basically, how it gets lived out, how it gets enacted, how it gets brought into some kind of effect.

FDR: The two chapters bring forward questions about bodies, how bodies reveal the tension between autonomy, heteronomy, and the common good. And these questions resonate with your earlier work, as well as with your more recent work on how bodies are incorporated into algorithms and military technologies, and how they deal with the question of the common good and autonomy. So, could you talk a bit about how the question of fragility can help us to think about this question.

LS: Well, I feel that we have started to touch on that. Maybe another way to put it is: How do we think about robustness in relation to the understanding of fragility that you're developing? And I think maybe, for me, that comes back to questions of sustainability and of this idea that maintenance is something more than mere reproduction. It is always involving inventiveness. This is an ethnomethodological premise—that every day social orders require continuous reenactment, not in the sense of repetition but in the sense of making something that is arguably the same happen across changing circumstances. In what way is what we're doing recognizably the same thing again? And how does doing the same thing again always require doing it across changing circumstances? What are the politics of reproduction and change? Moving away from this opposition of fragility and robustness, to the question: what's fragility's Other? We could argue that fragility is a kind of robust, an ongoing state of attention, of recognition, of the need to always think, always reinvent that which is of value in the face of different circumstances.

I can, again, turn this either way because if we're talking about artificial intelligence, understanding its reproduction is critical to showing how it keeps reviving itself. But if we're talking about the reproduction of things that we care about, the sustainability of the planet, then our modes of action are folded, enfolded in whatever logics of good we're participating in.. This goes back, in a way, to the opening of Annemarie's chapter in terms of innovation and the politics of those discourses.

DAVID PONTILLE (DP): This is really important. If I remember correctly, where Annemarie criticizes Hannah Arendt is precisely for thinking about reproductive labor as being purely reproductive. The whole point of her recent book, too—and this is mainly what maintenance and repair studies is about—is recognizing the kind of production that is made in reproduction.

LS: In a way, I think that we wouldn't even be preoccupied with maintenance and repair if we weren't immersed in the particular form of commodity capitalism that we are. I think about the case of how, famously, Cubans keep old American cars running. On the other hand, we have the peoples who have lived in what we now call North America before settler colonialism, who've had incredibly long, sustainable habitation with minimal destructive impact on the environment. We're preoccupied with repair and maintenance because everything has been built to fall apart.

FDR: So, we have a final question, which kind of dovetails on this last thought. What do you think about the overall intent of the volume to focus on fragility? Would you think that we can gain from such a move within something, or is there anything to be gained? And what do you think of the limitations or dangers that such problems can create?

LS: One thought is that we could get into trying to develop a vocabulary that distinguishes fragility, care, maintenance, and repair. And I say, *let's not do that.* Let's see how these terms work, what work they do in relation to particular analyses. I think of Steve Jackson and the work that he and colleagues have done to formulate new domains of discussion, of theorization, with respect to repair, in some really generative ways. I think it is best to foreground a concept like fragility so that we can see fragility in multiple places, in multiple senses. What I wouldn't want to see is that now we have new subgroups working on fragilities, and they have to distinguish themselves from the people working on repair or care.

FDR: Like fragility studies, or the fragility turn.

LS: Exactly. And, you know, certain people come to own a term, and instead this volume can help to keep open the question: In what ways are these terms working? In what ways are the connections and the distinctions between them actually helping us to think about the substantive things that we want to think about? Rather than an exercise in planting a new flag or making finer distinctions. So now, our students have to think, "Oh, god, is this fragilities? Or is it, you know, care? Or is it vulnerability?" That would be my one concern. That would be my only caution. But just looking at the way that you frame the volume, I don't think that's what you're up to. I think you're more into further elaborating and expanding the openings that the intersecting ideas of repair, maintenance, and care have generated, which I think is great.

FDR: Well, hopefully that's the case. We most certainly don't want to create the fragilities club or anything of the sort.

JD: There is something really interesting that you said earlier, which can also go with this last point. And this is that maybe fragilities is not an object or a domain but rather something like a concept *to think with.* The idea if we do that is we need to ask ourselves: What is fragility's Other? Because then we have to understand what robustness or strength can be. And we have to make them work all together.

LS: And maybe there's a way of resisting that, of saying, "Look, you know, we realized that offering a term such as this invites the question that I asked, well, what is fragility's Other?" And then if there's a way not to feel that you have to define what robustness would look like, but rather, to fold them together, because I think that's part of what we were getting at—it's the folding together of these terms, their co-constitution, and the way in which that co-constitution is not categorical or definitive, but both qualities are rather within any entity, simultaneously. Language is always asking us to set up these definitive opposites. But I know that part of what you're trying to work with is this space that is about thinking around and through such oppositions.

FDR: One of the things that we would like to do with the book is to invite people into a conversation, not to settle any conversation through definitions. We are trying to escape, as much as possible, from the either/or logic. It is either fragile *or* robust. Such logic misses the messiness of that distinction, and that is the messiness that is articulated in all of the chapters.

LS: That's right. And also recognizing, within that messiness, what work is done through the articulation of those terms, "Ah, you know, this is fragile," "Oh, this is robust," and what are the consequential effects of the articulation of things as one or the other?

FDR: In one of the chapters, Max Liboiron writes something that I really liked, which is that when people frame the Arctic region as fragile, that framing is doing a lot of political work. Because suddenly, that means that it's a space that requires a specific kind of intervention. The same goes for the figure of the kid. Describing a kid as fragile brings about a specific logic and framing of intervention or responsibility. We do not want to define what fragility is. We want to explore what happens when something is described as fragile.

LS: And for better or for worse, right?

II ENVIRONMENTS

5 THE FRAGILITY OF A MIGHTY PROCESS: CAPITAL AND CATTLE MUTUALLY ASSIST THEIR REPRODUCTION

MARISOL DE LA CADENA AND SANTIAGO MARTÍNEZ MEDINA

Lylehaven Lila Z is a Canadian Holstein also known as the "million-dollar cow."[1] Cows have a gestation period of nine months and have one calf a year. However, Lila has sixty-seven offspring registered in Canada and fifty more in the rest of the world, but she is only nine years old. Her secret? A multispecies bio-capitalist technology called "embryo transfer" *and* the value it places on the productivity of her ovaries. Responding to hormonal stimulus, Lila's ovaries generate many eggs, which, with unusual frequency, pair up with the inseminating sperm, resulting in an unusually high number of embryos. Extracted from Lila, these are transferred to other cows' uteri for their gestation; they will birth calves bequeathed with Lila's ovulatory quality (and superb milk productivity). Enabling Lila's embryo making—and her price tag—is artificial insemination or AI, also used in cutting-edge technologies such as CRISPR to produce genetically edited cows and bulls.

At its most quotidian level and simplest definition, AI is a human-mediated agricultural practice that uses genetically certified bull semen (extracted and turned into a commodity) to impregnate cows, reproduce cattle, and eventually improve the herd. Artificial insemination acquired recognition as an efficient agricultural technology throughout the 1930s. It peaked by the end of World War II, becoming a worldwide boom starting in the 1950s.[2] Confident enthusiasm met the emerging practice: "Some remarkable effects can be produced on animals now that human beings are learning to take charge of the directing glands" (Russell 1966, 336, cited in Clarke 2007, 319). Currently,

FIGURE 5.1
Lylehaven Lila Z, the million-dollar cow.

confidence in the benefit of artificial insemination is internationally shared, its science and know-how imparted in agricultural universities worldwide. A university extension center describes AI as "an Assisted Reproductive Technology (ART) used worldwide to deposit stored semen directly into a cow or heifer's uterus. It is a tool for improving reproductive performance and genetic quality of livestock. This technique is frequently used in the dairy and beef cattle industries to *more rapidly improve desired characteristics through intensive genetic selection*" (emphasis added).[3] The purported capacity to manipulate genetics to accelerate time to improvement may be the key to the popularity of artificial insemination: on farms, the acceleration results in "more productive cattle" and thus greater economic rewards.

Our chapter describes the many practices that compose "artificial insemination" as we saw (and, at times, performed) it on several Colombian farms. On all the farms—humble and wealthy—the goal of AI is to select the genetic makeup of herds to improve milk and meat production. Wealthy farms also use it in combination with embryo transfer to produce exemplars such as Lila, albeit not as extremely productive or internationally known. Thus, while we use the heading "artificial insemination" to name the technique of "deposit[ing] stored semen directly into a cow or heifer's uterus," as in the quotation above, we also include in our conception and description of AI the heterogeneous practices it requires and those that require AI. Among the former, we look at the detection of cows' heat and bulls' semen "collection" (obviously, there is no AI without both!). Among the latter, we look at embryo transfer—a practice that uses genetics to accelerate cattle reproduction by increasing its numbers.

Artificial insemination is indeed an "assisted reproductive technology" (as mentioned in the quotation above), but it is one that exceeds its description in the same quotation. The assisted reproduction of bovines is a complicated technology, which through a vast number of practices connects laboratories, heterogeneous markets, and farms through the animal and human bodies that work in all three. Through this thickly layered technology, cattle *and* capital *mutually assist each other's reproduction.* Using and revamping the shared etymology of these two words—cattle and capital—mutually assisted reproduction (MAR) is our ethnographic-conceptual tool to interrogate a multispecies technology whereby, through the skillful handling of life-producing substances (semen, ovulatory eggs, and embryos) as well as their lodging organs (uteri, penises, and vaginas) and enabled by a partnership with science, cattle and capital recursively become each other.[4] As semen and embryos extracted from bulls and cows (contained in small plastic vials called *pajillas* in Spanish, "straws" in English) circulate as commodities to reproduce cattle, they also reproduce capital: they assist each other's becoming. Potentially endlessly, parts of one become part of the other in mutual reproduction. Mutually assisted reproduction bears similarities with what Moore calls the "double internality" of nature and capitalism, whereby the latter reproduces itself by compelling the former to "work harder and harder for free or at a very low cost" (2015, 23). Similarly, mutually assisted reproduction describes a process through which capital enters "the web of life" (Moore's phrase) as it makes—and makes itself into cattle.[5] The photo of Lila Z bearing her price tag offers eloquent illustration! Yet, this photo suggests an ethnographic conceptual observation that adds to Moore's "double internality": as they recursively emerge from MAR, capital and cattle are themselves (and each of them) multispecies compositions.[6]

A circuit of humans and nonhumans capable of translating heterogeneities (bulls' and cows' life substances, human and nonhuman labor, and knowledges) into multispecies capital, assisted reproduction of cattle (and of livestock in general) is a potent biotechnology. At its inception is the fastening together of epistemic, biological, and economic conceptions of "cattle" shaping the reproductive possibilities of cows and bulls (and transforming farm life forever) is at its culmination.[7] Yet, nothing short of perfect human–cow/bull encounters—their flawlessness—is required for cattle to become capital and vice versa. The requirement of perfection extends to all that enables their encounter: tools, life substances, chemical mediums, infrastructures, bacteria. Not paradoxically, but not obvious either—for the practice exudes reproductive might—the encounters (and their sheer possibility of success) are also sites of the fragility of MAR. Chemical, photothermal, bacterial, temporal, and sensorial mishaps haunt the process, which thus needs to include protective measures. In the words of the university extension center cited above, "closely following the recommended protocol is essential for the process to be successful."[8] However, mishaps lurk and, worst of all, emerge from unknown (usually genetic) possibilities—those that protocols cannot control.

Take Arlinda Chief, a Holstein bull who (like Lila Z) was famous for his genetic prowess—used in insemination, his semen transmitted it. "Born in 1962, he produced 16,000 daughters, 500,000 granddaughters, and more than 2 million great-granddaughters. His sons were also popular sires." Yet, he is also known as "one of the Holstein bulls that caused the most damage to the breed."[9] Used year after year, at some point in its commercially expansive circulation, Arlinda Chief's successful semen inadvertently combined faultily to generate and introduce a lethal gene into the global Holstein dairy population that was identified after many generations had been bred with it. The discovery of the mutation revealed the possibility of controlling it (removing the allele that triggered the mutation), but by then it had caused an estimated half million spontaneous abortions worldwide. Genetic "flaws" such as Arlinda's can be retrospectively identified and repaired. Nevertheless, their unpredictability reveals the fragility of MAR, its powerful scientific and economic infrastructure notwithstanding. Clearly, the fragility of MAR does not necessarily indicate its weakness. Rather, it is an always-present possibility that manifests itself in a process which, robust as it is, may be exceeded in its capacity to know and control potential breakdowns.[10] This "excess"—that which slips out, sneaks in, or is unknown until it reveals itself—is an inevitable aspect of MAR as is therefore its fragility. Imponderable and ever present, excess usually dislocates the perfection of human–cow/bull connections that enable cattle as capital and vice versa. As the case of Arlinda Chief shows, fragility may have effects at any temporal and geographical scale, regardless of the size, materiality, or location of the "excess" itself. Shown by the same case, neither human utmost scientific practices nor the animals' experienced participation can shield MAR from excesses: fragility pulsates throughout this technology. Detailed protocols efficiently take this pulse but, as said, cannot predict the unknown, be it genetic, bacterial, or microbial.

Below, we describe the practices we learned in several Colombian dairy farms in order to discuss some of the fragilities that pulsate in MAR. All farms, wealthy and poor, artificially inseminate cows. Most farms buy "semen straws" produced nationally or internationally. Some wealthy farms use semen collected from their own bulls. Differently, less well-off farms stay away from embryo transfer, whereas well-off farms engage in it. In order of exposition, we discuss the detection of cows' heat, semen collection, artificial insemination, and embryo transfer. We have practiced each, talked to people, and spent time looking at and listening to cows and a few bulls. As a multispecies circuit, MAR necessitates cows' and bulls' flawless (even if many times unwilling) participation. Achieving it guides most practices and shapes human–nonhuman relations and farm life.

PRODUCING WHAT MAR NEEDS: MULTISPECIES OVULATORY AND EJACULATORY CAPITAL

A practice based on the sexual reproduction of cows and bulls, MAR rests on a heterosexual farm imaginary that it also creates. Contradicting it, however, farms are also everyday stages of frequent same-sex mounting among cows and among bulls. Farmers include this behavior (usually labeled "homosexual") in their technical toolkit. Among cows, mounting indicates heat and thus time to insemination (more about this momentarily). Young bulls known as teasers are used "to arouse mature bulls and collect their semen used for insemination," writes biologist Bruce Bagemihl (1999, 117). He adds:

> Homosexual activity is so routine among domesticated hoofed mammals that farmers and animal breeders have coined special terms for such behavior: mounting among male cattle is referred to as the "buller syndrome" (steers who are mounted are called "bullers", the males who mount them are "riders"), female sows who mount each other are described as "going boaring," mares who do so are said to "horse," while cows are said to "bull." (Bagemihl 1999, 117)

We have heard and seen similarly on farms. We do not use local terms to avoid extending histories of human sexuality for what may queer some human worlds we have seen as everyday life among bovines. Same-sex activities in corrals are joyous arousal and play—that is how we name them.[11] They call up human intervention toward fertilizing encounters between semen and egg, which, to state the obvious again, is not among the reason for the joyous play among cows or bulls. Such is, instead, the explicit goal of mutually assisted reproduction of cattle and capital: bulls' semen and cows' eggs must be channeled into sexual reproduction, even if it is not the inexorable destiny of these substances.[12] Yet, when thus intended, they must first be "collected" to then acquire value as they circulate in a bio-market and become "ejaculatory" and "ovulatory" capital—multispecies compositions that then enter the circuit of MAR to recursively make cattle (as said, also a multispecies composition).[13]

The recursive mutuality of cattle and capital reproduction is sustained by an obvious asymmetric multispecies connection: MAR requires human control of (and thus participation in) the bodily capacities of cows and bulls that produce the "raw materials" of reproduction and which capital appropriates. With Paul B. Preciado, we name those bodily capacities' *potentia gaudendi*, accordingly, the "strength of the body's (total) excitation," "an orgasmic force," and, we paraphrase, the capacity of a human or animal body to replete itself with joyful intensity throughout and to produce such joy endlessly without depletion (Preciado 2013, 48). As we see it, *potentia gaudendi* is a bodily faculty that, albeit differently, humans and cows/bulls share. On farms, it manifests as mounting sprees, joyous same-sex play which humans interrupt and channel into mutually assisted reproduction.[14] As the reader can imagine, arresting the intense joy vitalizing the body of a cow or bull to capture the substances connected to that vitality is difficult, rife with the tension of multiple risks: the human body has to interfere perfectly in the cows' joy, for an instant of failure, can risk reproducing cattle and, eventually, its mutuality with capital.

MAR requires and organizes reproductive heterosex: occupying different corrals, cows and bulls are classified as biologically females and males to be connected through a human-mediated, reproductive relation. Still, nothing in MAR is exclusively in human hands or will, and heterosexing is not an exception: it requires cows' and bulls' collaboration with their handlers.[15] And this needs the kind of relaxed mutual trust that results from the constant sharing (of spaces, schedules, actions) and familiarity with each other's habits, smells, sounds, and preferences. As we shall see, the know-hows and collaborations that MAR rests on—lay and scientific, or their combination—are textured by intimacy, which perhaps surprisingly is also an important protection against the fragility of the process.

DENOUNCING HEAT: ARRESTING JOY AND CAPTURING TIME TO FERTILIZATION

When cows are in heat, the corral is a mess. Cows in heat touch each other, rub their chins on other cows' butts, and moo frequently and loudly. Behind a fence, a human onlooker watches attentively, following expressions of joy in the corral, calculating which cow is the one in heat and when that heat started. He follows known signs: restless, a cow in heat suspends rumination and instead walks or runs incessantly, obsessively. Cows know when a cow is in heat, *en celo* and they have a distinct relation with her; contacts with her intensify, many cows want to play with her, and she willingly plays with them. For the human overseers, however, identifying "the" source of joy in the corral is a difficult task: what they may see is bodies knotted in movement, up and down, going in circles. The unequivocal sign comes when movement stops, as the cow in heat stands still, allowing her companions—one or many—to mount her. At this point, the human watcher decisively walks into the corral, moves among the cows dexterously, and pulls the cow in question away. This calls off all play.[16]

"To denounce heat is *ex-tre-me-ly-im-por-tant;* your farm's efficiency depends on it," says the leader of a workshop we attended along with employees of some big farms. Identifying the exact moment of each of their cows' heat (to "denounce" it) impacts their successful insemination, fertilization, and reproduction. "If cows are not in heat proper, nobody, not even a big bull, can successfully mount them, let alone inseminate them." A cow decides the moment of copulation by "standing still": "it is the moment when she shows complete acceptance of the bull." When using AI, a cow "standing still" for other cows indicates the moment for human intervention in the corral, the end of riotous joy. An egg is ready to meet a sperm—the moment has to be seized.[17] Cow stillness is a fleeting moment, our untrained eyes could not spot the still cow among the knot of bodies. "Denouncing heat is about catching *sólo tres segundos* (three seconds only), if you do not *see* [that moment] for *as many cows as you can* [relative to the size of the farm's herd], your insemination program fails." Missing this moment means a waste in the ovulatory cycle, a missed opportunity to inseminate, a longer interval between pregnancies for that cow. Known as "open days," the interval implies a cow's empty uterus.[18] Within the logic of MAR, unwarranted open days correlate negatively with the farm's economy. They reflect a waste of time in the procreative potential of a cow and indicate a timing error in the human–cow reproductive circuit. This upsets the opportune insemination of a cow, who, in the absence of timely assistance, fails to assist the reproduction of cattle/capital.[19] These temporal glitches are both controllable and inexorable. Apparent since this ground zero moment, shielding MAR from fragility (by controlling sites of known possible breakdowns) is also one of its constitutive features.

"To understand what is going on *outside*, it is important to know how a cow functions *inside*," the workshop leader tells the audience (us included.) He then translates heat/*celos*—what we have identified as the cow's joy—into medical reproductive language: "heat is produced by estrogen; it is how the cow expresses the estrus cycle." The best hormonal environment for egg and sperm to meet successfully and produce an embryo happens "twelve to eighteen hours after observing the *monta estática*," he instructs. Called "day 0 of the estrous cycle," *monta estática*, the moment when a cow "stands still" (and, we propose, reveals pleasure) tells humans to start the countdown to the exact insemination time.[20] Timing the fertilization of egg and sperm to produce an embryo—an impressive practice of control—needs to be tightly observed to reproduce cattle/capital successfully.

When onlookers "denounce heat," they tell which cow stood still and, just as importantly, *when* it happened. The timing of heat indicates when the egg will be at its most favorable position to receive the sperm and conceive an embryo—a future calf. The success of this encounter—the event of fertilization—demands constant surveillance of the corral: "at least thirty minutes, three times daily" is the recommendation we heard at the workshop. The attention to time that the human–cow reproductive coordination of MAR requires starts with absolute precision in "denouncing heat." "Insemination has to happen between twelve and eighteen hours after the *first monta estática*, and this means that we have to know, with close precision, the time when those three seconds of stillness happened," we hear the workshop leader again. Yet, the task is full of potential mishaps that can happen anytime and anywhere and which can originate with anyone in the process, including the cows of course. Cows have different personalities, "express their heat" (a frequent phrase in farms) heterogeneously in both duration and intensity. "Heat can last anywhere between eight to thirty hours, and during this period cows actively mount others and accept being mounted—but they are all different. In one hour, a demure cow will stand still to be mounted perhaps twice, not more; others accept being mounted much, much more—denouncing their heat is easier because you see them, but it is so often that then the difficulty is to know when the first *monta estática* was."[21] The exact precision that identification of heat requires in turn requires sharp human surveillance of the corral: "One needs a trained eye to both spot the cow and her few static seconds." Eyeing the particular cow amid twirling bodies is difficult, and it is even harder when all cows look the same (if they are all black for example) and the onlooker is behind a fence three hundred feet away. Adding to the challenge (and making surveillance—and thus human control of risk—insufficient!), some cows *muestran el celo*—show their heat at night when nobody is watching: the stillness of a cow at noon may not be the first of the day. Gauging incorrectly what appears to be a small detail is consequential to insemination.

Complications only multiply when, as happens frequently, several cows are simultaneously in heat. The corral is then chaotic with intense joy. "Guessing" which cow "stood still" twelve hours ago is not an option—the onlooker must know. How do they know? "Cows tell you if they had more than one standing heat: their lower back is chafed, the butt is dirty with all sorts or organic material, the vulva is swollen." But more is needed: to understand what the cows are telling them, the onlooker must learn to "see" signs that vary with the bodies; the onlooker's eyes, nose, and hands need to be familiar with the body and temperament of each individual cow in the herd. The more they know about each cow's personality, their bodies, their heat history, and how they express their joyous arousal, the more precisely they will identify an individual cow's "estrus moment." Familiarity also enables experienced workers to "see" the cow's body internally: when old farm hands (literally!) go inside the cow through their vagina, they can haptically tell the condition of the ovaries relative to the cow's estrous cycle and her readiness for insemination. Sometimes, hands touch the same cows repeatedly, more than once a year, frequently for more than ten consecutive years. Knowledge accrued in those hands (and arms—from fingertips to elbow!) enables "touch" to "denounce heat" for a timely encounter between eggs and sperm. In turn, cows learn to recognize *that* touch and will yield to it. Achieving cow–human haptic intimacy is precious toward sustaining the "mutuality" between cows and capital reproductive assistance. Controlling possible failures makes success possible: inside a cow's uterus, avoiding the fragility of MAR is at human fingertips.

SEMEN COLLECTION, A TENSE CHOREOGRAPHY

We are visiting La Paz, a semen collecting center and boarding place of genetically valuable bulls whose semen is to be extracted and commoditized. Owned by a well-known veterinarian, La Paz occupies a large extension of idyllically manicured lawns. The property includes pastures to house up to fifty bulls, infrastructure to extract semen, and a small laboratory that treats the semen immediately after its extraction and starts its transformation into a product to be sold. This facility is connected to a laboratory in Bogotá from where, upon arrival in frozen nitrogen containers, the semen is distributed into small plastic phials called "straws." Each phial contains a tiny amount of semen, an insemination dose. A human–bull production and vessels of ejaculatory capital, semen straws express a gathering of animal agriculture, genetic laboratories, and financial investment. In Colombia, they travel an expansive national market that includes poor and wealthy farms.

La Paz is a fictional name chosen to highlight the feeling of peace as a curated condition that this place uses to enhance the bulls' semen production. "When calm, a bull eats properly, gains adequate weight, his hormones are adjusted" (in Spanish *un toro tranquilo come bien, gana el peso adecuado, se "ajusta" hormonalmente*). Bulls spend kingly days at La Paz. Their veterinary care includes homeopathy, and their nutrition is calibrated considering the hormonal needs of semen quality—the valuable substance they harbor. Their daily routines are identical. With their handlers, bulls move from their individual nighttime indoor stables to their also individual daytime corrals: large patches of land with the right amount of shade and sun, where a Colombian peasant farm located in the same region could comfortably keep ten cows. At La Paz, bulls become familiar with their caretakers and vice versa. They mutually recognize their steps, sounds, voices, whistles, moos, bellows, and snorts. Caretakers do the rounds several times every day to feed them and refresh their water, and to prevent all possible harm, which intriguingly includes avoiding the bulls becoming bored. This can lead to self-stimulated ejaculation in the corral. Spilled semen is antithetical to the center's purpose; as the quotation above instructs, in this center, semen is destined for the insemination of cows: *No se puede derramar dinero* (money cannot be spilled). Likewise, electric fences separate bulls to prevent them from mounting each other: the ejaculation of two bulls is anathema to the purpose of this place. Of vital value for MAR, wasted semen subtracts from the human–animal potential to accrue ejaculatory capital. Thus, a paradoxical fragility envelops La Paz: the peacefulness necessary for semen productivity may bore the bulls and provoke their ejaculation, a semen leak away from the pipes of potential ejaculatory capital. Surveillance, as in the case of cows' heat, may be insufficient to control these outflows.

In Colombia, extracting semen from the bull's body is called *toma* (taking) or *colecta* (collecting). La Paz performs it with an artificial vagina or an electro ejaculator. With either contraption, semen extraction is exacting. To be successful—that is, to achieve a "good ejaculation"—extraction must be as smooth as possible for the bull. Yet, it is rough and trying for both him and humans alike. The huge body of the animal goes back and forth yielding to and rejecting the terms of a process humans need to firmly uphold. With either method, "extraction" becomes a perilous dance to adjust the disproportions of human–bull wills and bodily movements. A cue to the fragility of this moment: collecting semen—an imposition on bulls—requires avoiding their discomfort. This is a work of human talent, considering that the process both provokes and truncates the bodily intensity required for the bull's ejaculation. Bulls remember. The process is frequent. Their cooperation is necessary. It cannot be risked.

ELECTRO-EJACULATION, A ROUGH PROCESS THAT NEEDS TO BE MELLOW

"We use it with bulls that are big and heavy, when they are shy and their libido needs stimulation or if they have had a bad artificial vagina experience." Using the electro-ejaculator to collect the semen of immense bulls would be impossible without the invention of an ingenious chute that offers both sturdy comfort to the body of the bull it contains and security to the humans who, standing at intimate proximity, "extract" the bull's semen squeezing his glands with their hands. Soft but extremely strong straps immobilize the bull, resisting a body weight of between 1,200 and 2,400 pounds that may completely yield when the process reaches its peak. The bull knows the process; humans labor to deflect his dislike of it.

Semen extraction involves a gradual climax. Getting there using an electro-ejaculator requires the utter precision of at least three humans: one watches the bull's distress signals, one introduces the electro-ejaculator through the bull's rectum, and one observes bull and humans, anticipating the exact moment to activate the electric charge that will stimulate the bull's sexual glands and penis, provoking his discharge. Standing, the bull blows forcefully, his libidinal movements are smoothly and sturdily supported by leather straps, his enormity contained within the chute—nothing can tear, fracture, crash, or otherwise fail without resulting in great harm to all bodies involved and beyond. At this point, with things going well, the bull has an erection, his muscles tensely contract in a paroxysm that results from pleasure, we think. Semen starts to flow—an ejaculation provoked by a perfectly calibrated electric discharge, its intensity depending on the bull's size and temperament. The fragility of success requires perfection. A calculation error could impair the bull as a source of ejaculatory capital. The *centro de colecta* would have to compensate the owner for the bull's value. Most damaging, their harmed reputation would affect its worth in the circuit of MAR.

"We do not collect this transparent *líquido preseminal* (pre-seminal liquid)"—mixed with semen itself, it ruins the quality of the *pajillas*, the semen straws, and the final product of the collection process. "When the ejaculated liquid turns dense and whitish, we start collecting, that is when it is rich in spermatozoids." The transition from bad to good liquid happens in about two minutes and coincides with the moment of the bull's paroxysm. Located under the immense body that may give way (but will hopefully be sustained by the straps), the human hands on the penis (collecting the semen) swiftly switch bags—from the container of the initial pre-seminal liquid to the one that will contain the collectable semen. Sometimes, bulls ejaculate inside their bodies. In such cases, and still underneath the body of the bull, the human carefully massages the penis and the prepuce to squeeze out the very last drop of semen. "I am draining him," we are told. "He is ejaculating inside the prepuce, and if I do not drain, the pre-seminal liquid and semen mix up, the quality of his straws would be terrible. So, as soon as I see semen flowing, I have to drain and drain to separate the bad liquid but also so that nothing good stays inside—we need all he can give us." Reputation also requires the center to offer owners the most and best of their bulls' semen.

MIMICKING A COW'S VAGINA, A SEMEN-TRAPPING PROSTHETIC EXTENSION OF HUMAN HANDS

When bulls are small and "have good libido," humans extract their semen with an "artificial vagina." The control of wills and bodies occurs here without the chute and its sturdy straps separating them—hence the preference to perform this operation with small bulls: skilled human bodies can transact their movements better and avoid harm. The stage is a small open section on the collection center grounds. The participants are one bull, three humans, and a lure. Mutual familiarity among all is sine qua non. It allows trust and the ability to recognize, sometimes preempting harm, each other's bodily movements. As the process begins, the bull and the handler arrive connected by a rope laced around the bull's neck. The lure—in this case, a cow or bull tied very firmly to a pole—will incite the bull in question to ejaculate.[22] The process starts with both the handler and the bull carefully approaching the lure who, refusing to be mounted, moves relentlessly under the close watch of a second human monitoring both the tied lure's reactions and the ties themselves. A lose knot can cause a collision between animals and all humans involved—at this point, three (plus us watching). Eventually, the bull yields to the lure's attraction. Displaying signs we recognize as sexual arousal, he jumps to mount it. This is a hazardous, strenuous moment. The bull handler opposes the strength of his body to that of the bull: using the rope that connects both, he pulls the bull away from the lure while also leaving him close to it.

This choreography, the push and pull—away from the lure, but not much, then toward the lure, again away from the lure, but not much, and again toward the lure—lasts for a number of minutes and gradually acquires dramatic intensity. When the bull and the handler agree that the moment of mounting has arrived, the process reaches a high point. Its culmination requires human bodily dexterity, technical decisiveness, and—we think—experienced boldness. At the high point, the bull is ready to ejaculate, and the semen must be collected. With this intention, the handler forcefully—decisively, skillfully, smoothly—pulls the bull away from the lure, the direction in which the bull is forcefully jumping. Simultaneously—with exact precision—the human collecting the semen walks under the jumping bull and grabs his penis away from the lure and into the artificial vagina. The collector wants as much of the bull's vital substance as possible. The moment is fleeting and dangerous. The bull and the lure can harm each other, and the humans can be buried under the weight of either one. The human grasp of the bull's penis must be firm yet without pressure. The explanation for this is "when touching the penis, I cannot inhibit the bull's search reflex to find the artificial vagina that incites his ejaculation." The artificial vagina is a rubber receptable mimicking the texture, pressure, and temperature of a cow's vagina and must remain thus until the bull ejaculates. Held by humans, it connects their hands with the bull's penis and receives the ejaculation. If this choreography fails or the condition of the artificial vagina is altered, semen extraction collapses. Worse, an erroneous human movement may impair the bull's ejaculatory potential, ending his life purpose and possibly his life as well.

THE FRAGILITY OF SEMEN "IN TRANSLATION" AND "IN COLLECTION"

Once the collection ends, the human handlers free the bull (and the lure) and take both to their corrals. Attention is now centered on the semen: translating it into a laboratory substance is the first vulnerable moment for the semen, as it must maintain its condition as the bull's bodily substance. In a special sterile bag, it travels from the collection stage to an indoor laboratory. The technician pours the semen samples into petri dishes (with cell-protecting liquids) to evaluate its bio-marketable condition or impregnating capacity. Under the microscope, the technician observes the quantity, mobility, and motility of the spermatozoa, comparing it with those of other bulls. This will determine the price of each individual semen straw. As many as three hundred straws per ejaculation, all with the bull's name and date of extraction, will translate into ejaculatory capital as they travel through national (or international) AI markets. Innumerable and heterogeneous professional experts (biologists, accountants, truck drivers, refrigeration providers) and just as innumerable bio-technological instruments and sophisticated computer systems participate in the translation of bulls' semen into its commodity form. The process requires a chain of actions carefully conducted to maintain the substance's vitality. And indeed, at any moment, things can fail and harm the bio-commodity. An error in the temperature of the nitrogen refrigerating the straws is the risk that scares laboratory workers the most, but there are others: the straws can be labeled with an incorrect bull's name, or a power cut can stop the computers and the whole refrigerating system. With everything going well, the technoscientific achievement that extracting and translating semen into ejaculatory capital manifests rests on the bull's capacity for sexual joy. Achieving it, in turn, rests on the human ability to provoke and control it also by obtaining the bull's complacency: this moment of impressive multispecies intensity, and ideally success, is tremendously fragile, literally, as it can harm the enormous bulls and the extremely talented workers.

INTO THE COW'S UTERUS: ARTIFICIAL INSEMINATION AND EMBRYO TRANSFER

> Bull semen has one use: the insemination of cows.
> —*The Independent*, June 8, 1996[23]

Artificial insemination (AI) and embryo transfer (ET) are very different. The latter is a development of AI that uses genetics (and human–bovine asymmetric relations) to accelerate the reproductive pace of cattle as capital. While all cows can be inseminated, not all cows participate in embryo transfer programs. Cow insemination is but one practice in the embryo transfer sequence, with vulnerabilities at each step that do not exist when the practice is only AI. Perhaps the mightier the possibility of MAR—the more prodigious its practices—the more its sites of vulnerability. Similarly, unpredictable excesses to knowledge (or unknowns) may surface.

Indeed, protocols exist to protect AI and ET and to shield cows' organs and substances from damage. A cow's uterus is a structure from and into which AI and ET move bio-substances in a sequence of delicate practices. As the gestating chamber of the reproduction of cattle/capital, the uterus is both of the utmost importance for MAR and permanently vulnerable to the bacteria that (in poop, urine, blood, saliva, mucus, and hair) inhabit not only the milking parlors, stables, corrals, and chutes where both processes transpire but also the tools they use. Thus, a meticulous biosecurity protocol to protect cows' reproductive tracts from infection and to maintain their capacity to reproduce cattle is an enforced requirement. And then, as the quotation above reminds us, given that the only purpose of semen is to inseminate cows, a critical protocol during insemination (also necessary for ET) concerns semen straws. The protocol is nothing short of vital during the few seconds after removing each individual straw from the cryogenic tank where they are kept, thawed, and then placed in an AI gun. "This is AI's most vulnerable instant . . . we need all our attention; confidence can be deadly." Time and temperature are of the essence, and thus a farmer's rule of thumb is that when inseminating, "the tank has to be close to the cows" because "after forty-five seconds, the straw [and the semen it contains] will not be the same." Straws need to thaw at exactly 36°C and to be quickly placed in the catheter that goes in the gun, which, in turn, goes into the cow. When inseminating several cows, the process needs to be repeated one straw at a time, while also shielding them "from their enemies, light and water." Semen straws are as valuable as they are fragile participants in MAR.

GOING THROUGH THE CERVIX: IT CAN DECIDE ARTIFICIAL INSEMINATION AND THE COW'S FATE

It is 6:00 a.m. when we arrive at the dairy farm where Rodrigo has inseminated cows for ten years: "All these cows were born from a semen straw that I shot [in their uterus.]"[24] Our arrival corresponded to his AI schedule. The corral had been in heat chaos the previous day, and some cows were ready for insemination. Like us, the cows arrive at the site of the insemination: an open-air structure with a tin roof, cement floor, and several individual metal compartments parallel to each other. There, cows are partially restrained to allow Rodrigo to insert his hands through their rear openings, rectum and vagina, and toward each cow's uterus. Facing the only wall in the structure, during the procedure cows eat from individual buckets placed under their mouths.

Rodrigo starts. Dressed in clean overalls, his arms (covered hand to shoulder, in a plastic glove) are important in this human–cow connection. His right hand holds the AI "gun" carrying the semen straw, the other one is free. The right hand enters the cow's body through the vulva to reach the uterus where the gun "plants" the semen; the left hand enters through the rectum. The hands meet at the cow's cervix, "approximately twenty centimeters away from the vulva." "It is this long," says Rodrigo about the cervix, and he shows us the size of his index finger. "It has three hard little rings; [the gun has to] go through them." He describes cows according to the challenge cervixes offer the inseminator: "Many are easy, some are difficult, and a few are impossible." Cows' anatomies are diverse. Some cervixes are unworkable regardless of the inseminator's skills. "Some are like a Z, only a bull can impregnate that cow; no bull, the cow goes to the slaughterhouse." The cervix is a fateful site. Along with the failure of AI, it decides the cow's life. "Going through the cervix" allows inseminators to shoot semen to the uterine spot from where spermatozoa and egg have the most probability of finding each other. Failure to reach the uterus "passing through the cervix" wastes semen straws, wastes a cow's heat, and results in a cow who does not augment the farm's herd—a misuse of time and money that detracts from reproducing cattle/capital. Intriguingly, the cervix is an "obligatory passage point" (Latour 1988) on the route to mutually assisted reproduction of cattle and capital. In turn, a cow with a cervix that is difficult to negotiate with an inseminating gun is a cow that may be culled and may be discarded.

"Manipulating the cervix is key to insemination," Rodrigo says as he directs his left hand inside the cow and his eyes toward the ceiling. "Manipulation" is the right word for the process: it shares it root with *manos*, meaning "hands" in Spanish. Rodrigo uses his to *see* inside the cow as he searches for the cervix. Once located, he holds it to orient his other hand, the one moving the AI gun with the semen straw through the "three rings" all the way to the uterus. Inside the cow, the task is arduous. Her intestines engage the inseminator's arm, which she may expel (with her poop) if the arm provokes a bowel movement. Meanwhile, the other hand holds the AI gun as it touches the cow's reproductive tract, a precious MAR asset. Small mistakes may wound the cow fatally. A cow with a damaged reproductive tract burdens the farm's cattle/capital reproduction. Unable to assist it, she is a dead cow. The fragility of MAR is indeed consequential for the cow's life.

Of all four cows that participated in the process, three were "easy" to inseminate. The other one was a heifer. Unfamiliar with the heifer's internal organs, Rodrigo could not predict what his left hand would find; this made his right hand—the one holding the AI gun—wait (inside the cow) before finding the right spot to place the semen. Similarly, being new to the process, the heifer was uncomfortable. She resisted Rodrigo and needed restraint. This tensioned his organs and interfered with Rodrigo's haptic vision. Contrastingly, the insemination relation between Rodrigo and each of the other three cows was smooth. The cows recognized Rodrigo's touch, and he recognized their interiors. This afforded him good and quick haptic vision of each cow's reproductive tract. "Seeing inside the cow needs practice. Otherwise, when your free hand goes in, you only find poop," Rodrigo says. And there is plenty of poop. The first thing he does inside the rectum is to pull the excrement out to clear the movement of his hand toward the cow's cervix. This, plus the cow's spontaneous bowel movements and urination, transforms the insemination place into a huge bacterial petri dish. A meticulous protocol is enforced that shields cows from infection and maintains intact their cattle/capital reproductive capacity.

EMBRYO TRANSFER: MAKING THE CONCEIVING UTERUS INTO ALMOST MANY AND THE GESTATING ONES INTO ALMOST ONE

> Once we identify the elite cows . . . [we] subject them to a four-day hormonal treatment . . . with a *superovulation* injection that will allow them to produce from two to more than fifteen eggs. We then fertilize the eggs with semen of domestic or imported bulls [and] wait eight days before collecting the embryos, which we then take to a lab that goes to the farms . . . [there] we classify them with a special technique that guarantees that they will not be contaminated. Then we pack the embryos in straws, and finally we transfer them to the receiving cow who is *synchronized* with the donating cow for her estrus cycle to allow her pregnancy.[25] (our emphasis)

The author of the above quote is a successful Colombian veterinarian. He owns a cattle farm and is known for having performed more embryo transfers than anybody else in Colombia.[26] "Embryo transfer was a crazy adventure we engaged in years ago, fortunately it has been fruitful," he writes. Persuasively, he recalls the feat of another farmer who "imported four great cows and after eight years of intense work, owned one hundred genetically excellent cows."

The possibility of capital assisting cattle reproduction to achieve mutual exponential growth motivates the industry of embryo transfer. ET names a multi-sequence process. It starts with superovulation (see italics above)—a hormonal treatment to increase the production of a cow's uterus from one egg per estrus cycle to many more. (How many depends on the cow's response.) After insemination (frequently artificially but also by a bull yet always human mediated), spermatozoa will encounter not the usual one but many eggs and, conditional on their mutual reaction, make several embryos in one uterus.[27] These embryos are then moved from the conceiving cow to the uteri of many others that will gestate them.

Cows chosen for superovulation are selected among the best. They are considered "elite" and called donors, even if they do not own their embryos or willfully consent to treatments. Donors who respond positively to hormones are inseminated after a more attentive than usual observation of their heat period because superovulation may suppress its manifestation. Assuming successful fertilization, embryos must be removed before their "implantation" in the conceiving uterus: "eight days after insemination" recommends the veterinarian author of the quotation above. Errors in counting post-insemination days are consequential. At ten days, an embryo is implanted, and the elite cow will gestate one calf only—superovulation will have been lost. So, cows' bodies (and, at times, their will) have a say in the process. Although they are not asked if they want to be donors and human care and dexterity can make them such, this may mean that their bodily answer matters.

Embryo-collecting methods are heterogeneous. We are familiar with one descriptively called "flushing": using a catheter, liquid is flushed into the cow's uterus and then flushed out, bringing the embryos with it. The process needs a compliant cow and at least two humans: one takes charge of the catheter (hooked to an embryo-finding contraption), the other controls a "filter" that both flushes the liquid into the uterus and receives it back with the flushed-out embryos.[28] At this point, the filter becomes a vulnerable site: it needs a perfectly calibrated transparency both to allow the human a view of the liquid and to protect the embryos from excessive light. Simultaneously in need of attention is the liquid that, swirling vigorously, enters the filter. If it overflows, embryos can be lost: "spilling flushing liquid is like opening the corral door and letting the calves escape." If there is failure in any of these actions, the process falls apart: the cost of superovulation would be wasted, but the value that, resulting from human and cow labor, accrued in the embryos would also be lost.

Vulnerabilities continue as the embryos spend time out of the conceiving uterus. Protected in preserving substances, the living cells are placed under a stereomicroscope in petri dishes, where they are classified/selected to be then inserted one by one into plastic straws (like with semen) to be cryopreserved. These actions require nothing less than touching the embryos—bio-matter. Skill and precision are vital. An invisible splinter in the lifting tweezers, microscopic dust, undetectably wet hands/gloves—all of these can kill the valuable reproductive material. Just as damaging are slightly off temperatures, an extra second of exposure to light, or a slight decrease in the preserving liquid. Indoor laboratories require biosecurity routines to control similar risks. When laboratories are taken to farms—not an infrequent practice—biosecurity failure haunts the safety of the embryos.[29] Once successfully selected, the next hurdle is transferring the embryo. It must move between the conceiving and the receiving uteri without noticing the movement. This hinges on co-temporal precision. The estrous cycle of the conceiving and receiving cows must coincide and be exactly the same throughout, starting with the heat period. Temporal coordination is called "synchronization" (see our emphasis above). It is obtained through a rigorous hormone treatment administered to "donating" and "receiving" cows, and it crucially involves embryos. If transferring them between uteri is to be imperceptible, the condition of the receiving uterus and the embryo's stage must agree with each other. Accordingly, younger embryos go to the cows with the later heat; older ones go to the cows with the earlier heat.[30]

While this might sound easy, making actual matches is a juggling act of comparisons (time of heat, time of embryo formation) that risks all imaginable and unimaginable failures. Embryo transfer is an effort at co-temporalization that, starting with superovulation, makes the initially conceiving uterus into almost many and then, to enable the gestation of the transferred embryo, synchronizes all uteri involved into almost one. That the closure of the transfer must critically match the stage of the embryos highlights the fragility of the process: it requires an excellent response of the cows' bodies. They thus have an important say in the process that is unknown until expressed.

CHALLENGING MAR: WHEN CAPITAL AND CATTLE DO NOT BECOME EACH OTHER

Daniela is the owner of a small farm near Bogotá. Prone to technological innovations, she engaged in an embryo transfer program and even enlisted members of the dairy cooperative to which she belongs to join the same program. Extension workers of a nationwide *asociación ganadera* convinced her: they would bring hormones and embryos and perform the transfer at very low cost. Daniela and her fellow cooperative members would select among their cows those that would gestate embryos conceived (with selected semen) by the best cows of the *asociación ganadera*. Added to their excellent milk production, the new calves would improve the genetics of participating farms faster than they could ever do using AI only: non-exceptional cows would immediately birth exceptional cows! "We accepted and chose seventeen cows to gestate the embryos." Disappointingly, only two cows responded positively, and only two calves were born. Daniela blames this on synchronization neglect: extension workers only came once to work on embryo transplant. As is obvious to any farmer, not all cows are hormonally ready at the same time. Yet, what these farmers regretted most was that the hormonal treatment altered the (unsuccessful) cows' reproductive cycles. Their pregnancies were delayed, and their milk-production cycles were affected. The resulting bump in their incomes affected the quality of life on the farm—for cows and humans alike—and left a group of farmers determined against embryo transfer. Rumors of the experience quickly traveled across the region. An obvious conclusion was that poorer farms may restrict MAR's expansive might and signal a market fragility hard to repair, a condition without biosecurity protocol. This fragility of MAR may also signal these farms' distinctiveness and perhaps also their strength vis-à-vis the occupation of cattle by capital.

MAR is indeed our abstraction, but it is grounded in an empirical process in which cows/bulls and people are connected in heterogeneous technoscientific, economic, and affective relations. Thus, although a large majority of Colombian farmers (we are tempted to say "all"!) participate in the circuit of MAR, cows do not always become capital and thus are not always cattle. Sometimes, farmers are unable to achieve the transformation of cows into capital or of the latter into cattle. Other times, and most intriguingly, farmers are unwilling—or unhurried—to make their cows into cattle. Daniela is a good example again. She had a cow, Lupita, who she bought as a heifer attracted by the cow's good dairy ancestry. Although she knew Lupita milk's productivity would be good, Daniela took her time to inseminate her and instead learned about Lupita's personality by observing her cow's joyous heat cycles, watching her jump and be jumped by other cows. Lupita was making friends and "she was too young to be bred" was her explanation. Other farmers would disagree, even if some of them would perhaps skip their own cows' heat cycle once or twice "to give them some rest." Lupita and Daniela make each other through relations of mutuality. In that sense, they are like capital and cattle. Yet, the latter are different in that they do not relate cows and people. Relations among cows and people may include AI (or even ET), and the goal of cows' reproduction is certainly to obtain monetary income, but this money is used to reproduce mutually dependent livelihoods—those of farmer, cows, and even farm (soils, pastures tools, irrigation canals) together. Livelihood mutuality prevents the separation that alienates humans from cattle as well as the better income that such alienation may yield. And indeed, lower income may expose small farms to fragility, but rather than a forgone conclusion, that would be the subject of a different story.

NOTES

1. See http://www.thebullvine.com/investment-advice/lila-worth-1-15-million-dollars/.

2. Following the 1941 creation in England of the first center for the practice of artificial insemination, copious reproductive science research (always a practice) confirmed the benefits of artificial insemination for livestock breeding. A few decades later, a central intellectual of agriculture declared, "Some remarkable effects can be produced on animals now that human beings are learning to take charge of the directing glands" (Russell 1966, 336, cited in Clarke 2007, 319).

3. See https://nwdistrict.ifas.ufl.edu/phag/2020/05/29/tips-for-successful-artificial-insemination-of-cattle/.

4. An important qualification: our conceptualization requires distinguishing between "cow" or "bull" and cattle. The latter becomes through capital and its practices; not all cows and bulls do.

5. Our conceptualization also bears similarities with what Sahlins (2011) called "a mutuality of being." Using the phrase to discuss human kinship, he described such mutuality as "persons who are members of one another, who participate intrinsically in each other's existence" (2011: 2–3). Similarly in our conceptualization, as capital and cattle assist one another's reproduction, they participate in each other's being: their mutuality transpires through and makes a bio-capitalist multispecies kinship.

6. Donna Haraway's "value added dogs" is a source of inspiration. Our contribution, however, does not imply a value *addition* of capital to cattle but rather the mutual recursive becoming, and thus mutual value adding, of one to and through the other (Haraway 2008).

7. MAR is indeed a specific form of bio-capital (Helmreich 2008) that becomes multispecies life as it reproduces itself through the onto-epistemic occupation (and conversion) of cows/bulls into cattle (or multispecies life).

8. See https://nwdistrict.ifas.ufl.edu/phag/2020/05/29/tips-for-successful-artificial-insemination-of-cattle/.

9. See https://biology.ucdavis.edu/news/how-genetic-mutation-1-bull-caused-loss-half-million-calves-worldwide.

10. On discussing industrial pig production, Blanchette (2020, 30, 245) makes a similar point: fragility is a condition of the process, not a signal of weakness.

11. This sensual play may bear similarities with "petting" among humans—that is, "non-coital caresses, cuddles and amorous touching . . . across the site of their bodies and not restricted to the genitals (non-coital genital touching is given the phrase heavy petting)" Wadiwel (2017, 297).

12. Following Margulis and Sagan (1997, 17), we conceptualize sexual reproduction as the mixing of genes (DNA molecules) from more than one source that produces another similar living being. Accordingly, sexual reproduction does not need copulation, nor are practices with the organs used in copulation or for reproduction intrinsically linked to biological sex. In fact, they can be delinked and complexly linked again.

13. For the notion of "ejaculatory capital," see Preciado (2013, 50). We borrow it and add "ovulatory capital" to describe (and analyze) a process of industrial-scientific extraction of vital cells from cows that parallels that of bulls for purposes of market valorization.

14. The scientific-economic stimulation and appropriation of joyous intensity (Preciado's *potentia gaudendi*) that bodies (of bulls and cows in the case we discuss)

need to produce life-making substances/conditions is a specific trait of MAR's form of bio-capital. We describe this process, and all potential breakdowns, in the next two sections.

15. Caveats: cows and bulls are not born such; they are made such at farms. One of the practices through which this happens is heterosexing, which does not mean "hetero-sexualizing."

16. See https://www.fda.gov/animal-veterinary/product-safety-information/cattle-estrous-cycle-and-fda-approved-animal-drugs-control-and-synchronize-estrus-resource-producers.

17. The Spanish idiom naming this stillness is *monta estática*—literally, "static mount"; in English, "standing heat."

18. The standard recommendation for a productive farm is for cows to get pregnant fifty to sixty days after giving birth.

19. Standing heat is an important "control switch" for the multispecies circuit of mutually assisted reproduction. It prompts human intervention to select the cow to inseminate, thus arresting joy in the corral.

20. See https://www.fda.gov/animal-veterinary/product-safety-information/cattle-estrous-cycle-and-fda-approved-animal-drugs-control-and-synchronize-estrus-resource-producers#cycle.

21. See also https://extension.psu.edu/timing-of-insemination-for-dairy-cattle

22. The lure is diverse: "Some bulls mount frames covered in cowskin and ejaculate into rubber tubes with bottles on the end. Some mount other males, known as 'teasers,' only to be interrupted at the crucial moment (which arrives quickly and is over even more quickly) by a man with a rubber tube." See https://www.independent.co.uk/news/uk/home-news/bull-s-semen-10-things-you-didn-t-know-1336150.html.

23. See https://www.independent.co.uk/news/uk/home-news/bull-s-semen-10-things-you-didn-t-know-1336150.html.

24. We asked about the bull calves. "They do not keep them," he tells us. "This is a dairy farm. Only cows stay."

25. See https://www.contextoganadero.com/cronica/carlos-gomez-el-ganadero-que-mas-transferencias-de-embriones-ha-hecho.

26. According to the FAO, "The first transfer of a bovine embryo was reported in 1949 . . . and the first calf from embryo transfer in 1951. Application of embryo transfer to the cattle industry began in the early 1970s when European dual-purpose breeds of cattle became popular in North America, Australia and New Zealand." Motivating it was not only science, as "breeders and speculators sought means to circumvent the high costs and lengthy quarantine periods linked to the importation of European breeding stock and to capitalize on premium prices that progeny from these rare dams and sires could command." See http://www.fao.org/3/T0117E/T0117E01.htm.

27. This process made Lila Z, the cow in our introduction.

28. Throughout, the process must avoid bacteria and otherwise harming the donor's valuable reproductive tract.

29. Obviously, connecting cows' uteri with the laboratory requires human hands mastering their way through the cervix. Only inseminated cows and those whose embryos can be flushed can be donors, and only those with successful implantation can be receivers.

30. Embryos are classified by gauging the number and composition of their cells. This indicates the time lapse since the fertilizing encounter between egg and sperm.

REFERENCES

Bagemihl, Bruce. 1999. *Biological Exuberance. Animal Homosexuality and Natural Diversity*. New York: St. Martin's Press.

Blanchette, Alex. 2020. *Porkopolis: American Animality, Standardized Life, and the Factory Farm*. Durham, NC: Duke University Press.

Clarke, Adele E. 2007. "Reflections on the Reproductive Sciences in Agriculture in the UK and US, ca. 1900–2000+." *Studies in History and Philosophy of Science Part C: Studies in History and Philosophy of Biological and Biomedical Sciences* 38 (2): 316–339. https://doi.org/10.1016/j.shpsc.2007.03.003.

Haraway, Donna J. 2008. *When Species Meet*. Minneapolis: University of Minnesota Press.

Helmreich, Stefan. 2008. "Species of Biocapital." *Science as Culture* 17 (4): 463–478. https://doi.org/10.1080/09505430802519256.

Latour, Bruno. 1988. *The Pasteurization of France*. Cambridge: Harvard University Press.

Margulis, Lynn, and Dorion Sagan. 1997. *What Is Sex*? New York: Simon & Schuster Editions.

Moore, Jason W. 2015. *Capitalism in the Web of Life: Ecology and the Accumulation of Capital*. New York: Verso.

Preciado, Beatriz. 2013. *Testo Junkie: Sex, Drugs, and Biopolitics in the Pharmacopornographic Era*. New York: Feminist Press.

Russell, Sir E. J. 1966. *A History of Agricultural Science in Great Britain 1620–1954*. London: George Allen & Unwin.

Sahlins, Marshall. 2011. "What Kinship Is (Part One)." *Journal of the Royal Anthropological Institute* 17 (1): 2–19. https://doi.org/10.1111/j.1467-9655.2010.01666.x.

Wadiwel, Dinesh Joseph. 2017. "Animal Friendship as a Way of Life: Sexuality, Petting and Interspecies Companionship." In *Foucault and Animals*, edited by Matthew Chrulew and Dinesh Joseph Wadiwel, 286–316. Boston: Brill.

6 CONTAMINATION CHORES

MAX LIBOIRON

At the Civic Laboratory for Environmental Action Research (CLEAR), we study plastics that have been eaten by animals. Most of the plastics we find are the size of dust. We do much of this work in partnership with the Nunatsiavut Government in the subarctic region of Labrador, Canada. Nothing about this work, either in the lab or on the land, could be described as fragile. Nothing about our work is delicate, vulnerable, flimsy, insubstantial, or easily destroyed. The plastics in our sample are not fragile: they last forever. The processes that attempt to differentiate between plastics from the land and plastics in the air are not fragile: they are multifaceted, with various forms of quality assurance built in. The knowledge that comes out of these relationships is not fragile: the knowledge can shift as the plastics and processes exert agency, as this chapter will demonstrate, but it does not fall apart. Yet, at every stage, we are repairing, maintaining, and caring for pollutants. We repair, maintain, and care without the precursor of fragility.

The only time we hear the word "fragility" in our lab is when someone outside of our sphere misunderstands our research and calls the Inuit homelands from where we get our samples "fragile." Not only do the Inuit organizations and governments we work with denounce the term, but also using it in this way fundamentally misunderstands the relational nature of fragility. A brick isn't fragile. Unless you put it in the sight of a bulldozer. But calling a brick fragile in that scenario makes the relationship between brick and bulldozer seem like an inherent property of the brick while simultaneously failing to describe the bulldozer. Calling the North "fragile" fails to describe colonialism and other bulldozer relationships. In many narratives that use fragility to describe Indigenous lands, the settler state leverages that deficit framing for intervention, which brings in more bulldozers, making that brick seem ever more fragile. Such understandings of fragility can be described as fetishization, where certain characteristics are assumed to be the property of the thing, not its relations. Indeed, I invite readers to maneuver the text below to see how fragility is consistently and specifically a poor descriptor for our environmental pollution and contaminant work.

Instead, at CLEAR, we grapple a lot with purity. Like fragility, purity is not a thing but rather a set of relations, and we find ourselves caught up during our day-to-day science. This chapter aims to demonstrate how labor around an ideal but never real purity, what we playfully call "purity chores," acutely impacts knowledge production. I do not argue that this is inherently bad or good, but rather that it is a constant part of our research and thus must be accounted for.

Of course, purity, as an unadulterated state that maintains some type of clear dichotomy between pure and impure, is impossible. Not only does it not exist, since all matter and beings are always already part of complex relations, but when purity is evoked, it is often in the service of oppression and power moves, attempting to legitimize racism and white supremacy (Raffles 2017; TallBear 2013), the imperial and military state (Masco 2004), and industrial capitalism (Shotwell 2016), among other dominant systems and groups (Douglas 1966; Liboiron and Lepawsky 2022). In his essay, "Against Purity," Hugh Raffles writes about the fear of impure Jewish refugees to pure state bodies during Nazism and the similar ideologies used in biology to discuss invasive species of plants. He writes that in each case, the "particular senses of integrity and the wholeness and stasis they presume, [are] senses that run counter to a raggedy world in which all kinds of beings and phenomena—humans, animals, plants, landforms—refuse to hold still or keep pure" (2017, 181).

Moreover, as Alexis Shotwell has argued in a text also called *Against Purity*, purity is not only a way to describe matter but also a politics for action: "I argue against purism because it is one bad but common approach to devastation in all its forms. It is a common approach for anyone who attempts to meet and control a complex situation that is fundamentally outside our control . . . Purism is a de-collectivizing, de-mobilizing, paradoxical politics of despair" (2016, 8–9). That is, forms of action that rely on the integrity (and often the morality) of dichotomies create violent stalemates. I agree. We all seem to be against purity.

Imagine the awkwardness, then, when my work as a plastic pollution scientist is committed to models of purity. With others in CLEAR, I study plastics that are as small as a third of a millimeter—the size of a piece of dust. Indeed, dust is often made of plastics these days (Zhang, Wang, and Kannan 2020). A big problem for all labs that study microplastics is sorting out which microplastics are from your environmental sample and which are from the laboratory environment. Tiny plastics from dust, your clothes, your hair, your materials (petri dishes, bags, plastic caps on glass vials) and equipment (microscopes, trawl nets, ship rigs) are always getting into your samples (Prata et al. 2021). These are called "contaminants": they contaminate your pollution samples (hilarious logic, but scientific logic nonetheless). If you don't sort out the difference between plastic contaminants and plastic samples, which look identical, then your science isn't valid in the way it needs to be for pollution science, including justice-oriented science on, for example, Inuit food webs in Nunatsiavut.

This chapter is about doing scientific work using models of purity that require immense labor of maintenance, repair, and care while also being fully aware that purity is impossible and not a great model to believe in, even while it can be a good model for doing some kinds of justice-oriented science. Indeed, our lab membership reads authors such as Raffles and TallBear. So, there's some subtlety to how we simultaneously resist and reproduce models of purity. As such, this chapter has two goals: (1) to nuance a position on purity as a compromised but organizing model, and its implications for theories of change generally; and (2) to show how maneuvering the purity model through contamination chores directly impacts scientific knowledge production.

I start with a short review of how scientists already know that purity doesn't materially exist, even as we also use terms, standards, models, moralities, and theories of purity. CLEAR is not unique in dealing with the paradoxes of purity in mundane scientific contexts. Then, to affectively demonstrate the acute labor and frustration of doing purity chores, I have created a nonlinear Choose Your Own Lab Adventure based on real events and experiences from CLEAR lab members. Finally, we end with a discussion of lessons learned, mostly about relationality and compromise in the context of thinking about care, repair, maintenance, and fragility—this book's core themes.

LABORS AND HISTORIES OF PURIFICATION IN SCIENCE

There is a long history of scientists maneuvering the tensions of purity models, specifically the gap between the model and its material relations. In their first set of drinking-water quality standards, for example, the Committee on Standards of the National Association for Preventing the Pollution of Rivers and Waterways (USA) both wrote about the "original and natural conditions of purity" of waterways and stated that there was no "universal standard" of purity (1912, in Tarr, Yosie, and McCurley 1980) that would allow them to identify when that original and natural condition occurred. They echoed their British counterparts, who argued decades earlier that "there is no such thing as absolutely pure water in nature . . . there is actually no definite line of demarcation separating the purest spring water from the filthiest sewage" (Glen 1868: 75) and set out to demark exactly that through pollution controls. Early pollution scientists were tasked with finding a functional and feasible way to define pollution aligned with a model of pure dichotomies (drink this, do not drink that; this is safe, that is dangerous), even as they knew from the outset that this was a task of feasibility, not a discovery of "actual" purity. In *A Science of Impurity*, Christopher Hamlin outlines the efforts of scientists to understand polluted water and their creative scientific contortions to produce bright, white, demarking lines between pure and polluted drinking water they knew were fraught but necessary for public health and scientific achievement (Hamlin 1990, 2000; Pine and Liboiron 2015). They, too, were doing justice-oriented science.

Science and technology studies (STS) scholar Sebastian Ureta describes ruination science as that which "tends to be well adapted to engage with impurity . . . , ethically entangled, prioritizing attachment and compromises over the application of certain standard recipes or procedures" (2020: 1). While Ureta's case study is an extreme case of a falling-down, critically underfunded lab with failing equipment and acutely toxic samples, he argues that "in strict terms, any kind of chemistry-based toxicology practices a form of ruination science" (2020: 10). I agree and extend that argument to pollution science more generally. The first time I lost a sample because I laughed and the gush of air launched the tiny sample off the microscope slide and into the indoor floor dirt, the young scientist-in-training beside me said, "Oh yeah, whenever that happens, you just . . ." and then told me what to do with the sample, data, and write up to accommodate the loss. A normal part of scientific training is learning to deal with ubiquitous impurity as methods and materials consistently diverge from standards and specifications while also using and even creating standards and specifications so your work can move out of the lab (Bowker and Star 2000).

Simultaneously leveraging and disregarding purity models is not unique to pollution science. In his laboratory ethnography of material engineers, "A Little Dirt Never Hurt Anyone," Cyrus Mody writes that "practically all materials scientists with whom I have spoken readily acknowledge the role of considerations of purity and cleanliness in their work." He documents the many "pollution rituals" they use to produce knowledge about their materials despite and because of contamination (2001, 20). Mody and other laboratory ethnographers catalogue the exacting yet often bizarre labor of managing controls, blanks, sterility, quality assurance, background levels, and other techniques designed to uphold impossible dichotomies of purity (Cetina 1999; Traweek 2009; Utera 2020; Soto and Brilmyer 2020). These studies point out how scientists routinely make:

> ordinary objects and practices seem strange and exotic in much the same way I do as an ethnographer. This is particularly true of actors whose job it is to enforce standards of cleanliness. For example, operators of clean rooms have large manuals outlining how people in the clean room should accomplish such mundane tasks as pouring a bottle of water; the action of pouring might seem to be the same as outside the clean room, but operators need to impress on users of the clean room the necessity for care, diligence and vigilance (all terms, as Katz and Zabusky point out, associated with orientation to cleanliness). (Mody 2001, 21)

While Mody calls these "pollution rituals," in our lab, we call them "contamination chores." Together, the terms highlight the exquisite labor that goes into maintaining (and sometimes repairing) states oriented toward impossible purity, as well as the mental and bodily comportment scientists need to adopt to achieve a purity orientation.

I use the phrase "purity model" to denote a material orientation and its acknowledged impossibility. In *Models as Mediators*, Mary Morgan and Mary Morrison describe models as things that "represent, in some way, the behavior and structure of a physical system," whose status is somewhere between theory and data (1999, 5). They argue that models are not simulacrum, and when they use the term "representation" in their theory of models, they mean "a kind of rendering—a partial representation that either abstracts from, or translates into another form, the real [*sic*] nature of the system or theory, or one that is capable of embodying only a portion of a system," and never replaces the thing or perfectly stands in for the system it is supposed to represent (1999, 27; see also Soto and Brilmyer 2020, 7). It doesn't really matter that purity can't be achieved—the purity model brings out the salient material relationships that must be carried out, maintained, repaired, and cared for by scientists in a permanently and ubiquitously contaminated lab so our data can be valid. We deal in purity models, not purity facts.

Many researchers, including myself, have called working in this paradox "compromise," where you reproduce parts of the system you have a problem with while working to change the problematic system (Hale 2006; Shotwell 2016; Liboiron 2017). Compromise doesn't mean you're losing, nor is it a judgment of amorality. It's central to a theory of change and action that "accounts for the permeability of the apparatuses of power" where dominant systems "inadvertently support" nondominant goals and lifeworlds (la paperson 2017). Indeed, following Emily Simmond's concept of care, we can think of contamination chores as "an affective relation whose leading ethic is to create attachments within infrastructures of inequity" (Simmonds in Liboiron 2021, 115; see also Murphy 2015). Purity both sucks *and* is necessary for our justice-oriented science, and purity's relations—all its relations, good and bad and otherwise—are reproduced in laboratory chores.

So, what does that look like in practice? Specifically, how does navigating or failing to navigate a purity model in the lab change knowledge?

CHOOSE YOUR OWN LAB ADVENTURE

Welcome to CLEAR! In these next pages, you will become one of our "sample slingers," someone who looks in animal guts for microplastics. Our samples of guts come from animals caught for food in Nunatsiavut. Your job is to identify tiny microplastics smaller than a grain of rice in those guts. But beware! There are also microfibers (a subclass of microplastics that are tiny, kinked, thread-line plastics so small you can barely see them, like dust lint) that come out of your hair and off your clothes, fall out of the air, and land on your sample. They are as common as dust. These microfibers that contaminate the sample can increase in number if you breathe a certain way, touch certain things, move certain ways, or wear certain clothes. Yet,

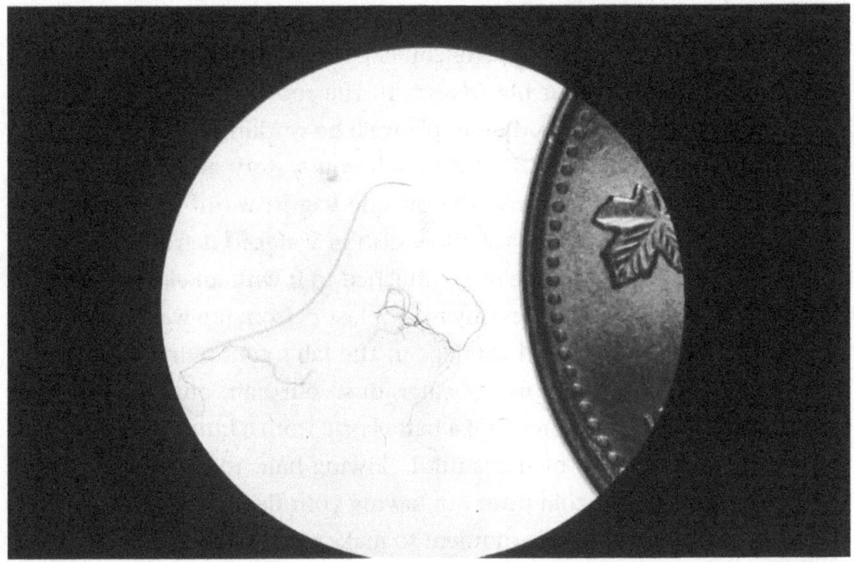

FIGURE 6.1
Microscope image (×10) of fairly large microfibers. Nickel coin for scale. Image is an example used in training in CLEAR. Image by the author.

microfibers are also found in the ocean and in animal guts—so you just can't discount them. You must figure out which ones came from the land and which ones came from the lab. Since they look the same, this requires some chores.

The following Choose Your Own Lab Adventure is based on real things that have happened in CLEAR, based on conversations and troubleshooting with lab members. Start reading and follow the prompts for how to move around in the text.

1. You're about to start your first day at CLEAR. As you approach the lab in the basement of the science building, you notice a sign in red block letters on the door that says NO FLEECE. You aren't sure whether the vest under your coat is fleece. Do you:

   A. Remove the maybe-fleece vest right there in the hallway and leave it outside the door, hoping that no one steals your nice fleece vest? Go to 2A.

   B. Step into the lab and ask if it's fleece? Go to 2B.

2A. Your fellow lab member and today's trainer, Kai, sees you setting down your things (minus a vest). "Welcome! Let's get you started!" They show you to one of the four big freezers in the room and remove a frozen bag of fish guts. "This is the sample we'll be working on. It's Arctic char from Nain, Nunatsiavut." As they tell you a story about the fish and its environment, they rinse the outside bag in warm tap water three times before resting it in a shallow dish of water to defrost. You notice the sink's faucet has a fine mesh attached to it with an elastic band. Kai tells you the mesh captures tiny microplastics from tap water, which the lab manager collects and catalogs in the lab's contamination archive. "Plastics are all around us, in water, dust, our hair, our clothes." Kai's hair is tied back, and they pull a hair elastic from a bundle near a pile of lab supplies for your own beautiful, flowing hair. You have a hard time listening, as you're cold from not having your fleece vest. "I'm going to work on this sample for a moment to make sure it's all defrosted—go get a sample for yourself from the same freezer," they tell you. Do you:

A. Tie your hair back, then go get the sample from the freezer? Go to 3A.

B. Get the sample from the freezer, then tie back your hair? Go to 3B.

2B. Your fellow lab member and today's trainer, Kai, sees you setting down your things. "Welcome! Let's get you started!" You ask if your vest is fleece, and Kai says yes. You quickly bundle the vest into your bag and zip it tight before Kai shows you to one of the four big freezers in the room and removes a frozen bag of fish guts. "This is the sample we'll be working on. It's Arctic char from Nain, Nunatsiavut." As they tell you a story about the fish and its homelands, they rinse the outside of the bag in warm tap water three times before resting it in a shallow dish of water to defrost. You notice the sink's faucet has a fine mesh attached with an elastic band. Kai tells you the mesh captures tiny microplastics from tap water, which the lab manager collects and catalogs in the lab's contamination archive. "Plastics are all around us, in water, dust, our hair, our clothes . . . See? There goes one now." They point to a piece of dust floating by that is the same color as your fleece vest. Hmm. Kai's hair is tied back, and they pull a hair elastic from a bundle near a pile of lab supplies for your own beautiful, flowing hair. "I'm going to work on this sample for a moment to make sure it's all defrosted—go get a sample for yourself from the same freezer," they tell you. Do you:

A. Tie your hair back, then go get the sample from the freezer? Go to 3A.

B. Get the sample from the freezer, then tie back your hair? Go to 3B.

3A. Your hair tied back in a no-nonsense style, you walk back across the lab to the sample freezers. You open the freezer door and locate a frozen Char sample from the same study. But when you try to take it out, the plastic bag is frozen to other samples and to the shelf! Looks like it was put away wet and has frozen to its surroundings. Do you:

A: Wiggle and gently tug the bag until it's loose? Go to 4C.

B. Go get some warm water to defrost the bag? Go to 4A.

3B. With your hair flowing free and beautiful in the lab breeze emanating from the ceiling ducts, you walk back across the lab to the sample freezers. You open the freezer door and locate a frozen Char sample from the same study. But when you try to take it out, the plastic bag is frozen to other samples and to the shelf! Looks like it was put away wet and has frozen to its surroundings. Do you:

A: Wiggle and gently tug the bag until it's loose? Go to 4C.

B. Go get some warm water to defrost the bag? Go to 4B.

4A. Kai looks at you curiously as you fill a spray bottle full of warm water and grab some towels, but nods knowingly as you gently spray the bag in the freezer until it comes loose on its own. You carefully clean up any water to make sure this doesn't happen to the next person. You bring the sample to the sink, rinse the bag three times, and then put it in a dish of warm water to thaw completely, just like Kai showed you. No water gets into the bag, so you know your thawing worked nicely and didn't result in any rips in the bag.

Kai then shows you how to make a control sample, or "blank." They attach double-sided tape to a petri dish and leave the top open, and they shake their hair into it and deposit a pinch of their lab coat lint. "We'll leave it open while we work, and dust will settle there." They tell you about how any type of plastic found in the control is discounted from the final analysis of the sample, since it is likely the plastic came from the lab environment rather than the original sample.

The next part of your training is to cut open the thawed guts over a set of sieves, washing all contents into them. You carefully make sure no water splashes out of the sieves, since you assume microplastics can surf (you are correct). Next, you and Kai bring the sieves over to a microscope and start looking in the gut contents for plastics. You slowly start a grid-pattern search, looking for plastics. A couple of minutes later, you catch sight of your own finger, enormous in the microscope's field of view—all covered in tiny black flecks! You realize that you scratched your leg earlier, and your black pants must be full of tiny lint—you have transferred them via your wet hands to the sample. Oh no! What do you do?

A. Run to the sink and rinse your hands, cover the sample you were working on so that no dust gets in, then carefully tweeze some of your black lint into the control sample? Go to 5B.

B. Cover the sample you were working on so that no dust gets in, run to the sink and rinse your hands, then carefully tweeze some of your black lint into the control sample? Go to 5A.

4B. Kai looks at you curiously as you fill a spray bottle full of warm water and grab some towels, but nods knowingly as you gently spray the bag in the freezer until it comes loose on its own. You carefully clean up any water to make sure this doesn't happen to the next person. You bring the sample to the sink, rinse the bag three times, and then put it in a dish of warm water to thaw completely, just like Kai showed you. No water gets into the bag, so you know your thawing worked nicely and didn't result in any rips.

Kai then shows you how to make a control sample, or "blank." They attach double-sided tape to a petri dish and leave the top open, and they shake their hair into it and a pinch of their lab coat. "We'll leave it open while we work, and dust will settle there." They tell you about how any type of plastic found in the control is discounted from the final analysis of the sample, since it is likely the plastic came from the lab environment rather than the original sample.

The next part of your training is to cut open the thawed guts over a set of sieves, washing all contents into them. You carefully make sure no water splashes out of the sieves, since you assume microplastics can surf (you are correct). Next, you and Kai bring the sieves over to a microscope and start looking in the gut contents for plastics. You slowly start a grid-pattern search, looking for plastics. A couple of minutes later, you catch sight of your own finger, enormous in the microscope's field of view—all covered in tiny black flecks! You realize that you scratched your leg earlier, and your black pants must be full of tiny lint. You have transferred them via your wet hands to the sample. Oh no! What do you do?

A. Run to the sink and rinse your hands, cover the sample you were working on so that no dust gets in, then carefully tweeze some of your black lint into the control sample? Go to 5B.

B. Cover the sample you were working on so that no dust gets in, run to the sink and rinse your hands, then carefully tweeze some of your black lint into the control sample? Go to 5B.

4C. You gently wiggle the bag back and forth, tugging on it to get it loose. Suddenly, the bag pops into your hands, free from its confines. It looks like some of the bag ripped, but the frozen sample looks to be completely intact. You bring the sample to the sink, rinse the bag three times, and then put it in a dish of warm water to thaw like Kai showed you. You notice that some water gets into the bag through the tear. Kai writes this on the data sheet. "We'll have to treat this water as part of the sample now," they say. "Microplastics could be moving in and out of the sample bag, and we'd never see them." They cover the thawing tray as best they can with a glass dish overtop. "To stop plastic dust from getting in," they explain.

Kai then shows you how to make a control sample, or "blank." They attach double-sided tape to a petri dish and leave the top open, and they shake their hair into it and a pinch of their lab coat. "We'll leave it open while we work, and dust will settle there." They tell you about how any type of plastic found in the control is discounted from the final analysis of the sample, since it is likely the plastic came from the lab environment rather than the original sample.

The next part of your training is to cut open the thawed guts over a set of sieves, washing all contents into them. You carefully make sure no water splashes out of the sieves and takes your sample with it. Next, you and Kai bring the sieves over to a microscope and start looking in the gut contents for plastics. You slowly start a grid-pattern search, looking for plastics. A couple of minutes later, you catch sight of your own finger, enormous in the microscope's field of view—all covered in tiny black flecks! You realize that you scratched your leg earlier, and your black pants must be full of tiny lint. You have transferred them via your wet hands to the sample. Oh no! What do you do?

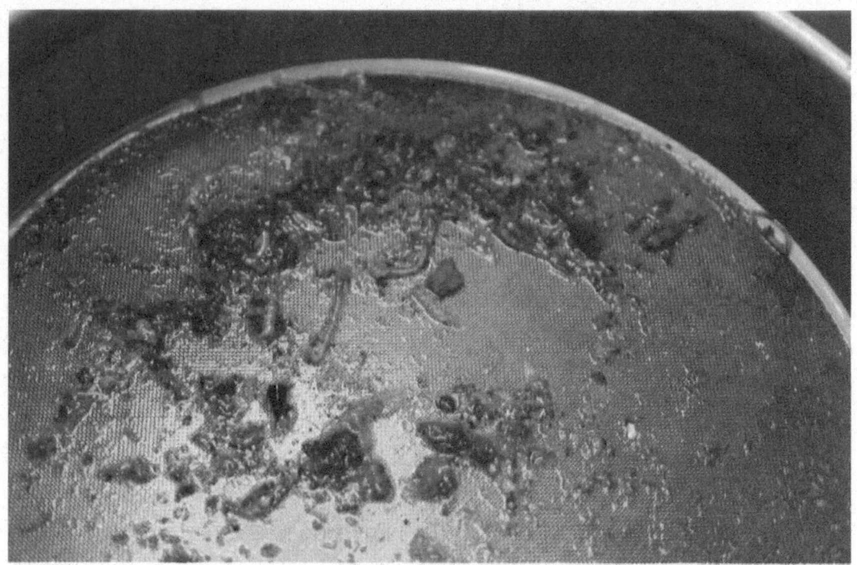

FIGURE 6.2
A sieve with gut contents in it. It's tricky looking for something the size of dust in here! This is why you're using a grid-pattern search.

A. Run to the sink and rinse your hands, cover the sample you were working on so that no dust gets in, then carefully tweeze some of your black lint into the control sample? Go to 5B.

B. Cover the sample you were working on so that no dust gets in, run to the sink and rinse your hands, then carefully tweeze some of your black lint into the control sample? Go to 5C.

5A. You're now very concerned that you have taken so long processing the sample that extra dust will get in. Do you:

A. Move quickly, processing the rest of the sample as efficiently as possible? Go to 6D.

B. Take your time, processing the rest of the sample as thoroughly as possible? Go to 6A.

5B. You're now very concerned that you have taken so long processing the sample that extra dust will get in. Do you:

A. Move quickly, processing the rest of the sample as efficiently as possible? Go to 6D.

B. Take your time, processing the rest of the sample as thoroughly as possible? Go to 6B.

5C. You're now very concerned that you have taken so long processing the sample that extra dust will get in. Do you:

A. Move quickly, processing the rest of the sample as efficiently as possible? Go to 6D.

B. Take your time, processing the rest of the sample as thoroughly as possible? Go to 6C.

6A. The habits you develop on your training day stay with you for the next few weeks when Kai and the lab director have a meeting with you. They pull out a spreadsheet on quality assurance and show you that, unbeknownst to you, many of the samples are spiked with a planted red microplastic they call Waldo. "If people find Waldo, we know they have processed the sample thoroughly. If they don't, we know they're missing plastics," the director explains. "You found all the Waldos! Also, when we look at the microfibers you found, after we subtract that black pants mishap, all your microfiber contamination was within normal ranges. Congratulations and thank you!" The data from the study you were part of reports the complete size range and types of microplastics that could be found in samples, including microfibers (after the types of dust-sized plastics in the control sample are removed from the study). In northern environments, microfibers are either from wastewater (usually via laundry), dust, or long-range transport from waters further south. The study finds that there are very likely two major sources of microfibers in the Inuit community the samples are from: one bay where the community's sewage discharges, and waters directly in the current coming from the south. This helps the local government make decisions about infrastructure and participation in national plastic policies.

6B. The habits you develop on your training day stay with you for the next few weeks when Kai and the lab director have a meeting with you. They pull out a spreadsheet on quality assurance and show you that, unbeknownst to you, many of the samples are spiked with a planted red microplastic they call Waldo. "If people find Waldo, we know they have processed the sample thoroughly. If they don't, we know they're missing plastics," the director explains. "You found all the Waldos! But there was something off about the microfibers from your samples, even after we subtracted all the short black ones from your pants and the blank. There were just a lot of other microfibers, much higher than in other samples. We think some contamination came in, but we can't pinpoint the source from the control. So, we're going to have to exclude microfibers from the study altogether. Otherwise, we'll overreport microfibers, and as scientists, our ethic is to discount potential false positives when we're not sure." The study is published, although without microfibers being reported, it is published in a less prestigious journal. The study can still be compared to older studies that were conducted before microfibers became a category of microplastic around 2016. When the lab director shares the results with Inuit partners, the director explains how this kind of work is tricky and that sometimes we have to remove microfibers to be sure of results. On the bright side, they can compare the results to older studies and see some trends in plastic abundance and distribution that the local government can use to make decisions later.

6C. The habits you develop on your training day stay with you for the next few weeks when Kai and the lab director have a meeting with you. They pull out a spreadsheet on quality assurance and show you that, unbeknownst to you, many of the samples are spiked with a planted red microplastic they call Waldo. "If people find Waldo, we know they have processed the sample thoroughly. If they don't, we know they're missing plastics," the director explains. "While it's normal to miss a piece once in a while, for some reason most of your Waldos are unaccounted for." This means there's an issue with quality control, and they cannot use any of the samples you processed in the study: "We just can't be sure how many plastics you didn't find! If you didn't find Waldo, you probably also didn't find other plastic pollution." Now, the lab will need to get more samples from Nunatsiavut to ensure a good sample size. The lab director talks to the funders and partners and tells them there will be a delay and starts applying for another grant to cover an extra season of fishing. You go back through basic training and practice on mackerel guts the lab director has left over from dinner until you start finding the Waldo plastics consistently.

6D. The habits you develop on your training day stay with you for the next few weeks when Kai and the lab director have a meeting with you. They pull out a spreadsheet on quality assurance and show you that, unbeknownst to you, many of the samples are spiked with a planted red microplastic they call Waldo. "If people find Waldo, we know they have processed the sample thoroughly. If they don't, we know they're missing plastics," the director explains. "We don't . . . really understand what happened here. Not only were your Waldos missing in nearly every sample, but there are all sorts of microfibers in your samples that weren't in any other samples or the control, and for some reason you have almost no fragment plastics either, which is one of our most common morphologies. We can't seem to pinpoint one source of error." Your sample plastics go into a special archive, and a chemist is hired to try to identify where they came from in the lab environment using spectrometry forensics, which will become its own study and paper (on which you will be a co-author), and results will also become part of new training materials (which you will be asked to test drive it as a key part of its evaluation). The lab director talks to the funders and partners and tells them there will be a delay and starts applying for another grant to cover an extra season of fishing. You're put on lit review duty and never touch a sample again.

CONCLUSION: NOT AGAINST PURITY

The Choose Your Own Lab Adventure results in four different knowledge outcomes based on the cascading ways that contamination chores were done. At no point does a study become invalid, but the terms of its validity—what it can and cannot reliably represent, for whom, and under what conditions—shift significantly. Chores make futures. The activities I've bundled into the term "chores" (maintaining controls, repairing unplanned contamination, and caring for the sample at its field of contamination generally) are not to stabilize an object or return something to a previous state in the way that repair chores do. Rather, they are designed to coordinate a field of possibility. In all cases, purity, or the idea of contamination versus an uncontaminated state, is a model, but it is never a doctrine, a morality, or something real. Elsewhere, I have written about scientific protocols as "orienting technologies, pointing us toward certain futures" (Liboiron 2021, 122). Contamination chores are an example of such orienting technologies.

These chores are about disciplining comportment (often a critique of purity but also a requirement of any methodology). CLEAR lab members often remark on how contamination chores come to change their perspectives on their everyday worlds. Now, they see "invisible" microfibers everywhere. One member who did plastic identification from home during a COVID pandemic lockdown remarked on how she became intimate with the scale of microfiber relations at her house, including the influence of her bedcover, bathrobe, and couch on her science. I now laugh, sneeze, and sigh out of the corner of my mouth so as not to disturb samples under the microscope, even when I'm not in the lab. CLEAR members notice when someone uses a lint roller, or not. We don't rub our arms against our lab coats when we walk. Our bodies and the ways we know our environments become tied into microfibers: sensing them, anticipating them, moving among them.

This work understands its relationship to purity much differently than most social science and STS literature. We do not seek to annihilate the concept of purity—in fact, we need it even if we also critique it. Indeed, we use purity as an orienting model to live among ubiquitous pollutants in a way that neither moralizes purity nor stigmatizes pollution (Murphy 2017). Even though they are fraught, we find that purity models are not fragile and can help us maintain a course in our research. Sebastian Utera has written that contamination chores, broadly conceived, are "care practices central to enacting waste regimes because, and in clear contrast with managerial optimism, they force us to 'give up dreams of perfection or control, but keep on trying' (Mol, 2008: 93)" (2021, 15). To return to Simmonds, purity models can guide affective attachments, given uneven power relations, and require neither annihilation of either purity or pollution nor an easy existence with them.

ACKNOWLEDGMENTS

Special thanks to CLEAR members Molly Rivers, Alex Flynn, Kaitlyn Hawkins, Domenica Lombeida, and Charlotte Florian for sharing their stories of contamination chores with me and for reviewing this text.

REFERENCES

Bowker, Geoffrey C., and Susan Leigh Star. 2000. *Sorting Things Out: Classification and Its Consequences*. Cambridge, MA: MIT Press.

Cetina, Karin Knorr. 1999. *Epistemic Cultures: How the Sciences Make Knowledge*. Cambridge, MA: Harvard University Press.

Douglas, Mary. 1966. *Purity and Danger: An Analysis of Concepts of Purity and Taboo.* London: Routledge.

Glen, Alexander. 1876. "Appendix B: Fourth Report of the Commissioners Appointed in 1868 to Inquire into the Best Means of Preventing the Pollution of Rivers." In *The Rivers Pollution Prevention Act, 1876, 39 & 40 Vict. C. 75: With Introduction, Notes, and Index*, 75–70. XXX: Knight & Company.

Hale, Charles R. 2006. "Activist Research v. Cultural Critique: Indigenous Land Rights and the Contradictions of Politically Engaged Anthropology." *Cultural Anthropology* 21 (1): 96–120.

Hamlin, Christopher. 1990. *A Science of Impurity: Water Analysis in Nineteenth Century Britain.* Oakland: University of California Press.

Hamlin, Christopher. 2000. "'Waters' or 'Water'?—Master Narratives in Water History and Their Implications for Contemporary Water Policy." *Water Policy* 2 (4–5): 313–325.

Liboiron, Max. 2021. *Pollution Is Colonialism.* Durham, NC: Duke University Press.

Liboiron, Max. 2017. "Compromised agency: The case of BabyLegs." *Engaging Science, Technology, and Society* 3: 499–527.

Liboiron, Max, and Josh Lepawsky. 2022. *Discard Studies: Wasting, Systems, and Power.* Cambridge, MA: MIT Press.

Masco, Joseph. 2004. "Mutant Ecologies: Radioactive Life in Post–Cold War New Mexico." *Cultural Anthropology* 19 (4): 517–550.

Mody, Cyrus C. M. 2001. "A Little Dirt Never Hurt Anyone: Knowledge-Making and Contamination in Materials Science." *Social Studies of Science* 31 (1): 7–36.

Morgan, Mary S., and Margaret Morrison. 1999. *Models as Mediators.* Cambridge: Cambridge University Press.

Murphy, Michelle. 2015. "Unsettling Care: Troubling Transnational Itineraries of Care in Feminist Health Practices." *Social Studies of Science* 45 (5): 717–737.

Murphy, Michelle. 2017. "Alterlife and Decolonial Chemical Relations." *Cultural Anthropology* 32 (4): 494–503.

paperson, la. 2017. *A Third University Is Possible.* Minneapolis: University of Minnesota Press.

Pine, Kathleen H., and Max Liboiron. 2015. "The Politics of Measurement and Action." In *Proceedings of the 33rd Annual ACM Conference on Human Factors in Computing Systems*, 3147–3156. New York: ACM.

Prata, Joana C., Vanessa Reis, João P. da Costa, Catherine Mouneyrac, Armando C. Duarte, and Teresa Rocha-Santos. 2021. "Contamination Issues as a Challenge in Quality Control and Quality Assurance in Microplastics Analytics." *Journal of Hazardous Materials* 403: 123660.

Raffles, Hugh. 2017. "Against Purity." *Social Research: An International Quarterly* 84 (1): 171–182.

Shotwell, Alexis. 2016. *Against Purity: Living Ethically in Compromised Times.* Minneapolis: University of Minnesota Press.

Soto, Ana, and Gracen Brilmyer. 2020. "On Language, Scientific Metaphor, and Endocrine Disruption: An Interview with Feminist Scientist Ana Soto." *Catalyst: Feminism, Theory, Technoscience* 6 (1): 1–8.

TallBear, Kim. 2013. *Native American DNA: Tribal Belonging and the False Promise of Genetic Science.* Minneapolis: University of Minnesota Press.

Tarr, Joel A., Terry Yosie, and James McCurley III. 1980. "Disputes over Water Quality Policy: Professional Cultures in Conflict, 1900–1917." *American Journal of Public Health* 70 (4): 427–435.

Traweek, Sharon. 2009. *Beamtimes and Lifetimes.* Cambridge, MA: Harvard University Press.

Ureta, Sebastian. 2020. "Ruination Science: Producing Knowledge from a Toxic World." *Science, Technology, & Human Values* 46 (1): 29–52.

Zhang, Junjie, Lei Wang, and Kurunthachalam Kannan. 2020. "Microplastics in House Dust from 12 Countries and Associated Human Exposure." *Environment International* 134: 105314.

7 CONVERSATION WITH MARÍA PUIG DE LA BELLACASA

FERANDO DOMÍNGUEZ, RUBIO (FDR): Can you tell us what you've learned from these two chapters and where you think the main points or connections or divergence are between them.

MARÍA PUIG DE LA BELLACASA (MPDLB): I think there are two interconnected lines of thinking that put these chapters in resonance. One is how both are exploring fragilities in the context of control. That's how it appeared to me. The first chapter—from Marisol de la Cadena and Santiago Martínez Medina—concerns control in processes of artificial insemination. "The second one" by, in turn, Max Liboiron's chapter, describes situations within the protocols of an experimental lab, in which people are controlling the contamination of a sample. I think this issue of control is important regarding the general intervention of this book. I'll get back to this point.

Another dimension that connects these two chapters is that they both approach fragility as an exception in a specific process. This somehow contrasts with other chapters in the book and with most research on maintenance and care that shows how fragility is ontologically wired to more-than-human worlds as we know them.

By apprehending fragility from these two perspectives—as an exception in processes of control rather than as part of the ontological fragility of a specific situation—I think these chapters add a level of complexity. Especially, what I learned from Marisol de la Cadena and Santiago Martínez Medina's chapter is that making someone or something fragile is political. In their chapter, fragility appears as what the processes of these artificial insemination techniques are trying to avoid at all costs: they are fragile because they can fail any time.

What haunts these manipulations is given in the title of the chapter: "the fragility of a mighty process." What they show is that the process requires nothing short of perfectly precise artificial human–cow encounters with the flawlessness required for cattle to become capital. What is significant is how the authors refer to *fragility* to qualify the impossibility of perfection in these forced adjustments. And yet, they show that the requirements of precise encounters extend to a variety of uncontrollable elements: the bodies, the tools, and the bacteria the cows' uteri, the joy of the cows . . . And they don't shy away from describing these processes in all their disturbing details (how the cows' bodies are manipulated, with the negation of their own fragility at play). What makes the process fragile here is that it can fail. Mistake and failure are felt as exceptions here. Fragility is not apprehended as a quality of the world but rather as an exception by the people enacting this process. This text shows a world in which fragility isn't meant to be happening.

When Max Liboiron speaks about the work of CLEAR, the Civic Laboratory of Environmental Action Research, they insist that nothing in this work is delicate, vulnerable, flimsy, insubstantial, or easily destroyed. These terms, which could be associated with fragility, seem pejorative in some ways. Liboiron somehow puts a defensive stance against fragility in a context where the idea of fragility diminishes the quality of things, and it's something to be avoided. Furthermore, as Liboiron shows, this lab is working with samples from Inuit homelands, that when qualified as fragile, it is by the settler state, mostly as a justification to intervene and advance settler colonialism.

I find this aspect really interesting. It reminded me of some discussions in the late 1990s, preoccupied with how the concept of "vulnerability" had become a category used to replace more implicitly critical notions of "excluded" or "discriminated" groups. Here, changing the category from "excluded" to "vulnerable" made invisible the act of exclusion—the fact that somebody or something may be acting to exclude a group of people. Instead, these are considered (intrinsically) vulnerable, and therefore their situation of needed some kind of assistance would be basically their responsibility. Keeping this in mind furthers the idea that fragility is relational. It can be interesting to projects with a specific perspective to claim a state of fragility, but in another situation, it can be a shifting quality, such as what Liboiron explains about the strength of a brick: a brick can be seen as something strong, but it can be *made* fragile by a bulldozer. Liboiron argues that there is a fetishization in making something fragile per se that may hide the relations at play in this qualification and which makes it a property of the thing itself. What is interesting here is not just that Liboiron makes an ontological statement about fragility, but also that there is always an ethical and political stake in qualifying something as fragile.

It is a lot like "care," and this is one aspect that connects with my own work. Care and fragility are highly charged concepts. More precisely, these two chapters highlight how exploring the field of fragility is ethically and politically charged. It is not an isolated concept. In other words, they reveal the ambivalence in reclaiming fragility, in the gesture itself of reclaiming fragility, which is one of the aims of this volume.

For me, recognizing fragility as a condition shared by potentially everyone is important because I have lived in a world marked by forms of power that have stigmatized fragility, excluding hose seen as fragile, increasing their exposure to the oppressive powers that have contributed to make them fragile in the first place. In such context, demonstrating that all things are fragile is a subversive project. Yet, in an ambivalent way, a feminist perspective also reveals what it means to live in a world that stigmatizes and demeans women as fragile. The subversive move then involves resisting that qualifier, demonstrating strength, and showing that, as women, we are not intrinsically fragile.

Standing against fragility and promoting fragility are questions of positionality.

So, these are important lessons from these chapters: fragility is ontologically relational, but it's also politically and ethically charged. And as such, the discussion gains from staying within these tensions.

FDR: Your own work has had care at the center of your inquiry. How do you think these contributions relate to your own work?

MPDLB: Both chapters expand and complicate the question of what counts as care practice and then the wider context of care. And this again is related to the context of control the chapters investigate.

In their chapter, de la Cadena and Martínez Medina discuss fragility in a context that would be very difficult to qualify as a caring context. The reproductive practices that are imposed on the cows are coercive. But on the other hand, even there, you could describe ways in which the people who are doing this are "careful" and show how they try not to hurt the cows. So, there is a lot of work of care put into taking care of this cow. But it is with the aim of maintaining these animals in a state of reproductive machines. And the way the lens of fragility is applied to the context of these reproductive technologies by the authors pertains to the process itself: they look at every moment of possible failure as a potential fragility of these life processes. Liboiron's chapter meanwhile does the opposite, since it takes the perspective of the attempt of purification rather than the possibility of failure. It's a completely different lens, I think, even if both chapters show technical processes that imply control, either of the purity of the experiment, of the sampling, or of the achievement of the objectives of the insemination.

In both cases, it is essential to acknowledge the ethically charged character of notions such as care and fragility by connecting the detailed empirical descriptions of what is happening on the ground to the larger relational contexts where they take place. It really is fundamental to see the broader consequences of a concept and of reclaiming that concept. This is what these chapters recall and how they complexify the idea that is at the center of this book, which consists in opening up the notion of fragility, which is and remains contested.

I think it's very much about acknowledging where one starts from, what specific trajectory means, when it comes to engaging with fragility. This is a way of enacting situatedness. Acknowledging that doesn't mean, obviously, that a concept works everywhere in the same way, but that it may allow you to open a number of concerns of problems. As I am myself writing about how we may hold ethical obligation to assist processes of material breakdown, I am also interested in how things can open up when you attempt connections between seemingly opposed projects of looking at the world from the perspective of caring for its fragility and simultaneously from the perspective of embracing the necessity and inevitability of breakdown.

Going back to de la Cadena and Martínez Medina's chapter, as I said earlier, when they talk about fragility, it's about the failure of a system. There's a mistake in the process. And several times, I was asking myself, reading it, do we want to call this fragility? And that's simply because I was reading from my own assumptions about what fragility does, what fragility says, how fragility becomes conceived as such, and so on. And that's probably why I flinch when I see it applied to talk about the failure of technical processes. But eventually, this is really interesting because it disrupts the way we see technology. It provokes friction. I probably would have expected the fragility of the cow to be discussed and highlighted in this context. Because what we understand, reading the chapter, is that the objective of the process of control is to produce a singular cow that can be inseminated. And as a reader, I may want the process to fail . . . I want it to fail, but the problem is that if it doesn't work, the cow is going to be killed. It's horrific—there is no escape for the cow. If the cow *fails*—and at some point, the cows have a say when their bodies answer and resist—the response is death. She gets slaughtered. This is why I wanted this fragility to be about the cow. I didn't want it to be about the technology. My reaction may be close to Liboiron's when they say they don't want us to talk about fragility in this context. In enacting these frictions, this text manifests and exposes sensitivities around this concept.

FDR: This is a great point that illustrates the relationality of the notion of fragility. Once you place fragility in the technical system instead of the cow, the ethical and moral claims are displaced. And naming something as fragile does something not only because it helps to describe it and to raise ethical and political question about it, but also because when you ask these questions, you also stop asking questions about something else (in this case, we stop asking questions about or from the cow). It will be interesting as a thought experiment to ask: If the question of fragility was about the cow, if we center the cow as the thing that is fragile and has to be cared for, what would the whole experiment look like? It would probably be entirely different.

MPDLB: Yes, absolutely. Because, again, this is enlarging the frame. There is no way that this whole technoscientific arrangement is not going to be about producing more cows. If we look at it from the perspective of the fragility of the cow, we will see that the fragility of the cow will always be recognized to be managed, so that she doesn't fall apart, so that she can still have babies. So, there's work of care here in some way. One cannot say that this is not about care. And then we have a perspective (on that form of care) and what we would want to do about it. What de la Cadena and Martínez Medina's chapter shows well is that the whole reproductive machinery is organized in a way that is completely antithetical to any welfare of the cows. And somehow, insisting on the fragility of the protocols, of this process, makes it appear unbearably shocking.

JÉRÔME DENIS: What you seem to imply is that we have to deal with the tension of reclaiming fragility as a "sensitizing concept," in Blumer's term—something that opens up the way we describe and apprehend practices, environments, realties, and fragility as an ethically charged concept. Which means that, even with our good faith of opening things up, we may be actually closing down ethically and politically important issues.

DAVID PONTILLE: What do you think about the overall intent of this volume to focus on fragility? What do you think we can gain from such a move? And what do you think could be possible limitations, shortcomings, or dangers?

MPDLB: First of all, I see a lot of strength in destigmatizing fragility. And I think this is what this book is doing, especially in eliciting the conditions that make someone or something fragile and another seemingly not, or less, fragile. This goes together with foregrounding that there is no space in our world that is not pervaded by unequal relations of power. This is something that always has to be elicited around a concept of fragility in a situation: who makes whom, or what, fragile. I cannot imagine fragility as something neutral anywhere. Particularly, I think that this concept can help to think of tensions that always worry me about care, which turn around the collusion between care and control. Focusing on fragility and reclaiming the notion, to me, is a way to make an opening in a world that is structurally built against it. A world that is organized around the fear of fragility, an abjection around the need to be cared for. These fears are at the heart of forms of domination. The same could be said about the ways some human bodies are shielded from their fragilities and made stronger and more destructive in their privileged endurance. That is something that I've been thinking a lot about with regards to the refusal of breakdown. The fact that some political and some historical logics, let's say white supremacist capitalism, have been constantly shielding themselves against breakdown by breaking down all others (making them fragile). However, breakdown is something that we can share in a world that is fragile by definition. A lot can be said about how what is made to endure and become sturdy in this world is made this way, against recognizing a predisposition to break, for many others and for ourselves.

It also may be that fragility can be articulated as a strength somehow. I don't know how far we can go with that. It's tricky.

Now, in terms of limitations, shortcomings, or dangers, in this conversation, I have thought as a theorist. I don't think these questions gain from being articulated as shortcomings or limitations. I mean, in terms of absolute limitation, they are about the ethical ways in which concepts oblige us and how the constraints of concepts, when we deploy them in a world, are teaching us something—they are potentially revealing aspects of a world, as much as of the ways in which we are implicated or involved in an intervention.

In reading the chapters and engaging with this volume, I think I have become more sensitive to how we specify what is meant by fragile in a particular context and what we are trying to say by eliciting the conditions of fragility. When discovering the chapters, I kept thinking, "What are the consequences of qualifying something as fragile? Where does it take us?" And if there is no absolute concept of fragility it's always going to be quite complex, by definition, to engage with fragility in the fraught worlds that we live in. So, engaging with fragility should never be easy. Maybe these feelings come from having experienced these ambivalences when engaging positively with the concept of care as a concept that had been criticized for its potential consequences, including by feminists. In this sense, it might also be interesting to think about the other concepts that we would like to associate with the notion: its conceptual relational space we could imagine for the thinking of fragility. Finally, if fragility, as I already said, is a question of positionality, then—like with the dynamics of care in unjust worlds—fragilities are inevitably unevenly distributed.

So, as a final note, I would say that an argument for fragility is generating an involvement. Because of this, the more situated and open this stance is, the more effective it will be. I think these two chapters open the possibilities not only of thinking from and with fragility but also of thinking against fragility—in different ways from those in which the status quo is against fragility. This is what is so interesting about these two chapters read together: they elicit and generate resistances and tensions about engaging with fragility in very different ways, thinking from worlds where fragility is meant to be avoided at all costs.

III LABOR

8 CARE IN FRAGMENTS: ECOLOGIES OF SUPPORT BEYOND REPAIR

TOMÁS SÁNCHEZ CRIADO AND VINCENT DUCLOS

> If "the world" is to be saved, this will be in each of its fragments. As for the totality, it can only be *managed*.
>
> —the Invisible Committee, *Now* (2017)

Writing almost two years into a global pandemic response gone wild (ripe with vaccine colonialism, securitarian nationalism, and blatantly unequal exposure to the virus), with public infrastructures in shambles, amid the splintering effects of decades of neoliberal policies and centuries-long settler and white supremacist violence, it seems pretty safe to suggest that care is falling to pieces. Care, a series of practices by which life is supported and made to thrive, is in fragments. When dealing with such a state of affairs, care thinking can become complicit with a tendency to subsume care, and indeed the organization of collective life, under a project of repair understood narrowly as a mere recovery of lost function. But what if taking care beyond repair entailed attending to fragmented lives without any hope of return to a lost unity or to a retrieved "normality"? Even in fragments, care demands to be defended—perhaps, even, *especially* in fragments.

The often disempowering or weakening effects of fragmentation are well documented. In this chapter, however, we examine how fragmentation may also give rise to, intensify, and pluralize the relations that hold and support lives—precariously composing what we call "ecologies of support" (Duclos and Criado 2020). When referring to fragments, we have in mind neither ruins nor parts of a whole that could be stitched back together. Rather, we are interested in the shattered parts that remain after wholes implode or are destroyed, be it by sheer violence, carelessness, or inattention. Against the persistent charms of unity, caring in fragments, bit by bit, activates a politics of groping for the appropriate supports: gauging whether singular forms of life might emerge, persist, and grow without compromising their life-supporting efficacy.

By exploring fragments and their afterlives, we aim to contribute to thinking about fragility not merely in the negative form of a loss, as the notions of ruins, degradation, or decay tend to pose. Rather than drawing from the reparative and restorative approaches that often haunt maintenance and repair studies, this chapter focuses on the endurance of fragments and how they may multiply and unfold in unexpected ways. In this sense, the language of the afterlife offers a powerful alternative to other terms that suggest a certain fall from a primordial unity. It opens up a way of thinking about fragility that allows us to see it as potentially—but not necessarily—generative and as something that can be embraced rather than avoided or fixed.

Hence, expounding the power of or rather lying within fragments, this chapter raises the question: How can continuity between fragments be cultivated? How do fragments endure? To examine this practical question, this chapter tells the story of two different ecologies of support, sharing similar concerns to articulate singular forces and situations with demands for continuity. The first story discusses MOS@N, a mobile health (mHealth) initiative that was implemented in Nouna, rural Burkina Faso. MOS@N was a network infrastructure that used mobile communication to improve medical follow-up and care. Central to MOS@N was the work of godmothers, who were selected and equipped with phones and bicycles to act as "community relays," following up with pregnant women in their respective villages. As is often the case with mHealth networks, MOS@N did not deploy as planned. Its everyday activities relied on a series of practices and relations of care that were gradually improvised over the course of three years—the most significant of which was the expansion of the role of godmothers to include the physical accompaniment of pregnant women to local primary care centers. MOS@N ran out of funding and was terminated in 2018. However, three years later, godmothers still carry care work in their communities. The project is over, but some of its most demanding activities endure and have taken on a life of their own—without any kind of formal or institutional support.

This chapter explores the afterlives of MOS@N, with particular attention to the continued work of godmothers and the related obligations. In this case, the notion of the afterlife is helpful to understand how a decaying project remains alive through the diffracting and diverging work of its fragments, not desiring to return to or restore a lost unity.

The second story features a particular form of design activism that emerged in Spain in the early 2010s, a time of a profound crisis of public care infrastructures: namely, harsh austerity cuts affecting the provision and the scope of private–public care technology markets as a result of the 2008 financial crisis. Activating a wide variety of embodied experiences and knowledge practices from do-it-yourself (DIY) amateurs, these initiatives, coagulating around a collective called *En torno a la silla*, didn't wish things to go back to where they were. Their workings appeared as the nemesis of standardized technical aids portfolios and of the ableist notions undergirding welfarist markets. In this chapter, we ethnographically follow traces of their inquiries and interventions that started after the *indignados* movement in the city of Barcelona. Discussing in particular the attempts at building a Tinkering Network, self-managing the making and repair of technical aids, we describe the challenge of ecologies addressing the almost impossible task of sustaining bodily diversity with fragmentary forms of DIY making. Although the Tinkering Network formally ceased in 2016, perhaps suggesting a process where nearly nothing remains, in this chapter, we also discuss the afterlives of its traces, through which some of its fragments endure, still being generative and productive in their own right.

Anthropology and science and technology studies (STS) scholarship have shown how infrastructures and networks tend to evolve slowly over time, and "how 'formal,' planned structure melds with or gives way to 'informal,' locally emergent structure," which may take hitherto unimaginable forms (Star and Ruhleder 1996, 409). Improvisation, tinkering, and open-endedness have been central to recent work on care practices (Mol, Moser, and Pols 2010), showing how togetherness or stability—technical or otherwise—is contingent on the continuous labor of social and material ordering (Denis and Pontille 2015; Simone 2004). As Annemarie Mol has suggested, care entails a continuous process of "attuning the many viscous variables of a life to each other" (2008, 54)—a task of handling life as a perpetual work to be done, which "goes on and on, until the day you die."

Very much in tune with these works, in the stories that follow, care entails learning how to cultivate continuity between fragments. However, in both stories, fragments only endure to the extent that they do not merely prolong or preserve past iterations of care. Rather, their afterlives generate openings and interstitial movements from which something new, still indeterminate, can grow. In either case, it is not possible to subsume the singularity of what care gathers under a larger totality or identity, to be managed by troops of experts and technocrats. In these stories, care appears as a process whereby disenfranchised actors seek to find endurance in uninhabitable domains—not an endurance that is about the "resilience of human life" but rather one that "entails the actions of bodies indifferent to their own coherence" (Simone 2019, 19). Care in fragments, to again borrow from Simone, "isn't just leaving things unfinished, it is not giving in to the constant of being incomplete or under duress, but rather creating conditions in which the disparate might stick together" (2019, 33). In telling these stories, our aim is to explore the stickiness of fragments and their afterlives, paying special attention to shared singularities, to confederacies of existence enabling the dissimilar to endure in its collective non-wholeness.

THE AFTERLIVES OF GLOBAL HEALTH (BURKINA FASO, 2014–)

> We are told that the project is finished but we cannot stop this work, we love this work, it is the village that chose us and it is not because the project is stopped that we will stop too.
>
> —Godmother E, Labarani

The next few pages discuss the implementation and afterlives of MOS@N, a mobile health project that monitored maternal and child health in the district of Nouna in rural Burkina Faso. MOS@N was implemented in a context where the proportion of women attending at least two antenatal care visits and delivering in a health facility remains relatively low. High maternal mortality rates also remain a major public health challenge in Burkina Faso. MOS@N aimed to use mobile technology to improve the medical monitoring and follow-up of pregnant women. Designed and launched by the Centre de Recherche en Santé de Nouna (CRSN), MOS@N was implemented in 2014 as a modest socio-technical infrastructure. It involved building a mobile network, including an electronic medical record system, which would send automated voice medical appointment reminders of upcoming (or missed) antenatal care visits. Central to MOS@N—and to this vignette—was the work of "godmothers"—community relays who would receive the appointment reminders and follow up with pregnant women in their respective villages. Until early 2018, MOS@N formally connected five health centers (CSPS) to twenty-eight villages in the district of Nouna in the Kossi Province in the western part of Burkina Faso. But as we shall see later, although the project is formally over, fragments of MOS@N have endured, maintaining and pluralizing relations that hold and support lives.

Over the past seven years, one of us (V.D.) has been working closely with researchers from the CRSN to document MOS@N. They have followed the design and implementation of the project, with particular attention to its impact on care infrastructure and practices in Nouna.

From its implementation, it was evident that people, devices, and data did not circulate smoothly along the network. Among many other challenges, MOS@N struggled particularly with technical issues. Phones, mobile connectivity, solar panels, and bicycles were frequently broken or failing. Sustainable communication required a constant additional effort of repair. When repair was not possible, godmothers had to come up with alternative solutions: charging their phones in local shops, for example, when the solar panels failed. Erratic network connectivity also plagued the mHealth infrastructure, leading godmothers to miss calls or delaying their access to voice messages.

As a response to these technical challenges, MOS@N's field coordinator, along with godmothers and health workers, altered the network. This was the case of the role of godmothers, which was considerably modified and extended in the course of MOS@N's implementation. In the initial design of the project, godmothers would receive the voice messages with automated reminders of antenatal consultations and then follow up with pregnant women. To do so, they were equipped with a mobile phone, a portable solar charger, and a bicycle to facilitate the communication of health information, as well as their own circulation, between the CSPS and villages. But as the automated reminder system faltered over broken equipment and poor network connectivity, the role of godmothers shifted from merely communicating information to pregnant women to *accompanying* them physically. A few months into the project, godmothers indeed started to accompany pregnant women for their medical visits at the CSPS, including being there for delivery. Godmothers and pregnant women started walking miles together, at times crossing watercourses on pirogues or on foot. But accompaniment meant more than just walking with pregnant women to the CSPS. When women gave birth, godmothers washed them, their clothes, and the room. They stayed with them through the night and called relatives to keep them updated. In case of complications, they accompanied women to the hospital in the nearest city (Nouna), sometimes for days. In the process, they learnt how to assist health workers in deliveries as well—none of which was part of their original job description. Accompaniment involved a great amount of labor.

Care relationships, not only between godmothers and pregnant women but also between godmothers and their phones, transformed MOS@N in ways that redesigned it altogether. Phones remained instrumental in the expansion of godmothers' roles, but they did so in unforeseen ways. Godmothers and pregnant women often traveled long distances together, often on foot. Under these circumstances, the phone's flashlight proved to be instrumental for walking in the dark. Godmothers would also use their phone to call ahead to the CSPS to make sure health workers were actually present or to be certain that the dispensary had the medication they needed. Not infrequently in Nouna, pregnant women would end up needing medical attention while on the road. On these occasions, phones were used to alert health workers and family. However, phones, batteries, and solar chargers often broke down and needed to be repaired. To perform their duties, godmothers cared not only for the women they accompanied but also for *things* that composed the network. Care, as anthropologists and STS scholars have shown (e.g., Mol, Moser, and Pols 2010), entails tinkering with what is present in a given situation, including the messy details of a socio-technical infrastructure: unstable network infrastructure, broken phones, or pregnant women walking down dirt roads on their own. In MOS@N, care materialized in fragments out of not only fragile, makeshift connections but also demanding, time-consuming work.

After three years of operations, MOS@N was discontinued in early 2018. Like the majority of mHealth projects, MOS@N had from the start been designed and funded as a pilot project, with a fixed beginning and ending. However, more than three years after the project was officially shut down, most godmothers are still accompanying pregnant women to the CSPS. They do so without institutional support—and without pay. One godmother summarizes the current situation, as follows:

> The project is finished but according to me the activity is not finished. Even tomorrow if I am not handicapped by any illness, if a woman comes to ask for my help, I will do what I can do. That is why I say that the activity continues. If I say that the project is finished and that everything is finished, and she was intending to ask for my support, she will not do it anymore.
> —Godmother D, Dara

The distinction between "activity" and "project" is important. Activity, for godmothers such as D, refers to a set of relational practices that do not follow any clear instructions as to how care should be practiced. Godmothers do not try to maintain the project as it used to be. They know well enough that MOS@N is not coming back in its previous form. They are not trying to fix or repair MOS@N as a project. They are working from some of its fragments to generate singular practices and relations, emerging yet diverging from MOS@N.

Commitments and habits do not magically evaporate as projects terminate. Care work carried out by the godmothers came with important affective and ethical implications. While some godmothers invoke moral or religious principles to explain their continued commitment to the accompaniment of pregnant women, most instead suggest that they aim to sustain relations of support that were developed over the past few years. For them, the ethical obligation to care relates to the material conditions of reproductive health in the district of Nouna. "Childbirth is a difficult thing, so if the woman asks for you, it is like an obligation for you to go with her, you can't refuse. Our communities consulted before choosing us, they believed in us, so we must take up this challenge," explains godmother N in Lekuy. Any formal contract linking godmothers to MOS@N is now terminated. Godmothers, however, feel that they remain responsible for life in their communities.

The obligation of care should be situated within the wider social structure of everyday life in Nouna. Accompaniment transformed the relationship godmothers had with fellow village dwellers. For many, being a godmother has brought a new social status, especially since accompaniment was introduced. They might be referred to as "Woman Doctor" (*dôgtôrô mousso* in Dioula), and the family of patients might bring them small presents such as soap, meat, peanuts, maize, fish, or candies:

> Many of us receive great consideration and respect thanks to this project. It has strengthened our collaborations, our friendships with many people and even

> among us godmothers. It is thanks to the project that we have known each other well enough to strengthen our relationships with respect. Before you could go a few years without seeing a person, but thanks to the project that person now might think of you and visit you to discuss. In my opinion this project has been very beneficial especially in our collaboration with each other and in the community. It has brought understanding and strengthened friendships. Anyone you have ever accompanied for childbirth, wherever she meets you, she will appreciate and respect you. This is very common now.
>
> —Godmother E, Dara

For some godmothers, the end of the financial compensation earned from MOS@N came with improved relations with women in their village. Compensation sometimes came with a sense of envy or resentment toward godmothers. Other godmothers noted that even when they disclosed the project's termination at the village level, many villagers still believed that they were being paid for their work. In some cases, this also led to conflict with extended family members, who considered that godmothers should not neglect their household duty to carry out their work, or that they should otherwise share the money that they, in fact, no longer receive. Other godmothers have simply not disclosed the termination of the project to people in their village, thinking that they would hesitate to ask them for accompaniment to the CSPS if they knew.

Care, notes María Puig de la Bellacasa, "is a force distributed across a multiplicity of agencies and materials and supports our worlds as a thick mesh of relational obligation" (2017, 20). This seems like a fitting description for the work of care in and beyond MOS@N. MOS@N's afterlives, in particular, invite us to attend to a craftwork that disrupts dominant modes of knowledge production in global health. For example, the production of scientific knowledge about mHealth is primarily concerned with finding models, or at least features, that can be scaled. Global health interventions generally come with identifiable criteria for success, as well as clear beginnings and ends. Imagined futures often make things seem whole. But what is interesting in MOS@N is not so much how the project could be scaled or how a better project could be designed. Rather, it is what could be learned from that which *escapes* the project per se (Savransky and Tironi 2021, 19). There was always, in MOS@N, a surplus that was not accounted for: habits, labor, and affective relations that exceeded the technical configuration of the project. This surplus is not simply waiting to be fed back into the system, making it more productive, better designed, or otherwise. MOS@N's fragments are not broken parts of a whole. As a matter of fact, the persistence of the godmothers' work suggests that fragments in MOS@N were not as fragile as one might think. Against the charms of unity, they exist and endure in their own way, taking on a life of their own. MOS@N draws attention to the messy and unsteady material ecologies—the labor, the bicycles and cell phones, the CSPS, and so on—that support life. These ecologies of support are not all-encompassing environments. Their protective effects are discontinuous, unevenly distributed, and cannot be taken for granted (Duclos and Criado 2020).

Then again, it is important not to romanticize the godmothers' commitment while neglecting the harsh material conditions under which they operate. Improvisation and the transformation of MOS@N should not be seen as a DIY success story, music to neoliberal ears, in which empowered actors can "do more with less." Care work in MOS@N's afterlives (re)produces gendered forms of social obligation. For example, the termination of MOS@N came as a huge financial blow for godmothers and their families. Money gained as godmothers was often used to buy soap, condiments, or kitchen utensils. But it was also often used to repair the equipment provided by MOS@N. Almost three years later, materials are in shambles. Most phones are out of service. Others are lost. Some godmothers still use a phone, sometimes borrowed from their husband or purchased with their own money. To keep their phone working, they need to constantly buy credits, as well as pay to recharge the phone in local shops. Most phones do not use the SIM card that was provided by MOS@N. Solar panels are also all broken. Bicycles are broken too, with punctured tires and inner tubes. Godmothers have always taken good care of the things provided as part of MOS@N. This care of things has kept MOS@N from falling apart. But the conditions under which this maintenance is now taking place, now that MOS@N has ended, appear to be exceedingly demanding, which might compromise godmothers' activities in the long term.

THE TINKERING NETWORK: BEYOND THE CATALOGUE OF TECHNICAL AIDS (SPAIN, 2011–)

The following pages tell the story of a very peculiar strand of collaborative work that emerged in Spain in the aftermath of the 2008 financial crisis: an underground network of low-cost prosthetic makers, DIY menders, and tinkerers—connected to the Spanish disability rights and independent living movements—who started politicizing themselves around design and making practices. Between 2011 and 2016, one of us (T.C.) was actively involved in this fleeting network, connecting existing elements—whose somewhat opaque existence was made visible by the crisis—with people who felt appealed by these challenges for the first time. This temporary endeavor gathered practitioners engaged in diverse material adaptations, knowledge sharing, and the production of networking events, while continually searching for a more stable way of operating. Ultimately, the aim of this collective was to tinker with various forms of mutual support in the midst of smashed public and collective care infrastructures.

Recounting the complex story of events that unfolded over more than five years is not easy. In attempting to do so, let us begin with a video that was shot for a mid-September 2015 TEDxMadrid talk starring Xavi Duacastilla, one of our associates at that time.[1] As is peculiar in TED-inflicted formats, in the talk, Xavi spoke with an autobiographical tone, incarnating the experience of being a post-polio syndrome sufferer and a wheelchair user. Besides, he was also speaking with a collective voice, describing attempts at building a network of care and support. Together with a group of people, T.C. had participated in co-writing the discourse and had traveled from Barcelona for that purpose. This had entailed working alongside Arianna Mencaroni to help script the talk and assist Xavi so he could learn it by heart, commenting on how to stage it, and watching him endlessly rehearse his shocking entry onstage from one of the sides: driving at great speeds, the DIY add-on engine gadget he had designed to "motorize" his manual wheelchair. The connection between the autobiographical and the collective element of Xavi's discourse was attempted by a repeated use in the talk of the notion of *trasto*, which in Spanish has an interesting double meaning: when addressed at children, it means "rascal," but when describing objects, it usually means something like "gadget" or "contraption." After his entry, Xavi excused himself for taking some time in removing the *trasto* he was wearing in his wheelchair and began his presentation while moving the wheelchair with his hands:

> Speaking of *trastos*, I was one when I was little, because I was naughty, but also because, if I got hold of a toy, I would take it apart completely. I would always put it back together. This tendency to take things apart today can be included within the "maker" movement . . . And, as it turns out, in the 1980s, well, I was a little bit of a "punk." And since I didn't have a cent to go to London, I made my own wristbands and belts. I had a little workshop with a friend. (0:19–1:35)

Xavi laughed as he showed a picture of himself looking like a Catalan Sid Vicious with crutches before continuing with his story: "And this characteristic of being a craftsperson . . . a customizer . . . has always come to me from the need to repair, in situ, the orthopedic devices that I've used since I was four years old" (1:38–2:00). He then went on to share many other references to that punk attitude he indeed embodies: "I wasn't born in a wheelchair. My mother didn't give birth to me and the wheelchair together . . . If you're 'weird', like I am, you find yourself subject to the orthopedic catalogue, the state portfolio of technical aids. If, for example, you need a wheelchair, you're subject to the ones that are in the state catalogue, if you want any refund at all, that is. But what if you don't like what they offer you?" (03:41–04:24). And calling universal design a "fairy tale," he proposed instead a more hands-on take: "The truth is, we need to make things pivot around our own needs and measurements [*hacerse la vida a nuestra medida*]. This is how my technical skills developed" (04:50–5:01). He described the reasons that impelled him to create the *Handiwheel*, the gadget he devised. As a performative dancer, he needs to travel very long distances, but he cannot afford, doesn't like, and cannot put a motor wheelchair into his flat. At that point, the story had jumped from the individual to the collective, in expressing the need to remake our *trastos*, our material supports, to live in diversity.

The whole talk resonated with the long tail of 2008's financial crisis. The situation was harsh for many, but austerity cuts especially impacted care infrastructures and hindered the workings of a largely publicly funded market of care technologies addressed at older and disabled people: a system allocating heavily standardized gadgets and contraptions to individuals "in need," whose purchase in privately run prosthetics shops is subsidized, subject to full or partial refunds from the state. These technologies are also subject to public production incentives, since they are created for a market segment of customers without purchasing power. The crisis led to payment delays or cuts. But what's more important, the crisis also made visible the cracks in a market-driven public system that was far from perfect: personal and urban technologies that are far too standard to be adapted to the needs and desires of singular bodies and which are always in need of many trials, tweaks, and adaptations, as amply made evident by Myriam Winance's (2010) work, but also gadgets and infrastructures produced in a technocratic fashion, many times conceived with ableist grounds (to "include" the "excluded" without changing much in that gesture).

Presenting himself as a "maker," Xavi was also signaling a different approach to this, where care as a practice of tinkering—as Mol (2008) has it—takes a more insurgent and nonconformist tone as a form of "critical making" (Criado, Rodríguez-Giralt, and Mencaroni 2016): taking the design and mending of these gadgets into one's own hands to alter them beyond what is given. But Xavi was also a "punk" in his disability politics. The network he helped construct wove together sparse and splintered activist initiatives: "It all started in 2011, with the *indignados* movement, in Barcelona's Plaça de Catalunya . . . There I found a group of people who were very tuned into my beliefs" (06:42–6:56). These diverse people—many of them long-time disability rights activists or professionals of health and social care sectors, as well as craftspeople and designers—felt mobilized around the concept of "functional diversity." The term acted as a democratic operator in many struggles against existing disability-specific organizations, whom they deemed too ableist and connected to biopolitical segmentations (forms of organizing the social deriving from medical readings of distinct bodily "impairments"). This notion signaled the pride of diverse bodies and their nonconformist forms of being and expression and was vindicated when engaging in devising alternative services in a country where residential care is still the norm. For instance, the term allowed the creation of a series of initiatives not "caring for the same," a wording that Domínguez Rubio uses to address "the mimeographic work of creating sameness by constantly regenerating and extending the life of something as a particular kind of object" (2020, 40). Indeed, something emerged in the *indignados* encampments. Life in common at the public sites of the encampment brought about many conversations on how to intervene in these urban arenas so that they would pivot around the needs of diverse bodies. Participants took these affairs into their own hands. This led to the creation of the Barcelona-based collective called *En torno a la silla* (a wordplay in Spanish, hinting at the need to situate around—*en torno*—wheelchairs—*sillas de ruedas*—to alter their environments—*entornos*). *En torno a la silla* did not only prototype and engage in material explorations. The attempt was, in the words of Alida Díaz, architect of the collective, to create *tecnologías de la amistad* (technologies of friendship): material interventions not only to get to know others across social and material divides but also to be able to prolong their relations in a world where everything has been conceived for that not to happen.

Beyond being simply functional "solutions," these technologies of friendship mostly elicited care as a "politics of wonder" around the design of our *trastos*, very much in tune with the work of Sara Hendren (2020)—that is, an interrogative mode of approaching disability-related design and making, speculating with the adaptations needed to forge collective and collaborative links, crafting forms of "mutual access," however difficult that might be. To ease up things a bit, Xavi mentioned one important aspect of *En torno a la silla*'s work on opening up design: "We reckon the importance of spreading these ideas, through thorough documentation, creating tutorials with building diagrams, with the most detailed diagrams, photos, and maps possible so that whoever could replicate them, improve them . . . take advantage of them" (15:38–16:02). But these technologies of friendship exceed the range of the objectual. *En torno a la silla*'s interest in these processes led the collective on many occasions to organize events, such as hackathons and public presentations or exhibitions, where the attempt was to mobilize the experiential knowledge and the small inventions of a collective used to needing many hacks to go on, not just to give them value but also to create a network of mutual support around making and repair. At some point, the idea emerged to put together a Tinkering Network (*Red Cacharrera*), a Barcelona-based workshop space to democratize bit by bit the making and remaking of personal and urban environments. In all of those events, to which Xavi also made extensive reference in his talk, we created gadgets and collected many ideas. These were powerful, energetic, and perhaps a tad hyperbolic times.

Although the attempt was to create a "care web"—an alternative space to enable "collective access" (Piepzna-Samarasinha 2018), asking after one another and making sure all needs and desires are addressed—this open and makeshift infrastructure broke into pieces. We envisioned a brand-new world, but we failed in all of our attempts at carrying it further: the city administration, to whom we requested funds, was not ready for something like that (as we found out, corporate and medical powers were always thwarting any attempt at stabilizing the co-creation of technical aids), and perhaps more importantly, in spite of the initial energy and enthusiasm, bodies many times didn't accompany the hard work of institutionalizing a workshop space where we wanted to start operating. After devoting great efforts to the project, now decimated, hope abandoned us. The aspirations and the fall of the Tinkering Network left *En torno a la silla* wounded to the point where the collective slowly and progressively deactivated.

Yet, fragments of what we experienced remain available, such as Xavi's. Beyond being an ethnographer through all these endeavors, T.C. also acted as *En torno a la silla*'s documenter. A better way to put this would be to say that *En torno a la silla* was the way he did collaborative fieldwork. Together with Arianna Mencaroni, T.C. curated the digital and audiovisual platforms of the collective, searching for the traces of what it had been doing, so that it could remain and last. Thanks to that work of constant maintenance and curation of those documents in an extremely volatile world with many platforms and social media dying—with stored knowledge and experiences being erased with them, perhaps forever—the traces and knowledge generated are still online, available for others. Fragments endure through the traces left by the things and people in the past.

En torno a la silla's digital platforms—webmail, website, social networks—have continued to exist, being regularly checked, even though no new information has been added for years. However, the open documentation that was gathered has continued to be consulted and downloaded according to the website's metrics. Indeed, in the winter of 2020, in the midst of the pandemic that was having a devastating effect on our independent-living friends, the collective received an invitation by Makea—an upcycling, reuse, and recycling design collective from Barcelona we knew from the time, and with which *En torno a la silla* always felt very much in tune—to contribute to their last project. Makea was updating its online platform: an open archive of DIY reuse "recipes" called *El recetario*. Beginning in fall 2021, it became part of the permanent exhibit of Barcelona's Museum of Design, and they requested our help to include several of *En torno a la silla*'s gadgets, tutorials, and documented processes. These traces will now perhaps be inspiring not just for activists, amateurs, and tinkerers but also for professional designers.

Although the end of the network crushed its collective aspirations, its existing fragments continued to operate in their traditionally underground manner. Some moved on to do other things, others remained tinkering as they had always been doing, resourcing to local craftspeople or developing their own contraptions to live by. For instance, Alida has continued to embody the knowledge and resources derived from these years in her work as an architect, becoming specialized in accessibility interventions and arrangements. She now services independent-living activists and promotes the smooth integration of accessible concerns in any private or public building project. For some time, Xavi became a local TV superstar, joining a popular morning show where he started going to different places in the city and speaking about everyday life and in/accessibility issues together with many of the functional diverse activists and colleagues he met at the time. So, while some of the relations that composed the network waned, some of the friendships remain, against the odds. Others were not so lucky, and many in such a frail movement have sadly disappeared. In fact, *En torno a la silla*'s archival remains have served on at least three occasions to put together obituaries for some of our colleagues, using traces where we wanted to celebrate their life and their joyous, struggling presence. The last one we worked on was Nacho's, better known in the Spanish disability rights scene from his Facebook page *Actúa con tu diversidad funcional* (act with your functional diversity). For a day, Alida and T.C. went through *En torno a la silla*'s materials to put together a collection of pictures and events in which Nacho had participated, reminding us of the words from Bakunin (or so he said—we never really verified) that he used to quote: "uniformity is death, diversity is life."

The Tinkering Network didn't last long, as activists and tinkerers didn't manage to create the supports needed at a local level to reclaim the industrial market of technical aids, which is still up and running. Who knows, maybe one day. But all of these traces nevertheless open onto another perspective: What if all of these remnants in our practices and ways of doing, as well as the traces of our undertakings, were nothing other than the operations of such a Tinkering Network, but in an underground mode, still enduring in us, between us?

CARE BEYOND REPAIR

"The fragment is what does not break, what remains when the whole is broken," suggested Javier Lezaún in discussions that informed this chapter. But perhaps, as geographer Colin McFarlane (2021, 3) suggests in a recent book, fragments are not to be treated just "as nouns but as verbs. Not just as things but as processes, doing different kinds of work, and sometimes in surprising ways." In this chapter, we've been particularly interested in the politics of care that fragments, as material processes, carry in their endurance—one that rather than addressing the negative contours of fragility, therefore inviting us to repair or restore, wishes to remain attentive to the generative and divergent prospects of fragmentary afterlives, what endures against the odds. As we hope our stories have shown, fragments are not conceptual abstractions. Personal, relational, technical, and knowledge fragments make life possible, or not. In both our stories, they constitute partially enduring, precarious ecologies of support—a precarity that has to be situated within broader normative and material forces.

In both our stories, fragments are not the parts of a whole in need of being fixed or restored back to unity. The fragment is not a faction or a group but rather the irreducible singularity of a broken existence, requiring a contradictory mixture of divergence and persistence. In our stories, fragments are better understood as singularities in connection with others (a relation of difference as difference). They are not to be confused with an act of identity boundary making, whose connection with others could only happen through the concertation of parts and wholes (a distributed relation premised on a certain degree of sameness, at least at a conceptual level). By contrast, we like to think that a politics of care in fragments is one of building interstices where the terms of the relation are not there ready-made. As Stengers and Pignarre signal in *Capitalist Sorcery*, "An interstice is defined neither against nor in relation to the bloc to which it nevertheless belongs. It creates its own dimensions starting from concrete processes that confer on it its consistency and scope, what it concerns and who it concerns" (2011, 110–111). Or, as John Holloway wrote in a similar spirit in *Crack Capitalism*, "The only way to think of changing the world radically is as a multiplicity of interstitial movements running from the particular" (2010, 11).

Exploring interstitial movements and spaces entails keeping a lookout for generative and divergent practices of care for the fragile that often go unnoticed. Let's take the example of MOS@N. Godmothers' makeshift accompaniment in Nouna, for example, remains invisible to the institutional stakeholders (whether in Nouna or in Ottawa) that were originally involved in the project. Fragments were salvaged from MOS@N that no longer fit the parameters of the project, with objectives, beginnings, and ends. They are also not enduring toward any predefined futures. Underlying godmothers' commitment to their work, there is a refusal, implicit but unequivocal, of the project's order of things. Funds, knowledge, and materials have stopped circulating between Ottawa and their communities. Godmothers' doings, in MOS@N's afterlives, are not accounted for in the production of global health knowledge. Yet, godmothers refuse to subordinate their activity to such considerations. For them, accompanying women to the CSPS appears as an immediate necessity, as the thing to do. Godmothers do not refuse mHealth projects such as MOS@N. However, they certainly are refusing to be enclosed by the temporality of the project, by a "projectification" offering only transient opportunities, which is dominant in global health (Prince 2013). The singularity contained in godmothers' doings, in their caring in fragments, is a world in itself.

Something similar can be said of the amateur designers that gathered in the Tinkering Network. Operating as fragments, living in the shadows of the standardized technical aids market, they tried to find ways of addressing how their bodily diversity could enable singular encounters. Activating frail and precarious technologies of friendship—in the form of tailor-made making endeavors, but also presentations, hackathons or workshops, and open documentation digital archives—the aspiration was to go beyond what is being offered to them as market segments of institutional welfare projects and infrastructures. The insurgent "punk" attempts Xavi embodied in his presentation, however, were not addressing survival. Rather, they meant to replenish or reimagine what living a good life in bodily diversity might practically mean, and what types of relations and technical supports would be needed for that to materialize.

To care in fragments might entail the need of constituting weird and precarious alliances that sometimes not only live through the ruins of caring wholes but also ruin and unmake those very wholes, as Rafanell i Orra (2018, 37) forcefully puts it. Caring in fragments hence refers to the processes by which the boundaries of the whole are disrupted, are unmade, implode, or are made to implode, enabling many possible afterlives. As we see it, caring in fragments means learning to inhabit the remains *as remains*, remnants supporting other remnants to endure in their divergence. In the stories we have told, fragments gesture toward underground, discounted forms of knowledge, as well as possibilities for caring and living otherwise that tend to go under the radar of dominant groups and actors. Ultimately, our stories show attempts at ensuring a certain degree of continuity between fragments, while refusing to subsume this continuity under a larger totality, inevitably waiting to be managed and repaired. By focusing on fragments and their afterlives, we wish to hint at a care politics for the fragile beyond repair, foregrounding emergent modes of crafting interdependences, interstitial movements, or ecologies of support that depart not from sameness but from the iridescent shape of singularity.

NOTE

1. The video can be seen here: https://www.youtube.com/watch?v=OY-0tG9bD-c&ab_channel=TEDxTalks. In what follows, we include fragments of the discourse, bracketing the times. For this, we have adapted the English captions, originally translated by Leyre Bastyr (shared with CC license).

REFERENCES

Criado, Tomás S., Israel Rodríguez-Giralt, and Arianna Mencaroni. 2016. "Care in the (Critical) Making. Open Prototyping, or the Radicalisation of Independent-Living Politics." *ALTER—European Journal of Disability Research* 10 (2016): 24–39.

Denis, Jérôme, and David Pontille. 2015. "Material Ordering and the Care of Things." *Science, Technology, Human Values* 40 (3): 338–367.

Domínguez Rubio, Fernando. 2020. *Still Life: Ecologies of the Modern Imagination at the Art Museum.* Chicago: Chicago University Press.

Duclos, Vincent, and Tomás Sánchez Criado. 2020. "Care in Trouble: Ecologies of Support from Below and Beyond." *Medical Anthropology Quarterly* 34 (2): 153–173.

Hendren, Sara. 2020. *What Can a Body Do? How We Meet the Built World.* New York: Riverhead Books.

Holloway, John. 2010. *Crack Capitalism.* New York: Pluto Press.

McFarlane, Colin. 2021. *Fragments of the City: Making and Remaking Urban Worlds.* Los Angeles: University of California Press.

Mol, Annemarie. 2008. *The Logic of Care: Health and the Problem of Patient Choice.* London: Routledge.

Mol, Annemarie, Ingunn Moser, and Jeannette Pols. 2010. "Care: Putting Practice into Theory." In *Care in Practice. On Tinkering in Clinics, Homes and Farms,* edited by Annemarie Mol, Ingunn Moser, and Jeannette Pols, 7–25. Bielefeld: transcript Verlag.

Piepzna-Samarasinha, Leah Lakshmi. 2018. *Care Work: Dreaming Disability Justice.* Vancouver: Arsenal Pulp Press.

Prince, Ruth J. 2013. Situating Health and the Public in Africa. In *Making and Unmaking Public Health in Africa: Ethnographic and Historical Perspectives,* edited by R. J. Prince and R. Marsland, 9–51. Athens: Ohio University Press.

Puig de la Bellacasa, María. 2017. *Matters of Care: Speculative Ethics in More than Human Worlds.* Minneapolis: University of Minnesota Press.

Rafanell i Orra, Josep. 2018. *Fragmenter Le Monde.* Paris: Éditions Divergences.

Savransky, Martin, and Martín Tironi. 2021. "Decolonizing the Imagination in Times of Crisis. Gestures for Speculative Thinking-Feeling: Interview with Martin Savransky." *Diseña* 19: 1–22.

Simone, AbdouMaliq. 2004. "People as Infrastructure: Intersecting Fragments in Johannesburg." *Public Culture* 16 (3): 407–429.

Simone, AbdouMaliq. 2019. *Improvised Lives: Rhythms of Endurance in an Urban South.* Cambridge: Polity Press.

Star, Susan Leigh, and Karen Ruhleder. 1996. "Steps Toward an Ecology of Infrastructure: Design and Access for Large Information Spaces." *Information Systems Research* 7 (1): 111–134.

Stengers, Isabelle, and Philippe Pignarre. 2011. *Capitalist Sorcery: Breaking the Spell.* London: Palgrave Macmillan.

The Invisible Committee. 2017. *Now.* Cambridge: Semiotext(e).

Winance, Myriam. 2010. "Care and Disability. Practices of Experimenting, Tinkering with, and Arranging People and Technical Aids." In *Care in Practice. On Tinkering in Clinics, Homes and Farms,* edited by Annemarie Mol, Ingunn Moser, and Jeannette Pols, 93–117. Bielefeld: transcript Verlag.

9 FRAGILITY, CAPACITY, AND THE WORK OF REPAIR IN THE TIMBER PLANTATIONS OF SOUTH AFRICA

THOMAS COUSINS

How are laboring bodies maintained in the timber plantations of South Africa? What effort is required to mediate the injuries that mark those bodies, and how do those workers endure the wounding and extractive histories of colonial and apartheid dislocation, fragmentation, and oppression? After uncertain liberation from apartheid in 1994, how are social projects of ethical and collective life composed, as waged labor disappears, displaced by machines? In this chapter, I turn to Algerian-French artist Kader Attia's notion of "repair" to reflect on the meanings and material effects of work in the postapartheid milieu of timber plantation labor. Specifically, I take up vernacular concepts of "capacity," "power," or "strength," captured discursively in isiZulu as *amandla*, to understand how laborers engage or undertake what I call, pace Attia, "the work of repair." It is this meta-reflexive concern with capacity as a question of how one engages the fragile filaments of ethical life that condenses *amandla* in political, ethical, and bodily registers in ordinary life. Indeed, as will become clear, rather than conceiving of fragility and repair in an antonymic pair–part structure, I draw on an extensive literature on care, repair, and maintenance to show how a different picture of ethical life emerges of techniques responding to a constitutive incompleteness that engages, in historically specific ways, with the wounding effects of plantation capitalism.

At the center of the account that I offer here is a group of twelve women who labored in the timber plantations around 2008–2010. Their ordinary concerns with *amandla* draw together agency and capacity, fragility and vulnerability. Among that group are Lindiwe, Nomvula, Zifikile, Thembisile, and several men, Luke, Gazu, Baba Njojo—laborers, team leaders, contractors, mothers, wives, daughters, and a thousand other names. The milieu is constituted by plantations, homesteads, pharmaceuticals, wetland conservation areas, human immunodeficiency virus (HIV) and demographic surveillance, a coal mine, and the fragments of ex-Bantustan "homelands" under customary authority and postapartheid municipal governance. *Amandla*, as a form of what Elizabeth Povinelli, in another context, might call "ethical substance," brings into alignment a disparate set of fragile, fractured, and wounding materials: the timber plantations, the conditions of labor, the nutrition intervention that was piloted and implemented during 2008–2010, the reactions of workers to the calculated calories, the wage, "traditional" curative substances, homesteads, kin relations, and the effort itself to maintain life and limb. The workers who build social projects in the shadows of a globalized regime of timber production contend also with the devastation of the HIV epidemic, and they do so in the remnants of the Bantustan state of KwaZulu, whose fragments are sutured by not only the values and norms but also the contradictions and failures of the postapartheid developmental state. Whether those materials cohere around something like a "social project" is an open question.[1] By attending to how this effort to augment the capacities of the constitutively vulnerable, incomplete, and exposed person is drawn together, I show how *amandla* arises as diagnostic and technique, resource and trope, in the effort to endure a labor regime that is coterminous with, and profoundly entangled with, the colonial and apartheid, and now the postapartheid, state.

REAPPROPRIATION, RECIRCULATION, REPAIR

The 2013 exhibition of Algerian-French artist Kader Attia, *The Repair*, has inspired a range of political and philosophical responses.[2] By juxtaposing, among other things, photographs of the disfigured faces of soldiers from World War I with severe facial injuries after having undergone plastic surgery (the "Broken Jaws") with fractured African masks, Attia reveals two pictures of repair, whose locations are suggested by the exhibitions subtitle, "From Occident to Extra-Occidental Cultures": a modern Western conception of repair that pursues an ideal of perfection by striving for the flawless recreation of the original state. In the consumer society cycle, for example, defective objects are disposed of and replaced by new ones. The repair itself remains invisible, amounting to an obliteration of history. On the other hand, the patched artifacts of ancient cultures openly show their sutures and clamps and thus the history of the object.[3] Such a notion resonates strongly with calls to attend to the invisible work of repair on machines and other artifacts, made by Steven Jackson, Fernando Domínguez Rubio, and Jérôme Denis and David Pontille, in which the almost-always-falling-apart world is always being fixed, maintained, reinvented, reconfigured, and reassembled.[4] In one sense, the mundane crises that timber plantation laborers contend with are produced by the timber corporation's maintenance of a machinic assemblage of working bodies, corporate calories, chainsaws, sprayers, trucks, and much else. For now, let's name the nutrition intervention as the corporation's attempt at repair, as mobilizing one aspect of this concept. *Amandla*, not as an untranslatable emic term but rather one already on the move in an intercultural space of translation, points in a slightly different direction.[5] Puig de la Bellacasa's description of a more-than-human ethics of care that embraces an ambivalent relation of mutual interdependence among things, objects, other-than-human animals, organisms, takes this ontological relation as fundamentally political. This is helpful, I suggest, in apprehending Attia's conception of repair, precisely because of the intimate traffic between people and things entailed in a critique of the postcolonial.[6]

"Repair," for Attia, points to the process of healing of a damaged state, whether in the form of bodily injuries, damage to cult or everyday objects, or the wounds of colonization that continue to make themselves felt today. Manthia Diawara draws out two levels of signification of Attia's work, both relevant to my argument concerning the work of repair. First, he says, we see that a broken body is a body that has had a weakness introduced into it—a hole that, if not repaired, becomes a sign of trauma. We need therefore to repair the hole, or the fissure, by covering it up, stitching it, or decorating it with other scars to reappropriate it and make it familiar. Second, we realize that the broken faces, of black and white, masks and people, utensils and human faces, are interchangeable because their scars are relatable: "They each construct a *lieu-commun*, the myth of which can be shared with the state in which the others find themselves."[7] Attia sketches out an arc from the "practical" notion of repair—redefined as the practice through which colonized cultures appropriate the symbols of the colonizing powers into their own cultural idioms—to the juridical realm of "reparation," as in the replenishment of a previously inflicted loss.[8] By showing the scar, the wound's stitching,

Klaus Gorner suggests, the concept of visible repair is thus directed against amnesia.[9] By embracing these disfigurations, argues Diawara, we change the way we see the victims of trauma by familiarizing ourselves with the victims, by embracing their scars and letting them embrace ours. "By licking the Other's scars and allowing him/her/it to lick our disfiguration . . . we engage in an exchange that changes us in the process."[10]

Finally, in speaking about "the repair," Kader Attia grounds the notion in a genealogy of the term "reappropriation," or rather, the "re-situation" of things as well as words—of both material and immaterial signs.[11] More specifically, he locates reappropriation in the thought of Pierre-Joseph Proudhon ("property is theft"), Oswald de Andrade ("Tupi or not Tupi: that is the question"), and Frantz Fanon (reparation and restitution of what people have been dispossessed of). While the term arose within European anarchism during the Industrial Revolution and developed within different colonial contexts, Attia suggests that reappropriation "governs all relations between modernity and tradition. It sheds light on the parallel relationship between power and modernity and, more precisely, colonization and modernity." How does this help to frame *amandla*, then, as an effort to repair capacity? I suggest it is both a modality of action that is oriented by a specific history of colonial oppression and corporate extraction, as well as a form of immanent critique that absorbs an older logic of exposure and vulnerability to others within a political history of southern Africa over the *longue durée*[12]—hence the political and ethical stakes of placing together reappropriation, recirculation, and repair.

Laborers in the timber plantations talk about *amandla* in a huge variety of contexts. I describe here two domains of life around the plantations in which fragility, as a quality of plantation exploitation in particular and an existential feature of life in general, is understood in relation to *amandla* and what I call "the work of repair." They are, first, the labor system itself, with the nutrition intervention at its center, and, second, popular curatives consumed by laborers to augment "capacity" and shore up bodily and social integrity. My argument is that, on the one hand, the people who work in the timber plantations must contend with a range of forces that splinter the effort to remain human: the fragmentation of spaces of habitation; the extraction of every ounce of labor power from the body; the wasting of the body by disease; the combined effects of many decades of impoverishment; and the erosion of trust, intimacy, and familiar modes of obligation and reciprocity, and the collapse of heteronormative ideals of marriage and lineal reproduction. On the other hand, the effort to augment one's capacity, in bodily and social terms, draws creatively on vernacular tropes to produce innovative forms such as industrialized curatives that cleanse the blood or expurgate a snake in the belly, or a "game of marriage" between women that queers customary kinship even as it provides camouflage for intimate alliance and subterfuge.[13] These creative responses, articulated explicitly around capacity, or *amandla*, counter an analytics of labor power, fatigue, and decay by producing new hybrid forms that restate a widespread African trope of constitutive incompleteness as the condition of personhood.[14] Attending to this concern with capacity points to the way in which the work of repair, as an existential and meta-reflexive project, threads together fragility and life as constitutively and ambivalently vulnerable and incomplete.

LABOR POWER AND SOUTH AFRICAN FORESTRY

From the beginnings of forestry as an organized sector in South Africa in the early twentieth century, labor has been a serious concern for large capital interests—the calculations of inputs and outputs, calories and costs, prices and profits, upkeep and supply, consistency and discipline—in short, its governability[15]. From the early history of forestry in South Africa, the plantation has been a racialized system of extractive relations—that is, a topos in which labor, territory, and value were forged in the making of capital. The techniques of dispossession of land are inseparable from the techniques of disciplining labor. The Dukuduku and Nyalazi timber plantations and surrounding communal areas are known for their proximity to the renowned coastal wetlands (formerly the St. Lucia wetlands and now governed by the iSimangaliso Wetland Authority) that separate the farms and homesteads from the sea. What came to be known as Zululand for much of colonial history was on the periphery of Zulu politics in the 1800s, although its incorporation into the Bantustan of KwaZulu and claimed genealogical proximity to the Zulu royal house is the story of conquest, strategic realignment, and state intervention over two centuries.[16]

Pre-Shakan political formations (i.e., before the Great Disruption of 1815) have been recently revitalized in both popular and academic registers.[17] Such reappraisals are helpful for understanding ongoing successional disputes around what is known as "traditional leadership," particularly given the fierce fights over mining rights, land claims, and small-scale timber stands in areas under customary authority, complicating calls for land restitution.[18] Who should "own" or govern the plantations and its milieux is increasingly contested as the large paper and pulp corporations put more distance between sites of primary extraction, urban beneficiation, and global distribution.

While indigenous forests had been exploited and mills established in other parts of Zululand since the late 1880s, it was not until 1926 that afforestation began and exotic varieties of tree species were introduced (initially pine—*Pinus palustris*—and more recently *Eucalyptus grandis*) after wetlands had been drained and indigenous people forcibly removed, initiating the profound reshaping of the landscape for profitable extraction.[19] Thus, allotments of surveyed land were added in 1928 to the forest reserve to enable it to abut the newly completed Zululand railway (and, in addition, avoid the East Coast fever restrictions on the movement of cattle). Seven thousand acres of forestland were "surrendered" to the sugar plantations on the Umfolozi Flats and alternate land swapped in return in 1946 and again in 1949 (as returning White soldiers from the War were rewarded with land to start sugar farming on the Flats). In 1934, A. W. Bayer and J. S. Henkel, as government-appointed foresters, conducted a series of ecological studies of the Dukuduku forests to determine the stage in the succession of the veld when afforestation could be undertaken without complete cultivation of the soil, the results of which were applied to all plantations along the Zululand coast.[20] As troublesome "squatters" were partially evicted from the Dukuduku forests and the swamps drained, making the landscape less deadly for both White settlers and Black laborers,[21] the growing plantations (both timber and sugar) soon encountered severe "shortages" of labor due to both malaria and "resistance to labor" among Black residents.[22]

While the timber sector grew first in the service of the "mineral-energy complex" with demand for timber coming mostly from gold mining and construction until the 1960s, demand from other sectors, in particular paper and pulp for boxes and print, grew substantially in the mid-twentieth century.[23] The state's direct investments in establishing large plantations helped to overcome many of the risks and costs inherent in a sector that takes many years for a return to be realized. Thus, from the 1960s onward, through a variety of subsidies and credit facilities, the state supported the growth of a paper and pulp industry, dominated in 2010 by two private companies, Sappi and Mondi, the latter a subsidiary of the Anglo-American group until

2007. The regimentation of the forestry labor regime was borrowed directly from that of the gold mines in concerns with housing, feeding, health care, and recreation. The availability and stability of labor and the articulation of health as a function of profitability were always central features of the system of apartheid economic and spatial planning. Thus, the establishment of Mondi in 1967 as a subsidiary of the Anglo-American corporation with key support from the state deserves special attention in the context of a crisis of reproduction and impoverishment that came to a head in the late 1960s as apartheid policies of spatial segregation took full effect.

It was at this point that the explicit concern with the raced "African" worker, less as an object of supply and demand and more as an active economic agent, was initiated and the contestations over wages began that transformed the problem of the wage into what Foucault called "capital-ability."[24] Thus, labor power was transformed from mere abstraction to ability—that is, from alienated commodity to the *capacity* to labor and to secure a future "earnings stream" as an investment in human capital. This production of the worker as subject depended on the regulation of the means of sustenance, the ingestion of a dietary regime, and the physical coordination of the racialized body. The concern with the capacity of the laborer thus emerged through the restructuring of the timber regime in response to the political and economic shifts that began in the 1970s and culminated in the transition to the new constitutional order of inclusive citizenship in 1994. The assumption that labor would provide the grounds for citizenship, as a condition of freedom, has a complicated relationship to productivist totalitarianism regimes of the twentieth century, and remained a troubling centerpiece of the post-apartheid social compact, as Franco Barchiesi has made clear.[25] This history is crucial for outlining how a topological space in which timber, labor power, disease management, and profits are assembled by tearing apart one milieu and transforming it into another.

CALORIES, CAPACITY, AND LABOR

I turn now to the first of the domains in which repair appears as a corporate concern, or care, for the laborer and their capacity: namely, the nutrition program. "Productivity" among timber plantation laborers in South Africa had been falling since the 1980s and accelerated in the 1990s after the end of apartheid. The industry blamed various factors, including the "contractorization" and outsourcing of labor, the opening of South Africa's markets to global competition after sanctions against the apartheid regime were lifted, and devastatingly high rates of HIV, particularly among young women. Injuries, absenteeism, and a general labor scarcity forced Mondi (PLC) to implement a suite of labor reforms from 2008, the centerpiece of which was a nutrition intervention that saw a carefully calculated, calorically enriched meal distributed to ten thousand laborers in the middle of the working day, deep in plantations across the province of KwaZulu-Natal. "Community-based" food suppliers were trained to cook and deliver calorically rich and "culturally acceptable" meals. For the company, the cost of labor power and its reproduction was key to global competitiveness, and the labor regime, by the 2000s, depended fundamentally on the idea that workers lived in rural homesteads adjacent to the plantations supported by an African mode of production, including the cultural ties afforded by clan, custom, and kin. By the late 2000s, most of those laborers were women, reflecting the feminization of the labor force in South Africa more generally since the 1990s.

By the time that Mondi began its nutrition program in 2008, timber had been produced on land from which Black African people had been forcibly removed for more than a century of colonial and apartheid dislocation and fragmentation. The nutrition intervention aimed at bolstering the productivity of laborers and shoring up falling profits because it was becoming clear that their productivity as a workforce was declining as the ripple effects of a generalized HIV epidemic began to be felt in all aspects of everyday life.[26] The plantation nutrition intervention, initially costing R50 million (USD 6.3 million) a year, on the one hand thus appears to bring together liberal compassion and corporate concern for an ailing, infected labor force that turns on the smooth functioning of a "human motor" metabolizing the hot cooked meals of calculated calories. On the other hand, to function at all, this system explicitly depended on the maintenance of a set thick of social relations between workers—of kin, neighbors, healers, and chiefs—that not only sustained their bodies but also coordinated the rhythms of the working day.

How does the organization of the working day make these laboring bodies fragile? For Marx, the "limits" of the working day provide the grounds on which to consider the extraction of surplus labor. For the women of Shikishela and Mfekayi who worked in the plantations, the day began at three o'clock in the morning, which gave them just enough time to prepare water and snacks for the day before walking for thirty minutes or an hour to a meeting point where the contractor's truck collected them. The rural paths and roads were dangerous in the dark, and they worried about falling prey to *izigebhengu*, thieves or criminals, along the way. Then, it was an hour on the tractor transport as it did the rounds of picking up laborers from the communal areas adjacent to the forests. The work started at six o'clock, when harvesting and silviculture contractor teams each headed off to their allotted forest compartment. Every morning as the sun rose, before setting to the work, the *induna*, or team-leader, led her charges in prayer and song, followed by a "toolbox talk" by the team's safety officer.[27]

Silviculture laborers planted, sprayed, weeded, pitted, hoed, or cleared. It was less intensive work than harvesting and thus more sought after. Harvesting teams, on the other hand, had a strict division of labor: chainsaw operating, measuring the timber into lengths, debarking, stacking, and loading. The same person performed each activity, repetitively. The most arduous of these activities was debarking, which entailed swinging an axe at the bark of the fallen tree to strip it, remaining bent at the waist for eight consecutive hours. Protective clothing was provided and had to be worn by all forest workers, but debarkers in particular had to wear shin pads, steel-capped boots, boot covers, rubber gloves, hard hats, and visors.[28] It made for sweaty, hot, and backbreaking work, the coordination, organization, and sequencing of which depended on the embodied, syncopated rhythms of capital, kin, and local authority.[29]

The silence of hard labor was broken when cooked food was delivered at ten o'clock by two small community catering companies that had been contracted to supply standardized hot cooked meals. They were mentored by ESS, a global food supplier that provided several million meals a day around the world to factories and hospitals, learning what it took to supply industrial quantities of food that were "culturally appropriate," "tasty," "nutritious," and profitable. In more remote plantation compartments, dry ration packs were given out—no less calculated for their caloric and nutritive value but far less popular or satisfying. Silviculture teams finished working by two o'clock on most days; harvesting teams were given until four o'clock to complete their quota for the day. Then, there was an hour's wait at the plantation gate or nearby filling station, waiting for other contractor teams to complete their tasks so that the transport trucks could efficiently return workers to their various pickup points, followed by the final walk home of up to an hour. It took fourteen hours on average from leaving home in the morning to returning in the late afternoon. Every weekday, week in and week out, the teams worked the trees, compartment after compartment.

As an interlocking community of small groups interacting closely through repetitive and dulling work, the women supported each other to complete tasks, to survive the physical demands of the labor, to endure the boredom of its repetitions, and to pass the time while waiting for transport home. Proxemic intimacies drew on and produced bonds of friendship, neighborliness, and kinship in enduring and surprising ways. The companies that operate the Nyalazi and Dukuduku plantations contract laborers from within a five-kilometer radius of the plantations, partly to maintain a corporate social responsibility profile framed by the Black Economic Empowerment (BEE) charter and partly to address the growing political pressure to resolve land compensation and restitution claims.[30] Thus, many worked alongside their mothers or daughters, such as Lindiwe and 'Sli, or fathers, brothers, lovers, municipal councilors, or chiefly subjects, such as Luke or Njojo. In this space of industrial production, authority and intimacy within the plantation overlapped with, reinforced, and pulled against authority and intimacy outside the forest: councilors, elders, children, occupational health officers, plantation security, auditors, neighbors, *izinduna* (chiefs), *izinyanga* (healers), *izintombi* (girls), and *izinsizwa* (boys).[31] At the same time, small-scale Black contractors who employed these workers were part of an emergent labor elite that represents a broader pattern of "accumulation-from-below."[32]

Most laborers were employed on a short-term contract that satisfied the existing labor law surrounding forest work. In 2006, the South African minimum wage was R834 per month (USD 122 in 2006); in 2009, the minimum wage had increased to R1,947 per month (USD 134), although forestry workers often went home with less than R1,000 per month (USD 69 in June 2009).[33] For a day's labor—that is, the completion of the daily quota—the wage in 2009 was around R55 (USD 7.20). The day's labor was recorded in a register, along with days absent, accidents, incidents, and the maintenance of equipment, all of which was used to calculate the forest worker's monthly wage. Workers who missed six consecutive days were dismissed as a breach of contract. It was possible to underpay for days because the "incomplete" days were recorded under "absenteeism." For harvesting contractors, the longer the timber sat stacked in the forest drying out, the lighter it became and the less they were paid upon delivery to the mill. The sooner the timber could be delivered, the closer it would be to the contracted price. On occasion, extra teams had to be hired to avoid defaulting on the contract. Strict auditing intended to minimize accidents and injuries often obscured all but the most serious infractions and injuries. The nutrition intervention and a concern with the ergonomic impact of heavy labor was thus one of a suite of labor reforms intended to maintain failing bodies and shore up falling rates of productivity and profitability. Complete mechanization of the plantations, while considered from the 1960s, did not begin in earnest until after 2012. In sum, the abstraction of lower power depended on an exacting system of exploitation premised on a flattened image of the worker, rendering invisible violent histories of apartheid and its dependence on ordinary and vernacular techniques of self and other for its profitable functioning.

FRAGILE CAPACITIES AND CURATIVES

At stake in the second domain in which repair and fragility meet is a set of commoditized curatives that hybridize popular notions of pharmaceutical, vitamin supplement, and "traditional medicine" (*muthi*). Here, a very different picture of repair emerges as industrial curatives such as *uVukahlale* ("wake up and go") and *uQhedizikinga* ("it finishes your problems") act on the body to augment the self. Francis Nyamnjoh makes explicit the logic of a constitutive incompleteness found in many societies across Africa, while Robert Thornton suggests that affliction in southern Africa should be understood in terms of modulating vital yet dangerous exposure to others.[34] If these efforts are framed as "techniques-of-self-and-other," then we can see how Attia's notion of visible repair premised on reciprocal wounding shifts away from a demand from machines or things for maintenance toward a profound political and ethical response to historical and existential conditions.

The hot cooked meals in the plantations were rolled out from 2008, just as a new, broad-based state HIV treatment and care program was becoming widely accessible across the country.[35] They intersected powerfully with a public crisis around HIV and the politics of nutrition, at the center of which lay a set of substances that had scandalized AIDS activists around the world: part vitamin, part traditional curative, manufactured in industrial conditions, and circulating through corporate pharmaceutical networks. The global controversy around the infamous claim by former state president Thabo Mbeki that HIV did not cause AIDS led in 2008 to a landmark study by the Academy of Science of South Africa on the relationship between nutrition, HIV, and tuberculosis. At stake, both politically and scientifically, was the question of how to consider the history of apartheid and the ongoing legacy of structural violence that unevenly distribute access to employment and nutritious food.[36] Relatively new then, as the report noted, was an uncertain science of the gut that suggested a subtle relation between the body's inner and outer worlds, and of microbiome and psycho-neuro-enterological relays that displaced the center of thinking, feeling, remembering, and acting from brain to gut, and which produced a new image of the hungering, diseased body situated in specific historical context. How, then, to consider together the plantation's nutritional meals alongside a set of popular curatives sold on the streets, in chemists, and in cosmetic stores around South Africa that operate in the registers of traditional medicine, vitamin supplement and herbal tonic, and are consumed by the same plantation laborers?

For Bashingile and other laborers in the timber plantations, popular curative substances that were vitally important to their well-being and capacity to work included *muthi* in its most elemental form, as raw plant material, and *amakhambi*, composed and prescribed directly by healers such as *izinyanga* or *izangoma*.[37] More mundane and cosmopolitan as impure signifiers of custom were the industrial hybrids circulating through cosmetics stores, pharmacies, and street stalls.[38] Both sets of "things" are what Puig de la Bellacasa might call lively actors in more-than-human, natureculture assemblages that are directly concerned with modulating ambivalent exposure to others. The origins of those hybrids can be traced to the industrializing centers in the late nineteenth century, such as Durban and Johannesburg and smaller, regional towns to which migrant laborers were drawn and pushed by the colonial system. Their archival traces suggest an enduring concern with capacity—specifically the capacity to labor for capital, in the sense of the alienation and embodiment of one's effort in commodities, but also to provide, to take care of, or to secure lineal reproduction and kinship relations—that is, the total life-giving effort toward which hunger directs the will.[39]

While the corporation's calorific interventions augment bodily capacities via the image of a "human motor," workers in the plantations talk about *amandla*.[40] One dictionary translates *amandla* as: "1. strength, power; 2. moral strength, power, authority, ability; 3. as an idiomatic expression of a man's virility and semen."[41] As capacity, strength, force, or virility, *amandla* is a vital quality of people (e.g., in the prophet Isaiah Shembe's ability to heal), things (e.g., pharmaceuticals), and actions (e.g., ritual healing or political utterances).[42] *Amandla* remains a particularly potent word in South African public life, from the mythology surrounding the early-nineteenth-century Zulu king Shaka kaSenzangakhona and the modes of power and virility associated with his rule through its explicitly political deployment in the antiapartheid struggle as a rallying cry at funerals and marches (as in the antiapartheid call and response of "*Amandla! Ngawethu!*" "Power! To the people!") and, from the late 2000s, in public critique of former President Jacob Zuma's personal life and the politics of redistribution. *Amandla* lives on as a polyvalent concept in everyday speech. In the timber plantations, *amandla* refers as much to bodily capacity to labor and pharmaceutical efficacy as it does to one's social and reproductive capacities, particularly in relation to earning a wage or ability to pay bridewealth. For example, Bashingile, one of my interlocuters, complained that the father of her children had been slow in completing his payments: "Hhawu amandla awasekho / Oh he had no power!"[43] The operative site of bodily intervention by which one's capacity is augmented as (what is named in English as) the gut. Indeed, a raft of classic structural functionalist ethnographies of "Zulu" healing, purity, and pollution suggest a concern with bodily fluids and the gut as a key site of action.[44]

Siyanda, who worked at one small pharmacy in Mtubatuba, described to me in detail how he had managed to expel a long, translucent snake from his belly by means of such substances, a response to an affliction sent by malevolent kin. As a potentially primitivizing image from southern Africa, such a snake is also an index of one's orientation to custom and its moral order. The women working in the timber plantations were deeply familiar with this snake, although they were clear it should not be confused with helminths that are common in this region, particularly schistosomiasis, and discussed in these terms.[45] Addressing their own afflictions in terms of this snake and other figures of distress, Lindiwe and others spoke in similar terms about the importance of treating the gut not only to heal broken kinship relations but also to attend to minor everyday ailments and enervation.[46] Techniques of the gut rebalance *inyongo*, bile, as a key materialization of the excesses of modernity, of poor diets, exhausting urbanity, and infected blood. Pretty, a pharmacy salesperson, explained in detail how bile and blood were rebalanced by popular, commoditized purgatives and emetics known as *izifo zonke* (all diseases).[47] The importance of purifying blood, cleansing the body, and strengthening the immune system (*amasosha omzimba*, soldiers of the body), as concerns of both kinship and lineage, were key tropes in the plantations, alongside ritually purified water, snake fat, purgatives, pain killers, and, later, antiretrovirals. As Karen Flint shows, the history of those scandalous substances, stretching back a century, is intimately entangled with mass urbanization, skirting the heavily policed boundaries of biomedicine and African healing and the devastations of migrant labor.

SHARED VULNERABILITY, INCOMPLETE REPAIR

Attending to the work of repair, with *amandla* as its central concern, reveals how labor power has emerged as a central node in the network of relations that structure the plantations and fragile life on its edges. The history of how this network of relations has emerged is crucial for understanding how *amandla* emerges from within, and subtends, the concern with labor power. Without effacing the broken fragments, the work of repair is at the heart of making the worlds around the plantations habitable—that is, it is profoundly conditioned by histories of dislocation and extraction. The lives of the twelve women I came to know reveal the fragile texture of struggles over territory, labor, and livelihood over the *longue durée*. Felling, stripping, pitting, planting, driving, managing, and guarding—in their work on the lines of zombie clones of eucalyptus trees, their lives sketch the "grounds of all making" in and around the plantations.[48]

Following the trajectories of cooked corporate food and popular curatives as they entered into the lifeworlds of Lindiwe, Zifikile, and others thus revealed a concern with "capacity" as a central trope through which people and relations are constituted and around which worlds are stitched in the ordinary work of repair. Capacity, *amandla,* is not a simple abstraction or calculation (viz. "labor power") nor some ethno-artifact of custom. Rather, it is a discursive and material source of value in itself with generative force emerging from its historically contingent fabrications. As calories and curatives worked in and through bodies and social projects, entangled logics of repair are mutually absorbed within the viscous folds of the gut. By attending to the wounding incorporations and exclusions of kin and corporation, a network of alliances begins to emerge that reveals the intimacies between self and gut, psyche and soma, and substance and kinship. The plantation laborers' concerns with the snake in the belly, medicines, calories, and kin relations brings into focus the gut as the site of the "enfleshment" of the social.

By tracing the circulations of commoditized curatives as they traveled through modes of industrial production, regional markets, and a domestic poetics of bodily care, a clearer picture of enteric mediation comes into view. The gut, as an unstable collection of organs, beginnings and endings, is thus both a medium through which signs are communicated and an active agent itself in shaping the meaning of health, as Elizabeth Wilson (2015) and James Wilce (2003) each suggest.[49] In Wilson's terms, ingestion and digestion are not metaphors for internalization, as some anthropologists have suggested (e.g., Coplan 1993; Mintz and du Bois 2002; Argenti 2007) but rather "actual" mechanisms for relating to others.[50] Gut pathology does not so much "represent" a breakdown in relations as enact it enterologically (Wilson 2004, 45) as a direct interruption to the process of remaining connected to others.[51] Gastrointestinal difficulties such as bloatedness, nausea, vomiting, constipation, and diarrhea are thus modes of distress, enacted enterologically. Interventions into the gut are thus modes of distress distributed in and across the social/political as moments of enfleshment.[52]

As a key site of bodily mediation and of existential exposure, the gut thus enables and invites both discursive commentary about and reflexive action on one's body and its relation to others and its context(s), thereby situating, enabling, and transforming relations. This is what Michael Silverstein calls "metapragmatic function" in the register of embodied action.[53] Thus, we can see how the manipulation of flows of substance in everyday life sets in motion presuppositional signs indexing a folded world of custom and righted relations with forebears and current kin. However, not only does the varied presuppositional material indexed by the production, circulation, consumption, and excretion of industrial curatives point to the retrospective folds of ritual thought as a problem of consciousness constrained by the structural contradictions of capital in postapartheid South Africa. Crucially, such ingestions, absorptions, and ejections are also indexically calibrated, (meta-)pragmatic gestures that bring together histories of violent displacement with contemporary struggles to engage the political economy of postapartheid life—that is, the cruddy crises of everyday life for surplus populations.[54] As such, these reparative gestures are ethico-political, embodied actions that mediate past and present, inner and outer, abstraction and concretization. We can thus speak of a complex of gestures, tropes, dispositions, and materials that the work of repair assembles, in widening arcs of concern, as world making. This is what Francis Nyamnjoh calls the "incomplete work of eating-and-being-eaten"—that is, the ouroboric, cannibalistic precondition of agonistic conviviality and of becoming.[55]

The work of repair at stake in *amandla* is thus not a labor of synthesis, integration, or resolution. As Jackson notes, "repair inherits an old and layered world, making history but not in the circumstances of its choosing."[56] Rather, the action at stake in repair folds healing and curing into a living politics, and a politics of the living—namely (the possibility of) shared vulnerability. To adapt Nancy Rose Hunt's formulation, the work of repair defends against the narrowing of the milieu of life.[57] *Amandla*, then, points to the possibility of shared vulnerability and its redistribution.[58] Robert Thornton's argument that *ngoma* is a figuration of exposed being that must be augmented is central here.[59] Anette Wickstrom points to another isiZulu form of life, *lungisa*, putting in order, turning to the image of "weaving together" as the action of producing space and relationships over time to exert some control over a life lived under political and economic circumstances that rip and rend.[60] Further away, James Fernandez shows how, in Bwiti, the "occult search for capacity" in Equatorial West Africa among the Fang is also concerned with "world reconstruction."[61] Hylton White's account of ritual action and its failures in northern KwaZulu-Natal is closer to the argument I have developed here in that he offers a picture of the vulnerability of action to misfiring that draws the fragility and powers of the dead intimately into the political economy of postapartheid South Africa.[62] It is in this context that the centrality of *amandla* as both bodily capacity and ethical aspiration elicits the acts of repair occasioned by the demands of the timber plantation labor regime.

On this view, fragility is thus not merely a quality of social and ecological life that bears the mark of colonial violence and capital's rapacious extraction. Rather, it is a political and existential fact that is absorbed and modulated in metapragmatic action in and on life around the timber plantations. *Amandla*, as the central concern of everyday speech and action, is that capacity to navigate the fragilities that place life in question—the life of the incomplete, "exposed" person as agent, as much as life as a relation between organism and milieu—that is at stake in the ordinary and ongoing work of repair.

In placing the corporation's nutrients together alongside the popular curatives, I have suggested two opposing views of how repair might be understood to order life in and around the plantations. One sees the workers' bodies as elements of a larger machine that produces paper, pulp, and profit, always breaking down, susceptible to fatigue and infectious disease, rebellious. The other sees repair as an existential and political effort mounted against the violence of (post)colonial extraction, operating as an ordinary and yet vital concern with life across material, ethical, biological worlds, working to remain open to the wounding and yet vital relations of others. This oversimplifies what is, in fact, much more entangled and blurred. Where labor power ends and another kind of work begins is not clear. The "work of repair" cannot be disentangled from, but rather is imbricated in, the colonial histories that have produced the very social forms that enliven the plantations—mothers, daughters, neighbors, lovers, kin, chief, boss, but also calories, *muti* (traditional medicine), *izifo zonke* (cures all diseases). Indeed, to draw on Jackson again, by appreciating "the ongoing activities by which stability (such as it is) is maintained," we might say that *amandla* names "the subtle arts of repair by which rich and robust lives are sustained against the weight of centrifugal odds."[63] *Amandla* is not merely discursive or symbolic, but rather it confronts the visible and invisible wounds of colonial violence. It is concerned with mutualizing capacity itself, across all registers of life, as the filament or tissue of political and ethical action. It is the concrete organization of ordinary materials and effort in the situated context of postapartheid South Africa. Not in the mouths of famous struggle icons but rather in the mundane efforts of ordinary laborers, the perlocution finds new force: the power is ours—*amandla ngawethu*!

NOTES

1. By "social project," I mean the sense of making social worlds otherwise, well described by Elizabeth Povinelli, *Economies of Abandonment: Social Belonging and Endurance in Late Liberalism* (Durham, NC: Duke University Press, 2011). Writing the social from the point of view of social projects, specifically the project of fashioning a world in and through the space of the plantation, puts into question sociological assumptions about the holisms of culture, society, and individuals and their fragile interrelations. It attends to the projects themselves, the effort to make the world otherwise, the compositional efforts of people whose capacity to endure is critically in question.

2. I am indebted to Todd Meyers for alerting me to Attia's work. See Kader Attia, *The Repair from Occident to Extra-Occidental Cultures* (Berlin: The Green Box Kunstedition, 2013).

3. Susanne Gaensheimer, "Forward," in *Kader Attia: Sacrifice and Harmony, Exhibition Catalogue*, ed. Susanne Gaensheimer and Klaus Görner (Frankfurt: Museum für Moderne Kunst, 2016), 4.

4. Steven J. Jackson, "Rethinking Repair," in *Media Technologies: Essays on Communication, Materiality, and Society*, ed. Tarleton Gillespie, Pablo J. Boczkowski, and Kirsten A. Foot (Cambridge, MA: MIT Press, 2014), 222. See Jérôme Denis, Alessandro Mongili, and David Pontille, "Maintenance and Repair in Science and Technology Studies," *TECNOSCIENZA: Italian Journal of Science & Technology Studies* 6, no. 2 (2016): 5–16; and Fernando Domínguez Rubio, *Still Life: Ecologies of the Modern Imagination at the Art Museum* (Chicago: University of Chicago Press, 2020).

5. Rather than invoke a pure incommensurability or nontranslatability, I use *amandla* to index those "invaginated" histories of invention, exchange, conquest, and resistance that precede the formalization of a Zulu polity, and an ongoing "mutuomorphomutation" of words and worlds across southern Africa, in which ideas about difference and language continue to inform debates about persons and polities. On (non)translatability, see William F. Hanks and Carlo Severi, "Translating Worlds: The Epistemological Space of Translation," *HAU: Journal of Ethnographic Theory* 4, no. 2 (2014): 1–16; John Leavitt, "Words and Worlds: Ethnography and Theories of Translation," *HAU: Journal of Ethnographic Theory* 4, no. 2 (2014): 193–220. On "invaginated," see Elizabeth A. Povinelli, "Routes/Worlds," *E-Flux* 27 (08/11) (2011): 1–10. On "mutuomorphomutation," see Peter McDonald, *Artefacts of Writing: Ideas of the State and Communities of Letters from Matthew Arnold to Xu Bing* (Oxford: Oxford University Press, 2017).

6. María Puig de La Bellacasa, *Matters of Care: Speculative Ethics in More Than Human Worlds* (Minneapolis: University of Minnesota Press, 2017), 41. See Achille Mbembe, *On the Postcolony* (Berkeley: University of California Press, 2001).

7. Manthia Diawara, "Kader Attia: A Poetics of Re-appropriation," in *The Repair, Poetics of Re-Appropriation*, ed. Attia, 13. *Lieu-commun* translates as "common ground" and "common place" and, further, as truism or topos. Diawara's reading of Edouard Glissant's *lieux-communs* is helpful here: "those sites where ideas emerge, illuminate and influence other ideas from other places of the world. In this sense, a common site is different from a commonplace, which is made out of naked truths and obvious statements. By contrast, a common ground . . . is a source of creativity and opacity, a fertile ground of inexhaustible energies, where relationships are continually generated between the ideas and poetics of one place and those of another (Diawara, *Poetics of Re-Appropriation*, 5).

8. Ana Teixeira Pinto, "In No Man's Land," in Kader Attia, *Signes de Réappropriation* (Dijon: Black Jack Editions, 2013)..

9. Klaus Görner, "Sacrifice and Harmony," in *Kader Attia: Sacrifice and Harmony, Exhibition Catalogue*, ed. Susanne Gaensheimer and Klaus Görner (Frankfurt: Museum für Moderne Kunst, 2016), 18.

10. Diawara, *Poetics of Re-Appropriation*, 13. Such an understanding of repair is quite different from Arendt's reading of the Christian tradition of forgiveness, as the grounds for relationships between individuals for whom "community" is an aspirational horizon and ontological premise for society (Hannah Arendt, *The Human Condition* (1958; repr., Chicago: University of Chicago Press, 1998, 236).

11. Kader Attia, "In Conversation: Kitty Scott and Kader Attia Discuss the Concept of Repair," in *The Repair: From Occident to Extra-Occidental Cultures* (Berlin: The Green Box, 2013).

12. In Robert Thornton, *Healing the Exposed Being: A South African Ngoma Tradition* (Johannesburg: Wits University Press, 2017). Thornton argues that the well-known "cult of affliction" of southern Africa, *ngoma*, is not only about social struggles for health, as John Janzen brilliantly showed, but also an older technique of modulating dangerous, but also vital, exposure to others.

13. I address these themes more fully in "Sex, Gender and Marriage in the Timber Plantations of KwaZulu-Natal, South Africa: A Minor Otherwise," *Social Dynamics* 42, no. 2 (2016): 218–236.

14. Francis B. Nyamnjoh, "Incompleteness: Frontier Africa and the Currency of Conviviality," *Journal of Asian and African Studies* 52, no. 3 (2017): 253–270.

15. The "timber industry" includes forestry and primary transformation industries (sawmills, pulp and paper, etc.). The term "forestry" covers the production cycle of timber, from growing trees (silviculture) to felling and debarking (harvesting), and transport.

16. See Jeff Guy, "Battling with Banality," *Journal of Natal and Zulu History* 18, no. 1 (1998): 156–193; Carolyn Hamilton, *Terrific Majesty: The Powers of Shaka Zulu and the Limits of Historical Invention* (Cape Town: David Philip, 1998); and Carolyn Hamilton and Nessa Leibhammer, *Tribing and Untribing the Archive: Identity and the Material Record in Southern KwaZulu-Natal in the Late Independent and Colonial Periods* (Durban: University of KwaZulu-Natal Press, 2016), 2.

17. The revitalization of pre-Shakan political formations and reexamination of those histories in the twenty-first century has recently begun to receive renewed attention, for example by Hamilton and Leibhammer's *Tribing and Untribing the Archive* and Mbongiseni Buthelezi's critical historiography of revitalized clan names emerging from the shadow of Zulu ethnonationalism, in "We Need New Names Too," in Hamilton and Leibhammer, *Tribing and Untribing the Archive* 2: 587.

18. Aninka Claassens, *Mining Magnates and Traditional Leaders: The Role of Law in Elevating Elite Interests and Deepening Exclusion, 2002–2018* (Mapungubwe: Mapungubwe Institute for Strategic Reflection, 2019); John L. Comaroff and Jean Comaroff, *Ethnicity, Inc* (Chicago: University of Chicago Press, 2008).

19. J. W. Turnbull, "Tree Domestication and the History of Plantations," in *The Role of Food, Agriculture, Forestry and Fisheries and the Use of Natural Resources. Encyclopedia*

of Life Support Systems Developed under Auspices of UNESCO, ed. V. R. Squires (Oxford: Eolss, 2002).

20. J. S. Henkel, S. Ballenden, and A. W. Bayer, "An Account of the Plant Ecology of the Dukuduku Forest Reserve and Adjoining Areas of the Zululand Coast Belt," in *Annals of the Natal Museum*, ed. R. F. Lawrence (London: Natal Museum, 1937), 95–126.

21. In this article, I use the capitalized terms "White" and "Black" to indicate the constructed nature of these racial categories (David Theo Goldberg, *The Threat of Race: Reflections on Racial Neoliberalism* (Oxford: Wiley-Blackwell, 2009); Achille Mbembe, *Critique of Black Reason* (Durham, NC: Duke University Press, 2017)). The postapartheid South African national census uses the categories "black African," "white," "coloured," and "Indian/Asian," which also appear in this article (Statistics South Africa, Republic of South Africa. "General Household Survey, 2019." Available online at Stats SA website, May 29, 2024, https://www.statssa.gov.za/publications/P0318/P03182019.pdf). At different points during the twentieth century, the state used different classificatory terms for racial categories. One of the more infamous pieces of apartheid legislation, the Population Registration Act of 1950, decreed that each citizen should carry an identity document that recorded their race as either "white," "coloured," or "native." This was later modified to divide the population into four groups: "African," "Indian" "Coloured," and "White" (Deborah Posel, "Race as Common Sense: Racial Classification in Twentieth-Century South Africa." *African Studies Review* 44, no. 2 (2001): 87–114). The anti-apartheid liberation movements used a more expansive conception of "Blackness" to build solidarity among all those discriminated against by the apartheid system and thus included "coloured," "Indian," and "Asian" people in this political category. In this article, the term "coloured" refers to the South African census category for people of mixed-race descent, and I retain this spelling to mark the specificity of term.

22. C. W. Marwick, *Kwamahlati, the Story of Forestry in Zululand*, Bulletin 49 (Pretoria: Department of Forestry, 1973).

23. Ben Fine and Zavareh Rustomjee, *The Political Economy of South Africa: From Minerals–Energy Complex to Industrialisation* (London: Westview Press, 1996).

24. Michel Foucault, *The Birth of Biopolitics: Lectures at the Collège de France, 1978–1979*, ed. Michel Senellart (New York: Macmillan, 2010), 225.

25. Franco Barchiesi, "Wage Labor, Precarious Employment, and Social Inclusion in the Making of South Africa's Postapartheid Transition," *African Studies Review* 51, no. 2 (2008): 119–142.

26. Jonathan Crush, A Jeeves, and David Yudelman, *South Africa's Labour Empire: A History of Black Migrancy to the Gold Mines* (Boulder, CO: Westview Press, 1991); Franklin Simtowe and F. M. Kinkingninhoun-Medagbe, "The Impact of HIV/AIDS on Labor Markets, Productivity and Welfare in Southern Africa: A Critical Review and Analysis," *African Journal of Agricultural Research* 6, no. 10 (2011): 2118–2131.

27. "Toolbox talks" are short, mandatory training sessions on such topics as hydration, nutrition, equipment maintenance, or safety around wild animals. See Hloni Nkomo, Ivan Niranjan, and Poovendhree Reddy, "Effectiveness of Health and Safety Training in Reducing Occupational Injuries Among Harvesting Forestry Contractors in KwaZulu-Natal," *Workplace Health & Safety* 66, no. 10 (2018): 499–507.

28. While much of the policy literature and many of the people involved in the forestry sector refer to "forestry workers," I have tended to use the term "timber [plantation] laborer" to refer to people employed in the timber plantations of northern KwaZulu-Natal, as the older sociological literature in South Africa on the "workforce" has a somewhat complicated relationship to the politics of critique. See E. C. Webster, "Race, Labour Process and Transition: The Sociology of Work in South Africa," *Society in Transition* 30, no. 1 (1999): 28–42. This does have the inadvertent effect of distinguishing this category of employment from other activities in the sector not directly concerned with the production of timber.

29. On the relationship between work and rhythm and the division of labor, see Gregor Dobler, "'Work and Rhythm' Revisited: Rhythm and Experience in Northern Namibian Peasant Work," *Journal of the Royal Anthropological Institute* 22, no. 4 (2016): 864–883.

30. To situate the politics of Black Economic Empowerment in post-apartheid South Africa, see Roger Southall, "Ten Propositions about Black Economic Empowerment in South Africa," *Review of African Political Economy* 34, no. 111 (2007): 67–84. On the forestry sector specifically, see Jeanette Clarke and Moenieba Isaacs, *Forestry Contractors in South Africa: What Role in Reducing Poverty?* (Cape Town: Programme for Land and Agrarian Studies, UWC, 2005).

31. Each of these terms for relations are highly situated indexicals key to both ordinary life and the "game of marriage," which I described in "Sex, Gender and Marriage." See Asif Agha, *Language and Social Relations: Studies in the Social and Cultural Foundations of Language* (Cambridge: Cambridge University Press, 2007).

32. There is a rich literature on emergent class striations in rural southern Africa. See Martin Legassick and Harold Wolpe, "The Bantustans and Capital Accumulation in South Africa," *Review of African Political Economy* 3, no. 7 (1976): 87–107; Timothy Keegan, "The Dynamics of Rural Accumulation in South Africa: Comparative and Historical Perspectives," *Comparative Studies in Society and History* 28, no. 4 (1986): 628–650; Ben Cousins, Alex Dubb, Donna Hornby, and Farai Mtero, "Social Reproduction of 'Classes of Labour' in the Rural Areas of South Africa: Contradictions and Contestations," *The Journal of Peasant Studies* 45, no. 5–6 (2018): 1060–1085.

33. In 2019, the minimum wage for the forestry sector was R18 per hour (USD 1.2 per hour), with monthly wages calculated as 4.33 times of a weekly wage. See https://mywage.co.za/salary/minimum-wages/6247-farming-and-forestry.

34. Nyamnjoh, "Incompleteness"; Thornton, *Healing the Exposed Being.*

35. Frank Tanser, Till Bärnighausen, Erofili Grapsa, Jaffer Zaidi, and Marie-Louise Newell, "High Coverage of ART Associated with Decline in Risk of HIV Acquisition in Rural KwaZulu-Natal, South Africa," *Science* 339, no. 6122 (2013): 966–971.

36. Didier Fassin, *When Bodies Remember: Experiences and Politics of AIDS in South Africa.* (Oakland, California: University of California Press, 2007); Thomas Cousins, "HIV and the Remaking of Hunger and Nutrition in South Africa: Biopolitical Specification after Apartheid," *BioSocieties* 10, no. 2 (2015): 143–161, https://doi.org/10.1057/biosoc.2015.8.

37. The range of associated meanings is important and would require more space than I have available here to explicate the glosses provided in the colonial moment of its translation. C. M. Doke, D. M. Malcolm, J. M. A. Sikakana, and B. W. Vilakazi, *English - Zulu, Zulu - English Dictionary* (Johannesburg: Witwatersrand University Press, 2006), 337: "1. Medicinal herb; herbal decoction used for medicinal purposes as household remedies; as opposed to amakhubalo, professional medicines. 2. The so-called intestinal beetle, believed by Natives to be parasitic in the intestines. 3. Large edible tree-caterpillar. 4. Nervous disorder, mental derangement. Lomuntu unekhambi (This person is mentally unsound)."

38. See, in particular, Karen E. Flint, *Healing Traditions: African Medicine, Cultural Exchange, and Competition in South Africa, 1820–1948* (Athens: Ohio University Press, 2008). ; Michelle Cocks and Anthony Dold, "The Role of 'African Chemists' in the Health Care System of the Eastern Cape Province of South Africa," *Social Science and Medicine* 51, no. 10 (2000): 1505–1515.

39. I am informed here by Audrey I. Richards, *Hunger and Work in a Savage Tribe; a Functional Study of Nutrition Among the Southern Bantu* (Glencoe, IL: Free Press, 1948); J. M. Garrido, *On Time, Being, and Hunger: Challenging the Traditional Way of Thinking Life* (New York: Fordham University Press, 2012).

40. See Anson Rabinbach's classic book, *The Human Motor: Energy, Fatigue, and the Origins of Modernity* (Berkeley: University of California Press, 1992).

41. C. M. Doke, D. M. Malcolm, J. M. A. Sikakana, and B. W. Vilakazi, *English–Zulu, Zulu–English Dictionary* (Johannesburg: Witwatersrand University Press, 2006), 9.

42. For descriptions of Shembe's power, see Elizabeth Gunner, *The Man of Heaven and the Beautiful Ones of God* (Leiden: Brill, 2004).

43. See Mark Hunter, "Fathers without Amandla? Gender and Fatherhood among IsiZulu Speakers," *Journal of Natal and Zulu History* 22, no. 1 (2004): 149–160. Here, Hunter describes how Zulu-speaking men struggle with their capacity to be fathers "without *amandla*."

44. Paul K. Bjerk, "They Poured Themselves into the Milk: Zulu Political Philosophy under Shaka," *Journal of African History* 47, no. 1 (2006): 1–19; Harriet Ngubane, "Some Notions of 'Purity' and 'Impurity' among the Zulu," *Africa* 46, no. 3 (July 1976):

274–284; Axel-Ivar Berglund, *Zulu Thought-Patterns and Symbolism* (Cape Town: David Philip, 1976).

45. At stake are the literalizing claims that the discourse of *izinyoka* is simply an ethnobiology of diarrhea. See Edward C. Green, Annemarie Jurg, and Armando Djedje, "The Snake in the Stomach: Child Diarrhea in Central Mozambique," *Medical Anthropology Quarterly* 8, no. 1 (1994): 4–24.

46. For a description of *Inkosi yaManzi*, King of the Waters, a giant snake in urban Soweto, see Adam Ashforth, "Reflections on Spiritual Insecurity in a Modern African City (Soweto)," *African Studies Review* 41, no. 3 (1998): 39–67. For a brilliant analysis of affliction and spiritual insecurity in post-apartheid South Africa, see Adam Ashforth, *Witchcraft, Violence, and Democracy in South Africa* (Chicago: University of Chicago Press, 2004).

47. On balance, see Kathryn Geurts, *Culture and the Senses: Bodily Ways of Knowing in an African Community* (Berkeley: University of California Press, 2003), 144–168. Cf. Harris Solomon, *Metabolic Living: Food, Fat, and the Absorption of Illness in India* (Durham, NC: Duke University Press, 2016).

48. Pamela Reynolds, "The Ground of All Making: State Violence, the Family and Political Activists," in *Violence and Subjectivity* ed. Veena Das, Arthur Kleinman, Mamphela Ramphele, and Pamela Reynolds (Berkeley: University of California Press, 2000), 141–170. This draws on Scarry's analysis of pain in her examination of the apartheid state's use of violence in breaking up families and the torture of young political activists: "The unmaking of civilisation inevitably requires a return to and mutilation of the domestic, the ground of all making." See Elaine Scarry, *The Body in Pain: The Making and Un-Making of the World* (Oxford: Oxford University Press, 1985), 45.

49. Elizabeth A. Wilson, *Gut Feminism* (Durham, NC: Duke University Press, 2015); James M. Wilce Jr., *Social and Cultural Lives of Immune Systems* (London: Taylor and Francis, 2003).

50. David Coplan, "History Is Eaten Whole: Consuming Tropes in Sesotho Auriture," *History and Theory* 32, no. 4 (1993), Beiheft 32: History Making in Africa: 80–104; Sidney W. Mintz and Christine M. Du Bois, "The Anthropology of Food and Eating," *Annual Review of Anthropology* 31, no. 1 (2002): 99–119; Nicolas Argenti, *The Intestines of the State: Youth, Violence, and Belated Histories in the Cameroon Grassfields* (Chicago: University of Chicago Press, 2007).

51. Elizabeth A. Wilson, *Psychosomatic: Feminism and the Neurological Body* (Durham, NC: Duke University Press, 2004).

52. Povinelli, *Economies of Abandonment.*

53. See Michael Silverstein, "Indexical Order and the Dialectics of Sociolinguistic Life," *Language & Communication* 23, no. 3 (2003): 193–229. For the uptake of Silverstein and her projection of metapragmatic action in corporeal terms, see Elizabeth A.

Povinelli, "Sexuality at Risk: Psychoanalysis Metapragmatically," in *Homosexuality and Psychoanalysis*, ed. Tim Dean and Christopher Lane (Chicago: University of Chicago Press, 2001), 387–411.

54. For a history of how "surplus" has been used in the critique of apartheid, see Surplus People Project, *Forced Removals in South Africa: The SPP Reports Volume 4* (Natal: Surplus People Project, 1983), 4.

55. See Francis B. Nyamnjoh, ed., *Eating and Being Eaten: Cannibalism as Food for Thought* (Bamenda, Cameroon: Langaa RPCIG, 2018); Marilyn Strathern, "Eating (and Feeding)," *The Cambridge Journal of Anthropology* 30, no. 2 (2012): 1–14.

56. Jackson, "Rethinking Repair," 223.

57. Nancy Rose Hunt, *A Nervous State: Violence, Remedies, and Reverie in Colonial Congo* (Durham, NC: Duke University Press, 2015).

58. While images of vulnerability can be found across the philosophical landscape from Hobbes to Hegel, Levinas to Foucault, often indicating a sense of bodily susceptibility to injury or of being threatened or wounded, I am less interested here in a Euro-American genealogy than the possibilities for a "Southern" reading of vulnerability. See Faisal Devji, "The Return of Nonviolence," *Critical Times* 4, no. 1 (2021): 93–101, for a critique of Judith Butler, *The Force of Nonviolence: An Ethico-Political Bind* (New York: Verso Books, 2020); see also Danielle Petherbridge, "What's Critical about Vulnerability? Rethinking Interdependence, Recognition, and Power," *Hypatia* 31, no. 3 (2016): 589–604. The uneven distribution of vulnerability has been well described in anthropological treatments of violence in various postcolonial contexts. See the landmark essays in Arthur Kleinman, Veena Das, and Margaret M. Lock, *Social Suffering* (Oakland: University of California Press, 1997); Veena Das, Arthur Kleinman, Mamphele Ramphele, and Pamela Reynolds, eds. *Violence and Subjectivity* (Oakland: University of California Press, 2000); and Veena Das and Clara Han, *Living and Dying in the Contemporary World* (Oakland: University of California Press, 2016).

59. Thornton, *Healing the Exposed Being*.

60. Anette Wickström, "'Lungisa'—Weaving Relationships and Social Space to Restore Health in Rural KwaZulu Natal," *Medical Anthropology Quarterly* 28, no. 2 (2014): 203–220.

61. James Fernandez, *Bwiti: An Ethnography of the Religious Imagination in Africa* (Princeton, NJ: Princeton University Press, 1982).

62. Hylton White, "Tempora Et Mores: Family Values and the Possessions of a Post-Apartheid Countryside," *Journal of Religion in Africa* 31, no. 4 (2001): 457–479.

63. Jackson, "Rethinking Repair," 222.

10 CONVERSATION WITH GEOF BOWKER

FERNANDO DOMÍNGUEZ RUBIO (FDR): Both chapters talk about care as a relational situated practice, specifically insisting on the unpredictability and openness of these relationships. Can you tell us what you've learned from them and what the main points of connection and divergence are between the two.

GEOF BOWKER (GB): I'm going give a couple of different answers to this. They both speak to a theme that's a little bit in the repair literature already, which is the concept of constitutive incompleteness—the fact that repair and care are never finished. Both chapters show that neither repair nor care are about making things whole. Rather, they are about making things work, making things possible. I thought this was a lovely idea. The second point is that both chapters underline the importance of the body, which is rare in this kind of literature. In Criado and Duclos's chapter, for example, the critique of the ableist version is not about making things whole but instead about understanding the role of the body in relationship. There's a way in which I'd say both chapters talk about the insides and the outsides of the body; they don't stop at the boundary of the skin. This reminded me of Taussig, when he makes the point that politics is centrally present when you're ingesting frogs and having a hallucinatory experience with the shaman. At the same time, you are enacting and dealing with vast political structures and capitalism.

I was also reminded of Marx's *Capital Volume 1*, where he discusses the cycle of money–commodity–money, as MCM, and then he flips into commodity–money–commodity. And he says, you get a very different analytic edge, depending on where you start that cycle. In both of the chapters, you could take it going away from the standard history of technology, history of infrastructure, just build, repair, build, to repair, build, repair and move toward starting with repair. When you start with repair, and the interstices, then you've got mediation as being a prior category. And I think what really came out in both of the cases was that mediation is not something that you do to make things work. Mediation is where it all starts. This thought came out absolutely beautifully in both chapters. I have a favorite phrase across both chapters, which was in Cousins's: "Gut pathology does not so much 'represent' a breakdown in relations as enact it enterologically." So, an exit through the gut.

JÉRÔME DENIS (JD): I think this idea of the cycle is really interesting. Beginning with repair and not with building is really important. It helps us to see that the finished form of something is not its final state but rather a moment in a cycle where repair is always needed but never completed. Related to this, what did you think about this idea of fragment in the Criado and Duclos's chapter? This idea of not only the cycle between repair and build and repair but of fragmentation—of fragments as starting points?

FDR: I think this related to what Geof said earlier about repair and care not being about making things whole but instead about making them work. But when they work, they do it in very different systems. For example, in Cousins's chapter, they are making bodies work in an exploitative system. In the case of Tomás and Vincent, it is about making fragments left *after* breakdown work in ways that actually defy established regimes of power or a confining definition such as ableism. It is interesting to see how making things or people work can be taken in completely different directions.

GB: I think that's absolutely right. I almost brought out from the Cousins's chapter as well where he says that the centrality of *amandla*, as both bodily capacity and ethical aspiration, elicits the acts of repair. And *amandla*, as he describes it, is both the capacity and aspiration, and they both elicit different kinds of ethics of care and repair. I think you're quite right about that when the ethics of repair driven by plantation owners are different from the ethics of repair when you need to get about a town and you can't get about the town, you know, without certain kinds of gadgets and fillings, you know, the bricolage that you're using.

FDR: One of the things what we want to do in the book is to push against the romanticization of these concepts. Because care and repair can also be used for the exact opposite purpose: to debilitate or make impossible resistance of other types of politics. I live by the US border. The US government puts a lot of work in caring and repairing the border as a way of creating and sustaining exclusion, separation, alienation.

GB: I mean that's a really beautiful analogy, and I think you're absolutely right. The wall is just like a totalizing infrastructure that can never be realized. However, there are forms of surveillance, which can be very powerful, such as those created by Peter Thiel, who is one of the founders of Cambridge Analytica, and Palentir, and a huge funder of Trump, who put in these series of really sensitive cameras and sensing devices along parts of the border with Mexico. And as put it, Fernando, all the care and repair that's going into making certain people don't cross. And at the same time, you had networks of people who were leaving food and water in the desert, for people who cross over illegally. So, both sides are doing care and repair work, if you like.

FDR: So, let's move on to the second question. Both chapters question fragility through the lenses of ecology in a variety of configurations—from project trajectories to labor and intimacies. You've developed ecological thinking in your own work. So, how do you think these contributions relate to your own work and the concept of ecological thinking as you have developed it?

GB: Both chapters really resonated me, especially Criado and Duclos's chapter and the idea that the failure of a project doesn't mean the end of the project. The question they raise: What is success? This comes out especially in the *En Torno a la Silla* project. This reminded me of Gina Neff's work on Silicon Alley, where all these people got laid off in the early 2000s, when the dot-com bust happened. And she said we can portray this as a narrative of failure of all of these different companies, or we can look at the success of the individual people who used the bust as a networking possibility or a chance to retool or a chance to gain new sellable skills. What she shows is that the dot-com bust was not only a site of enormous failure but also a site of continuing success. And that relates to a little bit of what I was saying in my answer to the first question: the idea of information infrastructure and about infrastructures that never get built. They're always part of a much longer and deeper ecology that accretes from the ruins of the old and the fragments of the new. The example I was thinking of is Starosielski's book on the undersea network, where she analyzes the undersea network and shows how it starts off as cable lines for telegraph in the nineteenth century. Then, you actually stabilize a set of political relations between countries, which agree on a right of way for cable networks. And then those same cable lines were later used for telephone, and now they're used for the Internet. And the point is that the political and social infrastructure we rely on today was already built for the telegraph network. It's very difficult to renegotiate a new path to lay a cable, even though it could be faster. That's why West Africa had such difficulty getting good Internet for the longest time. So, in a sense, we're building the new infrastructure of the Internet directly out of the ruins of the telegraph network. This reminded me of an architectural manifesto, which I love, called *Buildings Must Die*, by Jacobs and Cairns. What they argue is one of the problems that we have when we design stuff apparently de novo and assume it's going to live forever. We're no longer in that era of certainty. I mean, this is kind of an era of certainty that Timothy Mitchell was talking about in carbon democracy: the idea that the infrastructure in the 1920s was built to last forever. And then all these things crumble together in the 2020s. Today, any network must assume that the network is going to break, that things are going to break down, things are going to die. Death should be part of the design. Design should include fragmentation. Fragmentation is not an accidental feature. Fragmentation is always going to happen. And if it's always going to happen, why don't we design for it? Well, it's like, say, the iPhone. The iPhone is not designed for repair. It's designed to be thrown away. But we should be designing for repair? We just seem to have moved away from it, certainly in the West.

FDR: What happens when that design for fragments is reappropriated, domesticated, and neutralized? I'm thinking about concepts such as resilience, for example, which takes into account the possibility of collapse but enables the fantasy that we can plan for it, adapt, and keep going forever. Or think about sustainable architecture, which again acknowledges the possibility of collapse but never really has to confront collapse per se, since sustainability averts it. The point I am trying to make is that it is possible to design ways of assimilating, reducing, or governing collapse or decay and trying to keep things going. But how can you plan for actual collapse?

GB: There's a field in social informatics now called "collapse informatics," which is based on the idea that we're headed for a collapse economically, socially, politically. It's about how do we design stuff so that we can keep going after the collapse? And I think that's an interesting move, although I've got problems with the way in which they frame it. For another example, let's give you a cheap analogy from software from computing languages, between object-oriented programming and things such as COBOL. COBOL code for the grid network in Illinois, say, was one central program with eight million lines of code, but they were all dependent on each other. So, bugs had to be tracked down and then fixed along the whole set. The advantage of object-oriented programming was that you got modules. So, if any one module collapses, you don't need to redefine—you know, reinvent the whole structure. You just plug in another module with the same APIs. After 9/11 in America, there was very much a decentralization theme. That's one of the foundational myths about the origin of the Internet in Baran: that they didn't want something like the Library of Alexandria, where all the knowledge is constrained in one space, they wanted network knowledge networks so that bombing couldn't destroy it. And there was a discourse after 9/11 that now we need to dissolve Manhattan. It's too big, it's too concentrated a target. So, what we need to do is decentralize, just like the French have partially decentralized Parisian academia since the 1980s. In both the Internet case and the Manhattan 9/11 case, there is talk of designing for collapse and a recognition of the inevitability of collapse.

Now, the other point you were making Fernando, which I didn't respond to directly and want to now, is the issue of reappropriation. It's so amazing how good the fossil fuel companies are at reappropriating the dialogue about care for the earth and green technology. Chevron has a claim now that they're going to be carbon neutral within ten years. What does carbon neutral mean for Chevron, who are producing all this shit, which is polluting the world? And yet they say, "We will be clean and green and carbon neutral." When I was working in philanthropy around science and technology in Silicon Valley, there was very much the same thing. There's a reappropriation in what was called in business terms "the triple bottom line," which spelled out the need to be economically sustainable, socially sustainable, and environmentally sustainable. Interestingly enough, a lot—well, almost all—of the energy went to the economically sustainable. Some energy for the purposes of advertising went to the environmentally sustainable, almost nothing went to the socially sustainable—they're not interested in the socially sustainable. So, it's like the denial of unionization of Starbucks and McDonald's, the University of California or Amazon—they just don't want social sustainability. But taking, appropriating a notion. I mean, when have notions ever not been reappropriated? And I guess that's what I'd say: you come up with a radical idea and suddenly it gets reappropriated. So, you need to come up with another idea. That's just part of the dialectic. And then, I don't think there's any way to change that—without fundamentally changing the system.

JD: But there is another aspect, which is that maybe design could be something that accepts not only fragmentation but also transformation, which is not exactly the same—which is also to acknowledge that maintenance or repair is not making things exactly the same but rather always transforming them to get them to go on.

GB: I think that's really right. You're reminding me of the role of medicine. We actually know that every human body is going through transformations, but we know that ultimately it's going to collapse. Criado and Duclos talk about this very well when discussing the ableist mentality. But let's start from the fact that we're all disabled. That is actually the norm: to be disabled. So, the question is, How do we move from one set of being disabled to another? Or how do we maybe palliate it through transformation? But the idea of suddenly becoming a whole person—the whole complete, healthy person? We tend to think of transformation as smooth transformation. But transformation can also be a tipping point. You go completely from one place to another, and suddenly you're living in a different world. On the other hand, I mean, getting back to Cousins's case, there was a relatively smooth transformation between worker-based farming infrastructure in America and precision infrastructure. That was a smooth transformation, which left many people hugely suffering and much poorer in its wake.

FDR: Let's go to the third question. The two chapters bring forward questions about how fragments are related or not to a whole, revealing the incompleteness of repair. These questions resonate with your work, notably on information infrastructure, residual categories, and membership.

GB: I was involved for longest time in infrastructure studies, especially cyber infrastructure, information infrastructure. And it was really nice for me to see how this work has moved to physical infrastructure—for example, in Brian Larkin's work and the general turn to infrastructure in anthropology. Ideas that we've been using to analyze information infrastructure and are now being adopted to study physical infrastructure. Similarly, Steve Jackson's work on repair started in information technology, and then both Jérôme and David developed to looking at the that same work of repair in the physical world, the built environment and built infrastructure. The question for me is when it's useful to use a concept, that's what I've always said about infrastructure. It's not that infrastructure is a universally valuable concept. But sometimes I can use it to make links between studies in completely different areas. This reminds me of Yrjo Engestrom's paper "When Is a Tool?" and how he shows that not everything is a tool, but anything can become a tool in certain circumstances. And infrastructure, care, and repair can become really interesting tools, depending on the circumstances.

On residual categories, Leigh Star and I developed this concept in *Sorting Things Out* when talking about the concept of "being torqued" by a technology. Here, we wanted to get at how, while certain people are torqued by a given infrastructure—in our case, it was medical infrastructure—some sail along happily in that infrastructure. Everything's easy for them, they've got well-defined conditions. Whereas people who are in the residual categories live in the interstices. We could say that most people in capitalist systems have to make it look as if we fit within categories because we're not going to get cared for unless we fit in those categories. We need to twist ourselves or twist our description of ourselves to fit the categories. And that is much harder if you come from the interstices. That's something that Gloria Anzaldúa writes beautifully about the mestiza. She writes that there's no such thing as a pure X or a pure Y in racial terms. The standard, the norm, is to be mestiza, to be caught in this third space, in these borderlines. This is evident in Cousins's example, where the women on the plantation are being torqued by the system and need to contort themselves to fit. But they are being torqued into the system, they had been disfigured, attacked by the very system of apparent care.

One other thing I loved in both of the chapters is how they pay attention to the invisible work that happens after. In Criado and Duclos's chapter, they focus on the work that happens after the network has gone away, when godmothers are still continuing their work. But that work has gone from being visible, in a sense of being funded paid work, to being something that is invisible, in terms of nobody is going to document this, nobody's going to recognize it, you know, until the anthropologists come along.

FDR: This brings up the point of temporality. It is often the case that care and repair are associated with what we might call a "temporality of the return." They are understood as activities that return, or bring back, something to its original identity after they break down or fall apart. However, what both of these chapters do is to show us that there is nothing to return to—that repair and care are future-oriented or even future-making activities. They are about moving forward, changing, and moving things that are never quite what they once were, but something else that keeps working for whatever reason. So, it's not about recovering anything but about working with fragments. However, these are fragments that are seen not simply as the remnants of something that is gone but rather as seeds of something to become. And the work of repair is precisely the work that makes that passage possible. So, it is not about recovering, restituting, coming back, returning but instead about stitching things together to move forward. Which is counterintuitive, since we think about a design innovation as the only activity that moves forward, and repair is a merely restitutive past-oriented activity.

GB: I think that's a lovely point. Stuart Kaufman, who writes about complexity theory, talks about the adjacent possible as a solution, or transformation, that is always already there. You just need to find it and recognize it. I love that idea. Because for me, it's a very hopeful idea that we do not need to go out and seek for radically new solutions, which are going to change everything, but solutions that are already there. We just need to fight and sensitize ourselves to recognizing them. And for me, this is the sort of thing Leibniz meant when talking about compossibility, where the compossible is all things that can live together at the same time. We're talking about compossible worlds here and how they get built, how they get designed. This goes against the idea of repair as making whole again. Repair is bringing something new. This is sort of the reason of why for a number of years I've been into process ontology, especially Whitehead and Isabelle Strengers. There are never any fixed things in the world—only verbs, only things that are changing. This is what Pipek and Wulf said when they talked about infrastructuring as a verb rather than infrastructure as a noun. In the same way, Criado and Duclos talks about fragments not as a noun but as a verb. And I thought that was an absolutely beautiful point. The world looks differently if you turn your nouns, which seem to be fixed for all time, into verbs.

DAVID PONTILLE: Going back to something about this and all this transformation and process ontology with the topic of continuity. It is related to what Fernando says about the past and the future and continuity that is built, actually, in the present. When people think about repair, it is as the other of something. Often, as the other of creating or innovation, which are seen as the activities that produce new stuff in the world. But maybe repair is just another mode of building the world.

FDR: Let's go for the last one. So, what do you think about the overall intent of this volume to focus on fragility? Here's, by the way, where you have to lie and say that everything is great! What do you think we can gain from such a move? And what do you think could be possible limitations, shortcomings, and dangers?

GB: I think fragility has a very wide resonance now across a whole series of different disciplines. We used to think that the earth had a fairly robust climate, and now we realize that it's actually very fragile—that we could lose the trade winds, the circulation of the cold water from Antarctica, which makes the world feel much more fragile. I think we have a heightened awareness of fragility in the world. I am reminded here of Pete de Bolla's book *The Architecture of Concepts*, which has a really nice discussion of what he calls "load bearing concepts." A load bearing concept example for him would be Adam Smith's principle of the division of labor, which is central to the Industrial Revolution and also to the development of computing and Babbage or early bee studies. A load bearing concept does a lot of work when it's deployed within a given epoch. And I think fragility is a concept that can be that—that can speak to many contemporary discourses.

I think that it's a really important discourse for us to have because, quoting Timothy Mitchell, we've had a discourse of certainty, stability, you know, rock solidness. So, saying that fragility is a constant is really great. I think I've said this before, but I'll say it again, I liked it that neither of the chapters romanticize fragility and fragmentation. And I thought that was fantastic. And it's also clearly what you're doing in the volume. There's always that danger in romanticizing a concept that is probably best understood as sort of torquing in Leigh Star's sense. There's a danger if everything becomes fragility. For me, fragility and robustness always sit side by side. Yes, fragility and fragmentation are necessary. Yes, the work of repair is continuing and continuous. But there's always the possibility of a new kind of robustness emerging. And I think that gets back to, David, one of the points you're making that it is not the same robustness. We're not returning to an old robustness. But we are, at the same time, creating new robustness and new networks.

JD: I think this idea of dialectics and fragility and robustness is very important. And maybe a notion that we didn't mention regarding continuity is the idea of becoming, and the consideration that things that are fragility can become robust, for instance. And this idea of accompanying the becoming of the things or people acknowledging fragility but let some kind of robustness arise.

GB: I'm reminded here of Donna Haraway's wonderful phrase "staying with the trouble." Always stay with the act of becoming. We made this point many years ago in science and technology studies that far too much work looked at the creation of new stuff. It didn't look at the maintenance of old stuff. And Bruno Latour made this point in a different context, in Science in Action, where he makes the assertion that something like 80 percent or 90 percent of scientific funding is about the maintenance of standards. It's about the care for standards. But if I look at the history of science, there is very little about the care and maintenance of standards. It's all about the Higgs boson, mapping the human genome, and other bright shiny objects, just as far too much history of technology is about the development of the new. It's all about the new stuff that's being created. I think some of the work that you're doing here is presaged in that comment that if we understand science as being about care and maintenance as much as it is about innovation, then I think we understand science, technology, and society differently.

IV POLITICS

11 SOVEREIGNTY AND THE WEAKNESS OF THE KING: REGIMES OF CARE AT ROCHEFORT

CHANDRA MUKERJI

We may think that practices of care pertain to bodies and infrastructures, and we may assume that institutional power has no relationship to them. But the strength of political orders is always dependent on regimes of care, particularly modern Western states. Governments exercise power, at least in part, through the care of people and things in hospitals, schools, arsenals, military installations, and postal services (Joyce 2013; Joyce and Mukerji 2017). These sites of care are not powerful in themselves but instead provide scaffolding for dreams of good governance and collective purpose that give states their power.

Entangling cultural imagination with regimes of care is key to the administration of Jean-Baptiste Colbert, when he arguably created the first modern state to assert the sovereignty of Louis XIV. This chapter will focus on one of the state projects: the arsenal at Rochefort. As a center of shipbuilding, Rochefort not only illustrates the difficulty of tailoring reality to imaginaries but also shows how the "mindful hands" of artisans (Roberts, Schaffer, and Dear 2007a) could contribute to France's standing as a sea power late in the seventeenth century.

Like other sites of care in Colbert's administration, the arsenal was staffed with people of low rank, most importantly artisans. From a family of artisans, merchants, and financiers himself, Colbert understood that they carried expertise useful to the state (Bourgeon 1973). Talented artisans could dream up the political imaginary of the sovereign Sun King for Louis XIV and provide evidence of his glorious destiny in the magnificence and power of well-made artifacts and infrastructures. So, Colbert recruited artisans for his administration, but he understood that the king's dependence on their labor was an embarrassment that had to be concealed from public view. They made sovereignty seem automatic like the mechanical Turk (Irani 2015), creating the illusion of pure inevitability, not human effort and creativity.

When Louis XIV took the throne in 1661, the French monarchy had been weak for most of the century. French nobles were notably independent and powerful officials (Machiavelli 1966). The *noblesse de la robe* controlled the courts and local governments; the *noblesse d'épée* supplied and led the army. Nobles were part of local tax administrations, too, able to skim funds en route to the treasury. The religious divide between Catholics and Huguenots contributed to the tenuous power of the monarchy as well. Kings of France had to be Catholic, but Huguenots (French Calvinists) thought the king illegitimate. The territory that Louis XIV inherited was also physically and economically devastated by decades of religious violence. Towns were ruined, families homeless, trades disrupted, lands abandoned, people impoverished, and infrastructure shattered. And during Louis's childhood, a high noble faction revolted against the monarchy in the Fronde—even allying themselves with Spain, France's greatest enemy, to oppose the royal army. The movement failed. But the king remembered and sought power independent of the nobility. Colbert provided it with an administration of low-born, high-ability experts. They celebrated the king's sovereignty and set up regimes of care to attend to the well-being of the kingdom. The result was transformational. In a few decades, Louis XIV became one of the most powerful monarchs in Europe (Beik 1985; Clément 1979; Ranum 1993; Collins 2009; Mettam 1988; D. Parker 1983; Singer-Lecocq 1998; Mukerji 2017).

Foucault explains why. He argues that the institutional power of governments cannot be based on the laws or political ideas as we often assume. Both are forms of discourse that can be reversed, ideologies can be challenged, and legal principles can be reinterpreted. Institutional power rests instead on what Foucault calls "prophetic truths"—dreams of possibility that are hard to counter because they are fictions, albeit credible ones (Foucault and Davidson 2014, lectures 82–83; Stenger 2010; Reed 2020; Roberts, Schaffer, and Dear 2007a). Foucault thinks that these imaginaries can draw people together to give them purpose. But prophetic truths are still fundamentally fragile as fictions. So, they must be made credible with acts of care—in palaces, gardens, infrastructures, fortresses, weapons, and bodies—that seem to display evidence of prophecy. That is why Colbert's administration of experts would entangle imaginaries and programs of care to advance the prophetic truth of royal sovereignty (Joyce and Mukerji 2017; Maral 2013; Néraudau 1986).

Colbert had limited political options, even as minister of the treasury, minister of the navy, and director of the king's households. He could only exercise power in government by means of service. So, that is what he provided (Soll 2009; Clément 1979, intro.; Burke 1994; Da Vinha 2004; Weber, Roth, and Wittich 1978), Colbert's low rank made him too weak to insert himself into political arenas where noble officials governed through inherited offices. But the minister could deploy artisans, intellectuals, merchants, engineers, and others to change French material life, exercising logistical powers entangled with dreams. Colbert recruited the best talent he could find, bringing celebrated intellectuals and artists to royal academies, elevating their standing so they could gain credibility. And more radically, Colbert recruited artisans with great talent but no authority into sites of material care such as Rochefort to advance the sovereignty of the Sun King (D'Aubert 2014; Burchard 2016).

In this chapter, I will focus on the regime of material care that shipbuilders established at Rochefort, turning wood into warships, brush into ropes, and ores into cannon. They needed natural knowledge and experience to do this work. So, part of building the arsenal was acquiring and honing the necessary skills. Artisanal knowledge was embodied and uncodified so it could not be easily taught or managed from above. But it could be transformative, producing vital political tools such as a powerful fleet (Peter 2002; Smith 2004; Smith, Myers, and Cook 2017; Roberts, Schaffer, and Dear 2007b).

None of the work at Rochefort was glamorous or directly celebratory of the Sun King. Timbers for masts had to be located in the Pyrenees soaked in salt water so they would dry straight and strong; hulls had to be scraped and tarred to be waterproof; reeds and brush needed to be soaked and shredded so they could be twisted to make rope; ores had to be processed at high heat with chemical additives to make melts for cannon. The range of required practices made the work difficult, but it produced the great French ships of the line—impersonal displays of sovereign glory (Peter 2002).

Sovereignty was, by its nature, difficult to define and exercise. According to the Treaty of Augsburg (1555) and Peace of Westphalia (1648), sovereigns were supposed to be the supreme rulers with the moral and natural authority to govern their lands (Reed 2020). But sovereignty in this legal sense was an empty category (Milton, Axworthy, and Simms 2019). It was used in the Treaty of Augsburg as a generic term for the most powerful ruler—individual or collective. This generic "sovereign" was given the right to choose the religion for his, her, or its people. The point was to realign rulers with believers of the same faith in a period when people of one religion assumed that rulers of another were morally unfit for office. The Treaty of Augsburg was intended to restore moral authority in government, but it had no effect on the religious upheavals of the period. Overlapping jurisdictions and religious divides undermined the claims of any ruler to sovereignty. And the lack of precedent left it unclear what powers sovereigns should wield. So, kings remained in the eyes of their enemies and rivals simply nobles among nobles, subject to religious opposition and patrimonial pressures (Andrew 2011; Jackson 2007; Mukerji 2021; Strong 1985; Schmitt 1985).

Following the failure of the Treaty of Augsburg, the political philosopher Jean Bodin (1596) tried to clarify sovereignty by establishing principles of sovereign government. He argued that kings were ordained by God and should be surrounded by those with contingent rather than inherited powers. His principles of government were praised, but they failed to give princes the ability to stop religious warfare—and for just the reasons Foucault suggested. Legal discourse was just discourse. Sovereignty remained a category whose meaning could be contested. So, princes clashed over rights and lands, faiths continued to proliferate, governments rose against each other, peasants rebelled, and war spread through Western Europe (Andrew 2011; Jackson 2007; Mukerji 2021).

Almost a century later, the wars of religion were ongoing, and questions of sovereignty were still debated when the Peace of Westphalia was negotiated. It was not a single treaty but rather a set of agreements negotiated among combatants that tried to address local problems of jurisdiction and faith. The Peace of Westphalia accepted Calvinism as a legitimate form of Christianity and allocated territories and rights to sovereigns. Sovereignty was not an articulated principle of power and certainly not supreme power. Princes were subject to legal oversight, even in their own lands, and rulers could be sanctioned for breaches of the agreement. The Peace of Westphalia upheld the concept of sovereignty as the right to rule over a territory, but sovereign power remained problematic as both a political position and a practice of power (Peace of Westphalia 1648; Milton, Axworthy, and Simms 2019).

It was in this context that Louis XIV broke with tradition to assert his sovereignty by declaring personal rule. He refused to appoint a prime minister. He understood that a high noble official with that much access to information and power could threaten his autonomy—or worse, his throne. Louis XIV seemed to take to heart Bodin's advice to rule through officials with contingent authority and to act as a moral leader chosen by God, not just a noble among nobles (Reed 2020; Strong 1985).

Colbert's appointment as minister solved three problems at once. His low rank made his authority contingent on the king. And his programs of care characterized the sovereign a moral force: steward of his people and land. Plus, Colbert also had royal artisans develop the political imaginary of sovereign authority through the Sun King. None of these ways of expressing royal power was discursive.

Artisans at the Louvre were in charge of creating an appropriate device for Louis XIV. At first, Charles Le Brun wanted to depict the king as Alexander, a great hero, but this failed to give him moral standing. The king preferred Apollo, who was a god, a force of nature, and a figure from the ancient world. Apollo had the superhuman qualities to revive France's heritage from Gaul and bring in a new dawn. Apollo's rise was a dream of enlightenment before its time (Mukerji 2021; Burchard 2016; Singer-Lecocq 1998).

Artisans placed seductive images of Apollo everywhere in the king's households and in public art too—from gardens to triumphal arches and to ships launched at sea. It was a modernizing vision despite its ancient referent because it disrupted patrimonial assumptions. It provided cultural scaffolding for innovations grounded in ancient precedents, defining sovereignty in historical terms that weren't present in the legal tradition or the patrimonial order (Apostolidès 1981; Mukerji 2017, 2021; Burchard 2016; Strong 1985).

The king revealed this historical logic of sovereign power in the Carrousel of 1662. This ritual contest of military might was staged as a struggle among historical empires. High nobles were enrolled to be leaders of the empires: Turkish, Indian, American, and Persian. The king of France would lead the forces of Rome. The event was public—enacted in front of the Louvre in Paris—to manifest the king's ambitions. The elaborate costumes, sets, choreography, and music brought the fictional contest of empires to life. The event was a political demonstration of royal ambition that was given material form and credibility by artisans (Perrault 1670; Néraudau 1986; Rosental and Porter 2021).

Perrault (1670), in his memoir of the event, argued that it was more than a traditional carrousel that enacted military virtues:

> It would not be enough for posterity only to know [Louis XIV's] great achievements in war and peace; the hurt he could inflict on his enemies through force of arms and the good he did for his people through assiduous care and the example he set with his own conduct. . . . It is important that [posterity] learn that he was not only the most valiant and wise of princes of our times, but that he was also the most adroit and magnificent, and that the nobility of his court always [put France above] over all the nations of the world.[1]

The event served as prophecy, projecting the glory that Louis XIV would bring to France as sovereign. Louis XIV would not only honor France with military successes but also improve it with his wisdom, magnificence, and generosity. The grandeur of the event itself seemed to demonstrate the scope of the young king's dreams, and it thematically tied military might with excellence in the arts and engineering—all achievements worthy of Rome.

The imaginary of the Sun King was most aggressively asserted at Versailles by the artisans of his household and royal workshops. They made him glitter like the sun with golden clothes and sparkling jewels, filled his chateau with light using mirrors and tall windows, gilded his luxury goods such as clocks and inlaid chests to shine, and represented the sun god in fountains in his gardens that reflected the sky. In the *levée* each morning, the king rose like the sun, transformed by valets from man to Sun King. His *valets de chambre*, many of them artisans, turned his vulnerable human body into a godlike figure of unassailable power. The Sun King was a fiction, of course, and ridiculed as such. But visions of sovereignty conjured up by artisans made his grandeur seem palpable and drew nobles to his court (Singer-Lecocq 1998; Apostolidès 1981; Da Vinha 2004; Maral 2013; Néraudau 1986; Mukerji 2021).

Artisans gave substance to the king's glory beyond Versailles too. The improvements they made in war-torn France became a measure of his moral standing. So, artisans in the administration repaired damage by building new roads, canals, and water supplies. And engineers helped to sustain claims to France's heritage in Rome. Sébastien de Prestre de Vauban, François Blondel, and the Chevalier de Clerville marked territorial borders with star-shaped fortresses and cities such as those in Vitruvius ([1521] 1960). These and other public works projects became enduring parts of the landscape—seemingly ordained, natural, impersonal, unassailable, and necessary (Konvitz 2020; Lynn 1997; Mukerji 2015).

Where discourses of sovereignty had failed, the Sun King succeeded in shifting relations of power and promoting religious peace. Artisans and the laborers transformed France with regimes of care. They were modest social actors but brought into government material abilities that helped shore up the weak king (Scott 1985; Roberts, Schaffer, and Dear 2007a). Their accomplishments were entangled with the powerfully organizing imaginary of the Sun King, shaping a dream of possibility outside discourse. This political constellation allowed Louis XIV to amass unimaginable power—so much that his enemies called him a tyrant (Foucault and Davidson 2014; Mukerji 2017, 2021).

CARE AND REGIME POWER

In his "Age of Louis XIV," Voltaire (1752) argued that the king himself was not the source of the greatness of his age. Rather, it was the creativity unleashed around him by ordinary people aspiring to new heights. Patronage in the arts, letters, sciences, and the military affected multiple domains from war and geopolitics to science, poetry, and gardening. The desire to embrace ancient levels of achievement and excel in all fields spread beyond the court. Artisans working in regimes of care for the administration took the goal of excellence into the countryside (Academie royale de peinture et de sculpture 1669; Bertucci 2017).

Foucault suggested that social affirmation was crucial to making prophetic truths forceful. He put the act of prophecy in the Greek chorus, a community foretelling of what was to come. In his theory, prophetic imaginaries were objects of concern that drew people together to manifest their common destiny. But such unity of purpose was not possible in France. Ravaged by war, religious divides, and jurisdictional disputes, France could not speak with one voice (Mettam 1988; Beik 1985; Latour 2004; Foucault and Davidson 2014).

Artisans in the Louvre, Gobelins, and Versailles were successful in drawing high nobles to the court with a glittering political stage and glimpses of the magnificent future that the king offered. But the magnificence of the court did not draw all the kingdom into the royal orbit. Some nobles in the countryside and Huguenots throughout France were not proponents of the Sun King's rise. They nurtured their independence and were wary of the crown. Still, as Voltaire argued, Louis XIV spawned an "age." The question is how (Apostolidès 1981; Beik 1985; Néraudau 1986; Burke 1994; Voltaire 1752).

The overflowing creativity that Voltaire observed was unleashed not by affirming voices of destiny but rather by "mindful hands" (Roberts, Schaffer, and Dear 2007a). The cultural outpouring was the product of modest social actors that aspired to do extraordinary things—if not to affirm the superiority of the sovereign then to restore Gallic greatness. The artisans who Colbert assembled in royal workshops, academies, and manufactures rushed to invent a culture worthy of Rome. They were required to make the court and king magnificent because positions were contingent on the king's largesse. But artisans also had a distinctive relationship to Rome. Families of them lived among the ruins and remnants of classical arches, bridges, roads, and walls—all artifacts made by artisans, many of whose techniques they still employed. The Gallic heritage was theirs to revive and improve upon with the natural knowledge they had acquired through experiment.

But how could such "mindful hands" making artifacts and installations contribute to state power? Michel Serres (1983) suggested a way in his book on Rome. He argued that the Roman Empire was a product of two quite distinct processes: violent struggles for domination and material creation of habitat—forms of strategic and logistical power (Mukerji 2010). The growth of the Roman Empire required aggression on the part of leaders, but its success depended on settlers claiming territory with habitat. Disbanded soldiers and slaves put the stamp of empire on the ground by using knowledge of the hands and eyes.

The political significance of habitat to regime power is more obvious when settlements seem to defy the political order. Antoine Hennion (2018) demonstrated this in his study of the migrant camps at Calais. A despised minority caught between France and the UK began to build residences and other structures in their encampments, creating amenities to sustain themselves. The migrants produced a modest regime of care. Unable to leave or improve their lot by migrating further, they created settlements to ameliorate their suffering; they had no power other than their embodied abilities to engage with nature and materials. They employed these "weapons of the weak" that did not depend upon the largesse of social superiors (Scott 1985). But the settlements were claims to territory that France could not tolerate. It bulldozed the encampments to realign regime power with habitat.

Claiming places through material labor had different effects in San Diego when a freeway interchange was laid over a Chicano neighborhood. The land under the freeway "belonged" to the state, but artists, activists, and neighborhood leaders claimed it as their own with art, producing a community park: Chicano Park. Officials opposed the park as an unsightly and illegitimate settlement of poor people under a freeway, but members of the community were able to defend the installation. The freeway had divided their neighborhood, and they were simply mending it. So, the park remained and became a tourist attraction, defining San Diego as a center of Chicano activism and art (Henke and Sims 2020).

These cases illustrate that ordinary people can exercise logistical powers that are independent from regimes but integral to their legitimacy and identity. So, when Colbert introduced artisans into his administration and entangled their work with images of the Sun King, his policies transformed the state, giving substance to royal power and echoing the logistical foundation of Rome (Roberts, Schaffer, and Dear 2007a; Denis and Pontille 2011; Mukerji 2015).

THE SETTLEMENT AT ROCHEFORT

The town of Rochefort itself exemplified the practices of care and cultural aspiration animating the administration. Rochefort was an "ideal city" in the Italian military tradition. It was designed by the French engineers François Blondel, the Chevalier de Clerville, and Sebastian Le Prestre de Vauban. Ideal cities were based on ideas by Vitruvius about social engineering and urban design (Vitruvius [1521] 1960; Rosenau 1959; Konvitz 2020). The walls, bastions, and moats were meant to protect inhabitants, while the interior geometry of streets would teach rationality and promote peaceful social relations. It was a material regime of care based on classical precedents intended to achieve a superior way of life (Konvitz 2020; Rosenau 1959).

Rochefort exercised care in other ways as well. It was located up the Charente River away from the Atlantic and behind an island off the river mouth. The site was not visible to ships traveling along the coast, and so it was protected from attack. The bastion walls also protected the installation not only from foreign enemies, as all ideal cities did, but also from Huguenots, who were plentiful in the Aunis and Saintonge regions of the Atlantic coast. The Huguenot population in this part of France was large and generally hostile to the crown. So, a royal installation there was vulnerable (Konvitz 2020; Mukerji 2010, 2017; Peter 2002; Rosenau 1959).

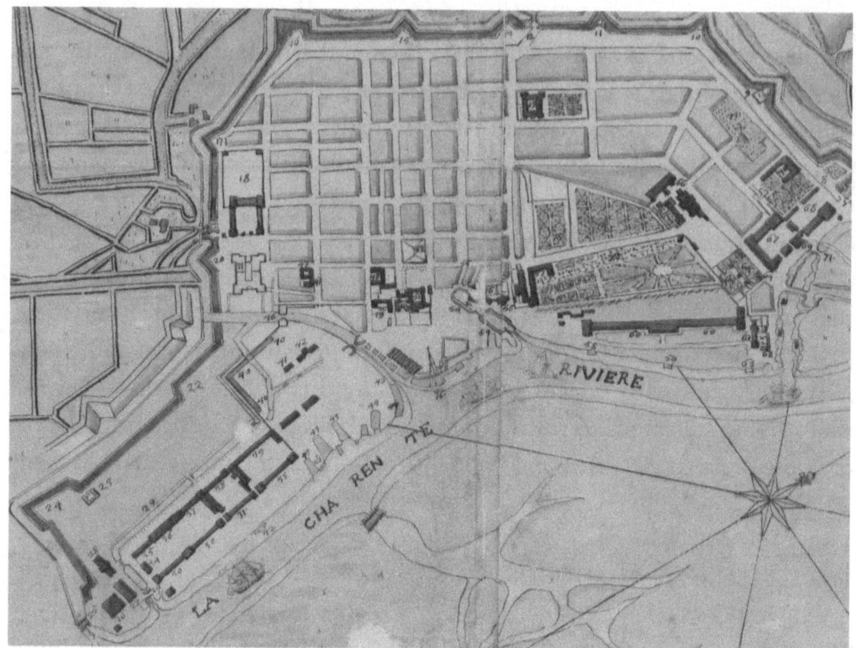

FIGURE 11.1
Map of Rochefort.

The map of Rochefort in figure 11.1 illustrates the details of this ideal city. There are few doors and many bastions to the city. And the residential settlement at the center of the port is a grid of streets—a model of geometrical rationality. The areas to the right and left are geometrical, too, but rotated to fit the curve of the river. The streets on the right are laid out as radial lines; the buildings on the left are rectangular (Rosenau 1959; Konvitz 2020).

It is a city designed for independent manufacture and commerce. The administrative area on the plan is small (figure 11.1, #47–50). Only a commissioner and an engineer in chief are in residence to supervise the work. There are guards and naval officers, too, but they do not have supervisory status. It is a town for artisans, who are given the independence typical for experts in the trades (Schaffer 2007; Peter 2002).

If the administration is small, the facilities for creating the fleet are extensive and spread along the Charente River. The arsenal provides extensive infrastructure to turn water, wind, ores, and fibers into tools of sovereign power, caring for the fleet. The main warehouses and workshops are located in the rectangle of buildings on the left side of town (figure 11.1, #26–45). Behind them are forges and bunkers (figure 11.1, #21, #41, and #42). On the opposite side of town in front of the gardens, the long building is the rope manufacture or *corderie* (figure 11.1, #60). In the center is a double dry dock for ship repairs (figure 11.1, #54). Nearby, there is a small port with docks for receiving and storing timber (figure 11.1, #45).

The shipbuilding took place in the open space on the riverbank in front of the rectangle of warehouses and workshops (figure 11.1, #26–40). This is where mindful hands did the caring labor for the incipient fleet. The largest warehouse (figure 11.1, #26) was where mast timbers were dried after they had been cured in basins of salt water for three years. This building was also where mast pieces were joined and then shaped into long spars to be raised with yards or crosspieces to hold the sails (Mémain 1937, 109). In the main workshops (figure 11.1, #38 and #40), carpenters prepared parts for the hull and decks, sailmakers sewed canvas (figure 11.1, #36), coopers assembled barrels for provisions (figure 11.1, #3 and #5), and gunmakers crafted and assembled parts for artillery (figure 11.1, #39). Behind these hangers were bunkers for storing powder (figure 11.1, #21), barracks for the soldiers (figure 11.1, #18), and a set of forges (figure 11.1, #41 and #42; Mémain 1937, 107–109). There were slips next to the river, too, where ships could be careened (turned on their sides) to seal the hulls with tar, and where the ships could be towed on rolling timbers into the river. Only after it was successfully floated would a ship be outfitted with spars, yards, and rigging and equipped with batteries of cannons.

The right side of town was home to the royal rope-making factory (figure 11.1, #60). Here, tangles of fibrous materials such as hemp, reeds, and so forth that had been soaked and prepared were braided together under tension into strands of rope. Thicker ropes—ones strong enough for anchors and rigging—were made by braiding thinner ones together in multiple iterations (Peter 2002).

The *corderie* had to be a long building—spanning much of the right riverbank—because ropes were manufactured under tension. So, the building had to be longer than the desired ropes. A stationary machine at one end of the *corderie* fed out strands of fibers or thin rope to be braided. A machine on wheels at the opposite end of the building twisted the strands, moving along the floor to keep tension because the rope shortened as it was braided. When the great ropes for rigging and anchors were made thick and strong, they were treated with tar to reduce deterioration and unraveling (Peter 2002). Through this regime of care, weak fibers became strong tools of sovereignty.

The settlement at Rochefort, then, was set out according to principles of design from Rome and was outfitted to pursue an imperial destiny at sea. And as a settlement, it claimed territory for the sovereign. But the state had a fragile hold on the region, and the Charente River area had no tradition of shipbuilding to provide scaffolding for naval construction. Almost from the beginning, Rochefort was plagued with problems because it lacked experts (Acerra 1993, vol. I; La Roncière 1919; Verge-Franceschi 1997; Clément 1979, vol. III: ii–iii; Martin 2015).

MINDFUL HANDS AND REGIMES OF CARE

The navy was in terrible disrepair when Louis XIV took power. The French fleet had just eighteen vessels, many of them not seaworthy and most of them bought from the Dutch. Throughout the seventeenth century, the French navy borrowed warships from allies when it needed sea power. Richelieu even leased ships from the Dutch and England's East India Company for his assaults on Huguenots. Leasing was expedient because the army was engaged in costly battles, but it left French shipbuilding in a sorry state. As a result, even French merchants preferred Dutch ships to French ones. If Louis XIV was weak, his navy was a clear measure of it (Clément 1979, vol. III: ii–iii; Meyer and Acerra 1994).

Building Rochefort into a manufacturing center for warships was not a quick or easy process. The original foundations for the *corderie* started to sink into the mud on the riverbank. In 1671, the architect, Louis Le Vau, observed that Rochefort still did not have a forge capable of making anchors. And although ships' timbers were arriving from the Pyrenees, per instructions by Colbert, the soaking ponds for masts were not finished until the Reglèment of 1674. Worse, the arsenal had to buy its anchors from the Dutch because the local forge would not get hot enough to cast them (Mémain 1937, 107–109; La Roncière 1919).

But the main problem for the arsenal was the labor force. Master builders for ocean-going vessels were in short supply. The arsenal at Toulon had Rodolphe Gédéon, who oversaw construction of the flagship for that fleet, *Royal Louis*, in 1688. Brest had Laurent Hubac, who designed and oversaw construction of the *Vendome* in 1651 and the beautiful but neglected *Soleil*

Royal in 1670. Rochefort had no comparable master and only launched the *Grand* in 1680 (Peter 2002; Meyer and Acerra 1994).

There was no reservoir of experienced engineers or master carpenters around the Charente. But Colbert still insisted on establishing an arsenal and port there because France lacked a port on the Atlantic for trade with the colonies, and it needed warships to defend the merchant marine. Brest could not become a major port because the harbor had a rocky entrance and was often shut down by fierce Atlantic storms. So, the minister continued to rely on Brest and Toulon to build up the fleet as he tried to help Rochefort work properly. The lack of a skilled labor force made France weak, not just Rochefort. So, he was determined to train the French in this form of manufacture.

Colbert treated shipbuilding as comparable to lace manufacture. There were local traditions for making lace, but the products were not as good as foreign goods. So, the minister established a policy of import substitution, training French workers under foreign artisans to make something like the desired goods. In lace making, the result was a distinctive French product but a more refined and desirable one. Colbert sought something similar in shipbuilding (Cole 1964).

Colbert sought talent in Italy and the Netherlands in light of their vital shipbuilding industries. He had greater success in the Netherlands, where Protestant artisans were being persecuted by Spain and wanted to start new lives. These foreign shipbuilders were not well accepted in Brest and Toulon. But Rochefort was more accepting—perhaps because Huguenots preferred working with Dutch masters or perhaps because workers in the arsenal simply wanted guidance (Acerra 1993, vol. I; La Roncière 1919).

The labor-force problem was probably exacerbated by Rochefort's location near La Rochelle. That Huguenot stronghold and port had no love for the Catholic monarchy. The town had been sieged by Louis XIV's father and Cardinal Richelieu. They blockaded the port, and half the population starved. So, it was likely difficult to recruit skilled carpenters from La Rochelle for Rochefort (Accera 1993).

Local resistance to Rochefort was clear. As they started building smaller vessels, Colbert needed sailors but could not recruit them from the region. He offered good wages and guaranteed time off, making the navy a popular place to go for people in Brest. But in Rochefort, there was little interest. So, Colbert told estate owners to send peasants. This had little result. In frustration, the minister started a draft, but many conscripted sailors deserted. In a rage, the minister made desertion a capital offense, but enforcing it was hard. Half the sailors from Rochefort still disappeared en route (La Roncière 1919).

More carpenters and metallurgists came to work at the arsenal than sailors came to the harbor. Colbert told Toulon to send people, but the best had no intention of leaving. In this period, when families were displaced by religious warfare and roaming the countryside, a number of carpenters could have arrived at the new port. Perhaps some local Huguenots signed up too. But the labor force did not immediately have the expertise to build effective vessels.

Colbert tried to help by offering a wider view on problems. The minister called upon the mathematicians of the royal academy to determine the proper shapes for hulls and to calculate the best proportions of hulls to masts for French ships (Peter 2002 Wilson 2003; Schaffer 2007). In addition, Colbert asked successful engineers and masters in all the arsenals to circulate and to share their ideas. But shipbuilding required mindful hands as well as measures, methods, and materials.

The first ship produced in Rochefort apparently never left the Charente River. The *Victorieux* was badly built and had to be broken up. The first cannons cast in Rochefort fared equally badly. They blew up when they were tested (Acerra 1993, vol. I; Mémain 1937).

Colbert could only set parameters for naval vessels. First-rank vessels were to have three decks with a forecastle and poop deck, carrying between eighty and a hundred cannons; second-rank warships were meant to have two decks or were three-decked ships that had been downgraded, carrying between sixty and seventy-six guns; third-rank ships had two decks and between forty and sixty guns; and fourth-rank ships had two decks with between thirty-five and forty guns. Even with the variability within ranks, ships rarely turned out to fit them precisely. They often needed to be modified too—reconstructed, rejuvenated, and reclassified. Mindful hands had limits (Acerra 1993, vol. I; La Roncière 1919).

At Rochefort, artisans and engineers without experience experimented. So, the port was outfitted with dry docks that looked like a double canal lock. The interior could be flooded with river water to float ships in and then drained to repair the ships. The rope factory was innovative, too, and even more so when part of the building started to sink into the soft riverbank. The foundation was rebuilt partly on a wooden platform that would float like a ship in the mud. Such a floating foundation had ancient precedents but also took advantage of shipbuilders.

After years of floundering and experimenting with ships of lower rank, the master carpenter, Honoré Malet, designed and constructed Rochefort's first great ship of the line, the *Grand*, followed by the *Intrépide*. There were now enough "mindful hands" at Rochefort to contribute to the "age" of Louis XIV (Roberts, Schaffer, and Dear 2007a; Mémain 1937, 103–104; Clément 1979, vol. III: intro).

PROPHETIC IMAGINATION IN THE *ALBUM DE COLBERT*

The image of the sovereign Sun King was not simply burnished at court with depictions of Apollo bringing light, warmth, and abundance to the earth. It was also furthered by the accomplishments of regimes of care set up by the administration. But the feats of artisans in the countryside had to be products of sovereignty, not labor. The fine vessels that started to sail from the Charente were appropriately magical because they appeared to come from nowhere. The wind impelled them from France itself into the Atlantic. It was ironic but the labor force Colbert carefully assembled and nurtured at Rochefort and other arsenals had to be just ascarefully concealed from public view. For sovereign power to be prophetic, it had to seem ordained rather than manufactured.

We can see how this sleight of hand was realized in the *Album de Colbert* (Service Historique de la Marine n.d.). The *Album* was a collection of drawings depicting the steps for assembling a first rank ship of the line. It contained more than a hundred drawings depicting all the pieces for the vessel and illustrating where they should go (like a Lego manual). But despite its detail, the *Album* never displayed artisans at work. The mindful hands that would design such a vessel, shape the pieces for it, and assemble them properly were absent. The ship sailed off at the end of the *Album* as a product of impersonal forces.

The *Album de Colbert* was found in the minister's papers without any explanation of its origins or accompanying text to suggest the book's purpose. It was certainly not an instructional manual for artisans, since that would have included details of the labor. It may have been produced for Colbert to help him understand the complexities of shipbuilding. He commissioned comparable drawings of locks to instruct himself about the construction in the Canal du Midi. But it was more likely a document Colbert could use to explain shipbuilding to the king. Whatever the case, the artisans of the Sun

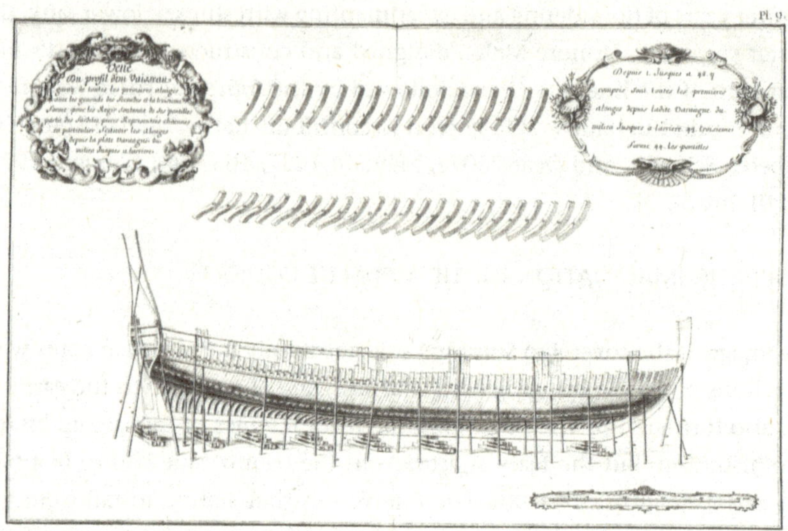

FIGURE 11.2
Album de Colbert. Building the hull.

King were like the elves for the shoemaker in Grimm's fairy tale. They labored out of sight. The result at the end of the *Album* was a glorious vessel and pure expression of sovereignty (Clément 1979, vol. III: iii–iv; Mukerji 2015).

The first images show a modest hull rising from stacks of wood and balanced between timbers. Like a Lego instruction manual, the pieces needed for each stage of construction are laid out at the top of the page and numbered. Underneath, a picture of the vessel shows where the numbered pieces should go. There is no indication of where the parts come from, or how they are to be put together. It is not a "how-to" book. Instead, it resembles a natural history volume. The images are comparable to period illustrations of dissections: the parts are arrayed around a central object. This form used in the *Album* naturalizes the process of construction, and makes the absence of artisans less surprising. Like an animal or plant, the ship seems to arise spontaneously, responding to the Sun King as a force of nature (Roberts, Schaffer, and Dear 2007b; Smith 2004; Guerrini 2015).

As the hull rises in subsequent illustrations, decks appear with openings for ropes, spars, and ladders. Cutaways of the vessel show barrels in the interior without evidence of where they came from. Ropes are coiled on the decks and connected to anchors, appearing in the ship as inevitable, necessary rather than made. It is a self-organizing ship.

The eerie vision of autonomous growth is suddenly disrupted in figure 49 when the vessel is "careened" or turned on its side. At this point, the hull is made watertight with hot tar. And men appear. They are scraping the hull and applying the tar. Who are they? And why do they appear now? The most likely answer is that they are sailors that do not build ships, but care for them. Crews need to careen ships on long voyages to strip the hulls of barnacles, repair damage to their underbellies, and reseal the bottoms of the ships with tar. So sailors can be represented when artisans are not. Sailors serve, while artisan create. Artisans would disrupt the illusion of the sovereign's creative power to usher in a glorious future.

The few later figures in the *Album* also seem to be sailors. They do the work of sailors, raising the spars, yards, and rigging. Finally, when the vessel is almost ready to be launched, naval officers in uniform appear on deck. In all three cases, the human figures in the *Album* serve the sovereign rather than construct his sovereignty.

The *Album de Colbert* provides insight, then, into the entanglement of prophetic truths and regimes of care. The mindful hands of artisans are needed to create the magnificence of the sovereign in things but their creative abilities have no place in the cultural imaginary of the sovereign. His glory is natural, inevitable, and moral. But even hidden from view, the shipbuilders' labors add to what Voltaire calls the "spirit of the age."

CONCLUSION

The fragile dream of the sovereign Sun King could become an effective tool for amassing power for Louis XIV when embedded in things. The cultural imaginary could not in itself gather France around the king, but the art at Versailles rallied nobles at court. And dreams of royal glory were credible when manifested in warships. Conceiving of the sovereign as a force of history made his prophetic destiny a matter not of debate but of evidence. And Colbert's administration produced the evidence with achievements worthy of Rome. Artisans brought natural knowledge, understandings of precedent, and mindful hands to the administration, aspiring to greatness in ways that served their sovereign. But the prophetic quality of the Sun King's glory depended on artisans being invisible (Reed 2020; Irani 2015). Hidden from view in places such as Rochefort, artisans and laborers—the weak—made the king strong.

FIGURE 11.3
Album de Colbert. Trial Run.

Pierre Clément, Colbert's compiler and biographer, explained the transformational nature of this administration: "An excess of trouble (mal) often gives rise to energetic and decisive moves for the better. This characteristic marks the end of a regime which cannot be restored anymore"[2] (1979, vol. III: iii–iv).

By January of 1677, there were three hundred ships of all ranks in the navy and fifty-two thousand sailors to man them (Clément 1979, vol. III: iii–vi). The labor of artisans at Rochefort and other arsenals may have disappeared behind the glow of the Sun King, but their experiments in naval engineering were impressive. The beauty and agility of French warships embodied their dreams and physical evidence of their knowing hands.

NOTES

1. Il ne suffit pas que la Posterité sçache ses glorieux travaux de Guerre & de Paix; le mal qu'il a fait à ses Ennemis par la force de ses Armes, & le bien qu'il fait à ses Peuples par les soins assidus & sans exemple q'il prend luy-même de leur conduite: il fait qu'elle ait encore la safisfaction de sçavoir quels étoient ses relâches dans ses occupations importantes. Il est bon qu'elle apprenne qu'il n'a pas été seulement le plus vaillant & le plus sage de tous les Princes de son Siécle, mais qu'il a été aussi le plus adroit & la plus magnifique, & que la Noblesse de sa Cour est toûjours en possession de ces avantages sür toutes les Nations de la Terre.

2. De l'exès de mal naît souvant (III) l'effort énergique. décisif, vers le bien. Cet état de choses caracéristique marque la fin d'un régime qui ne devait plus revenir.

REFERENCES

Academie royale de peinture et de sculpture. 1669. *Conferences de l'academie royale de peinture et de sculpture pendant l'année 1667*. Paris: Frederic Leonard.

Acerra, Martine. 1993. *Rochefort et la construction navale française, 1661–1815, Tomes I & IV*. Paris: Librairie de l'Inde Éditeur.

Andrew, Edward. 2011. "Jean Bodin on Sovereignty." *Republic of Letters: A Journal for the Study of Knowledge, Politics and the Arts* 2(2): 75–84.

Apostolidès, Jean-Marie. 1981. *Le Roi-machine: Spectacle et politique au temps de Louis XIV*. Paris: Editions de Minuit.

Becker, Peter, and William Clark, eds. 2001. *Little Tools of Knowledge: Historical Essays on Academic and Bureaucratic Practices*. Ann Arbor: University of Michigan Press.

Beik, William. 1985. *Absolutism and Society in Seventeenth-Century France: State Power and Provincial Aristocracy in Languedoc*. Cambridge: Cambridge University Press.

Bertucci, Paola. 2017. *Artisanal Enlightenment: Science and the Mechanical Arts in Old Regime France*. New Haven, CT: Yale University Press.

Bodin, Jean. 1596. *Les six livres de la Republique de Jean Bodin Angeuin*. Geneva: Jacques Gamonet.

Bourgeon, Jean-Louis. 1973. *Les Colbert avant Colbert*. Paris: Presses Universitaires de France.

Burchard, Wolf. 2016. *The Sovereign Artist: Charles Le Brun and the Image of Louis XIV*. London: Paul Holberton.

Burke, Peter. 1994. *The Fabrication of Louis XIV*. New Haven, CT: Yale University Press.

Clément, Pierre. 1979. *Lettres, instructions et mémoires de Colbert* (Vol. 3). Paris: Imprimérie Impériale.

Cole, Charles W. 1964. *Colbert and a Century of French Mercantilism*. Hamden: Archon Books.

Collins, James B. 2009. *The State in Early Modern France*. Cambridge: Cambridge University Press.

D'Aubert, François. 2014. *Colbert*. Paris: Perrin.

Da Vinha, Mathieu. 2004. *Les valets de chambre de Louis XIV*. Paris: Tempus.

Denis, Jérôme, and David Pontille. 2011. "Materiality, Maintenance and Fragility: The Care of Things." 'How Matter Matters' Third International symposium on Process Organization Studies. Corfu, June 16th-19th.

Foucault, Michel, and Arnold Davidson. 2014. *On the Government of the Living*. Translated by Graham Burchell. London: Palgrave MacMillan.

Froidour, Louis de. 1892. *Memoire du Pays et des États de Bigorre*. Edited by Jean Boudette. Paris: H. Champion et Baylac.

Froidour, Louis de. 1899. *Les Pyrenées centrales au XVIIe siècle; lettres écrites . . . à M. de Héricourt . . . et à M. de Medon*. Auch: Impr. et lithographie G. Foix.

Guerrini, Anita. 2015. *The Courtiers' Anatomists: Animals and Humans in Louis XIV's Paris*. Chicago: University of Chicago Press.

Henke, Christopher, and Ben Sims. 2020. *Repairing Infrastructures*. Cambridge, MA: MIT Press.

Hennion, Antoine. 2018. "Faire Face, Pour le saisie politique de la question des migrants." *Tumultes* 51(2): 173–189.

Irani, Lily. 2015. "Difference and Dependence among Digital Workers: The Case of Amazon Mechanical Turk." *The South Atlantic Quarterly* 114 (1): 225–234.

Jackson, Robert. 2007. *Sovereignty: The Evolution of an Idea*. Cambridge: Polity Press.

Joyce, Patrick. 2013. *The State of Freedom*. Cambridge: Cambridge University Press.

Joyce, Patrick, and Chandra Mukerji. 2017. "The State of Things." *Theory and Society* 46 (1): 1–19.

Konvitz, Josef. 2020. *Cities and the Sea*. Baltimore, MD: Johns Hopkins University Press.

La Roncière, Charles de. 1919. *Un grand ministre de la marine, Colbert*. Paris: Plon-Nourrit et cie.

Latour, Bruno. 2004. "Why Has Critique Run Out of Steam?" *Critical Inquiry* 30: 225–248.

Lynn, J. A. 1997. *Giant of the grand siècle: The French army, 1610–1715*. Cambridge: Cambridge University Press.

Machiavelli, Niccolo. 1966. *The Prince*. Translated by Daniel Donno. New York: Bantam Dell.

Maral, Alexandre. 2013. *Le roi, la cour, et Versailles 1682–1789*. Paris: Perrin.

Martin, Sébastien. 2015. *Rochefort arsenal des colonies aux XVIIIe siècle*. Rennes: Presses Univérsitaires de Rennes.

Meyer, Jean, and Martine Acerra, 1994. *Histoire de la Marine Française*. Rennes: Editions Ouest France.

Mémain, René. 1937. *La Marine de Guerre sous Louis XIV: Le Matériel Rochefort, arsenal modèle de Colbert*. Paris: Librarie Hachette.

Mettam, Roger. 1988. *Power and Faction in Louis XIV's France*. London: Basil Blackwell.

Milton, Patrick, Michael Axworthy, and Brendan Simms. 2019. *Towards a Westphalia for the Middle East*. Oxford: Oxford University Press.

Mukerji, Chandra. 2010. "The Territorial State as a Figured World of Power: Strategics, Logistics and Impersonal Rule." *Sociological Theory* 28 (4): 402–424.

Mukerji, Chandra. 2015. *Impossible Engineering*. Princeton, NJ: Princeton University Press.

Mukerji, Chandra. 2017. "Artisans in the Construction of the French State." In *National Matters: Materiality, Culture and Nationalism*, edited by Geneviève Zubrzycki. 21–36 Stanford, CA: Stanford University Press.

Mukerji, Chandra. 2021. "Sovereign Sun King." In *Crafting Enlightenment*, edited by Lauren Cannady and Jennifer Ferng. 29–48. Oxford: Oxford University Press.

Néraudau, J. P. 1986. *L'Olympe du Roi Soleil*. Paris: Société des Belles-Lettres.

Parker, David. 1983. *The Making of French Absolutism*. London: Edward Arnold.

Perrault, Charles. 1670. *Courses de Teste et de Bague faites par le Roy et par les Princes et Seigneurs de sa Cour en l'Année M.DC.LXII*. Paris: Impriméric Royale.

Peter, Jean. 2002. *Le Port et l'Arsenal de Rochefort sour Louis XIV*. Paris: Economica

Ranum, Orest. 1993. *The Fronde: A French Revolution 1648–1652*. New York: W. W. Norton.

Reed, Isaac. 2020. *Power in Modernity*. Chicago: University of Chicago Press.

Roberts, Lissa, Simón Schaffer, and Peter Dear. 2007a. *The Mindful Hand*. Amsterdam: The Royal Academy of Arts and Sciences.

Roberts, Lissa, Simon Schaffer, and Peter Dear. 2007b. "Introduction." In *The Mindful Hand*, edited by Lissa Roberts, Simon Schaffer and Peter Dear, 1–10. Amsterdam: The Royal Academy of Arts and Sciences.

Rosenau, Helen. 1959. *The Ideal City: Its Architectural Evolution*. Boston, MA: Boston Book and Art Shop.

Rosental, Claude, and Catherine Porter. 2021. *The Demonstration Society*. Cambridge, MA: MIT Press.

Schaffer, Simon. 2007. "The Chater'd Thames." In *The Mindful Hand*, edited by Roberts, Schaffer and Dear, 279–308. Amsterdam: Royal Academy of Arts and Sciences.

Schmitt, Charles. 1985. *Political Theory: Four Chapters in the Concept of Sovereignty*. Translated by George Schwab. Chicago: University of Chicago Press.

Scott, James, 1985. *Weapons of the Weak: Everyday Forms of Peasant Resistance*. New Haven, CT: Yale University Press.

Serres, Michel. 1983. *Rome: le livre des foundations*. Paris: Grasset.

Service Historique de la Marine. n.d. *Album de Colbert*. Printed reproduction of manuscript cote140.1513.

Singer-Lecocq, Yvonne. 1998. *Quand des artistes logeaient au Louvre, 1608–1835*. Paris: Perrin.

Smith, Pamela. 2004. *Body of the Artisan*. Chicago: University of Chicago Press.

Smith, Pamela, Amy Myers, and Harold Cook. 2017. *Ways of Making and Knowing: The Material Culture of Empirical Knowledge*. University of Chicago Press.

Soll, Jacob. 2009. *The Information Master*. Ann Arbor: Michigan University Press.

Stenger, Isabelle. 2010. *Cosmopolitics II*. Minneapolis: University of Minnesota Press.

Strong, Tracy. 1985. "Foreword." In *Political Theology: Four Chapters in the Concept of Sovereignty*, edited by Charles Schmitt, translated by George Schwab. VII-xxxiii,. Chicago: University of Chicago Press.

Verge-Franceschi, Michel. 1997. "L'amirauté de France dans la deuxième moitié du XVIe siècles; un emjeu entre catholiques et protestants." In *Coligny et les protestants et la mer*, edited by Marine Acerra et Guy Martinière. Paris: Presses de l'Université de Paris-Sorbonne.

Vitruvius, Marcus. [1521] 1960. *The Ten Books of Architecture*. Garden City: Dover.

Voltaire. 1752. *Histoire du Siècle de Louis XIV*. La Haye: Benjamin Gilbert.

Wilson, Timothy. 2003. *Flags at Sea*. Newbury: Greenhill Books.

12 THE FRAGILITY OF ICE: CRYOHUMAN RELATIONS IN TIMES OF COLLAPSE

CYMENE HOWE

On the southern edge of Iceland, you might find Sigrún Thorsteinsdóttir standing atop a glacier, sweeping away. Her broom gripped in both hands, she brushes at the layers of earthen matter that have settled over the glacier's surface over time. With each stroke, she finds herself clearing away the accumulation of industry and consumption, scouring away the layers of soot that paint the time between centuries. To tend the glacier, Sigrún will bend to pluck something from its surface, or she will reach to dust its blackened edges. Her glacier is clothed in volcanic matter: tiny black stones it has gathered on its path to where it now sits, covered by a mist of ash that has settled across its peaks and fissures. In the grayscale landscape she occupies, Sigrún performs these acts of care for glaciers that here, as everywhere, are becoming more fragile. As a warming atmosphere steadily melts the ice of the world, Sigrún sweeps that which is being swept away. A metaphorical actor in a staged act[1] of response and acknowledgment, she is called "The Custodian"—one who has the responsibility to look after something that is fragile: to guard, protect, and maintain it.

Iceland's glaciers have forever been a central feature of the country's landscape. Over time, they have literally shaped the topography of the island, etching themselves across its surface, carving valleys, and contouring mountains into form. More recently, Iceland's 400+ glaciers and 130 volcanoes have come to represent a kind of geologically inflected national character for the country, captured in the appellation "the land of fire and ice." But glaciers have not always been celebrated in Iceland. For most of the last twelve hundred years that humans have inhabited the island, they were a source of fear: a looming, destructive, and uncontrollable embodiment of nature's force. Icelanders who have lived in proximity to glaciers have seen their farms washed away and their homes destroyed by glacial outburst floods (*jökulhlaups*). They remember the stories of people and animals washed far out into the frigid waters of the North Atlantic. These were events where human fragility was exposed. Only in the nineteenth century did glaciers begin to be redefined as valued features of the Icelandic landscape and sites of cultural heritage. And it was only in the twentieth century that Icelanders began to venture into these glacial environments for recreation and retreat from the bustle of the terrestrial world. In the twenty-first century, the meaning of glaciers is changing once again. With the Arctic region heating at somewhere between two and three times the global rate,[2] the preservation of glaciers seems increasingly impossible. Infusions of cold are rarer and rarer, snow is reduced, and the ice that resides on both land and sea is in a state of demise, disintegration, and debility. Where they were once fearsome forces threatening human life on the island, glaciers are now seen as themselves vulnerable to human impact. Transformed by the steady pulse of anthropogenic warming, human encounters with ice that were once grounded in trepidation have now become centered on protection. Those imposing, massive bodies of ice are now fragile bodies in need of care and maintenance; they are victims of a vanishing equilibrium.

The retreat of glaciers can be seen everywhere across Iceland for those who are willing to look. As an anthropologist, I became very interested in what we might call "the social life" of ice in Iceland, and I began a research project to better understand how Icelanders were responding to the loss of ice on their island (Howe 2018, 2019b). I wanted to know how the relationship between people and the bodies of ice that they have called neighbors for the last twelve hundred years might now be changing. Glacial retreat is evident across Iceland's landscape, but more recently, a new phenomenon is afoot: not just the shrinking of glaciers but their total disappearance or "death." In the summer of 2019, I found myself reckoning with these deaths and creating a memorial for the first of Iceland's glaciers to be felled by climate change.[3] Over several years, as I was speaking with Icelanders about their thoughts and experiences with ice—and, critically, how they imagined its future—I began to think of the relationships between people and ice as a "cryohuman" encounter. My thinking about cryohuman relations has drawn inspiration from work in the human sciences about climate change, environmental conditions, and adaptation to what has been called "the Anthropocene" (Barnes et al. 2013; Chakrabarty 2009; Howe 2019a; Boyer 2019). Whether or not we subscribe to the term "Anthropocene," the results of anthropogenic impacts upon the Earth system are showing themselves everywhere. Industry (Linnenluecke and Griffiths 2015), security programs (Heininen 2015), markets, and infrastructures (Strauss and Orlove 2003; Watson and Adams 2010) are all implicated in, and attempting to adapt to, unprecedented environmental change (Zolli and Healy 2013). Climate models demonstrate that weather events will become more virulent in the future (Edwards 2010; Hulme 2011), and the reports from the United Nations Intergovernmental Panel on Climate Change (IPCC 2021) warn, in unparsed terms, that increased climate disasters are "locked in" for decades, even if we were to cease emitting greenhouse gases immediately. As Timothy Morton (2014, 126) has put it, "There is no away."

The political, economic, and scientific prognostications about climate change provide a critical context. But with cryohuman relations, I am also interested in a more intimate dynamic of acknowledgment and response to fragility. Donna Haraway (2015) has proposed that "response-ability" is a way to gauge our capacity to relate and act upon interlocking forms of fragility, both social and ecological.[4] In our response to, and with, glaciers, a trans-corporeal (Alaimo 2008) challenge is put into place. Our sympathies and relationships with nonhuman neighbors become tested (Behar 2016). In this chapter, I consider responses to melting ice as they are enacted by both humans and nonhumans. Response, as I see it, is both a reaction and an attempt at an answer, but response is also a profound acknowledgment—an acknowledgment of the continuum between human and material worlds, or a relational ontology of care and attention that becomes manifest in distinct ways (Puig de la Bellacasa 2012, 2017). In the process of response, I argue, multiple fragilities become apparent. As glaciers melt, they undergo an ontological "phase change"—a fundamental transformation in their material state. For living beings, such as humans, glacial phase changes can be known through affective encounters, scientific accounts, and meditations upon ecological futures. For nonhumans, glacial phase changes are more likely to be felt through corporeal experience. One seemingly singular source of fragility, the melting of glacial ice, generates a field of "divergent fragilities" that require different response-abilities, practices, and logics to address them. With the growing awareness that human behaviors, past and present, are deeply impacting ecosystems that sustain biotic life and give shape to geological form, the trans-material qualities of ice highlight the tenuous space between living and dying. Our responses can be many in a world of multiply entangled fragilities.

FUNERALS ARE FOR THE LIVING

For seven hundred years or so, Okjökull (Ok glacier) lived atop Ok mountain. There, it accumulated snow and ice, and it crawled—not quickly, but persistently—down the face of the shield volcano where it made its home. In summer 2019, a large group of people gathered in the place where Okjökull had whiled away the centuries. They had come for its funeral. A funeral for a glacier had never taken place before; in many ways, this is because it had never needed to happen before. Okjökull was the first of Iceland's major glaciers to be killed by climate change. And its passing, it seemed to me and my collaborators, deserved recognition. It demanded a response. And while it is true that there is a first time for everything, it is also true that that this will not be the last memorial for a glacier lost to climate change.

Five years earlier, in the summer of 2014, a team of scientists led by the glaciologist Oddur Sigurdsson had climbed to the top of Ok mountain. They were there to measure the remaining glacial ice and to determine whether the "remnant" ice was still thick enough to be considered a glacier. Sigurdsson suspected that Okjökull had expired several years prior based on aerial footage he had been monitoring. The unique crystalline structure that signifies glacial ice was still apparent in the remnant pieces, as were the firn lines—spiral-like tree rings to indicate where snow accumulation had hardened into glacial ice over each passing year. The scientists found that Okjökull's mass had shrunk to the point where it could no longer move under its own weight. It was, therefore, no longer a glacier. It was instead what glaciologists call "dead ice."

How do we memorialize something that was never, in truth, "living"? Okjökull, in its time, moved across the stony face of Ok mountain. Gravity pulled at it, and the weight of its corpus allowed it to inch across the landscape. Although it moved, it was not—at least through the logics of Western science—alive. And yet Okjökull's expiration and its memorial service, once the news was widely circulated, inspired an outpouring of mournful commentary in social media outlets and traditional news sources. Thousands of news stories around the world, in hundreds of languages, announced not only that Iceland's first major glacier was gone but also that, for the first time in known human history, a funeral would be held for a glacier-that-was. What do we say, or do, in response to the "death" of ice?

Creating a letter to the future is one response.

FIGURE 12.1
Okjökull memorial plaque installed in August 2019 on top of Ok mountain, Iceland. The plaque reads, first in Icelandic and then in English:
A letter to the future
Ok is the first Icelandic glacier to lose its status as a glacier.
In the next 200 years all our glaciers are expected to follow the same path.
This monument is to acknowledge that we know
what is happening and what needs to be done.
Only you know if we did it.
August 2019
415 ppm CO_2

Ok mountain is not a particularly steep mountain, but it also has no path or trail to the top. It is rock all the way up and all the way down. A year earlier, we had climbed Ok mountain in an event we called "The Un-glacier Tour"—a spoof on the many glacier tours available in Iceland and a commentary on the country's quickly disappearing cryosphere. On that hike, with about thirty vigorous members of the Icelandic Hiking Society, we identified a large basalt stone that was monumental in its own way: a dusky pink obelisk with a slight tilt to its facade. It was a good location to place a plaque. On our journey to the top of Ok mountain for the funeral a year later, we are a group of about a hundred scientists, artists, journalists, activists, politicians, and others. On that August morning, among us, there are a few septuagenarians, at least one eight-year-old, and half a dozen youth climate activists carrying bright homemade signs. The rest of us are every age in between. As we reach the peak, Andri Snær Magnason, the Icelandic writer and filmmaker, reminds us of an old Icelandic tradition. When ascending the sacred mountain Helgafell, walkers must go forward together in total silence, never looking back. If we hold good in our hearts, the folk legend goes, we will be granted three wishes. And so, we do.

Public recognition of a death is an important human act. Honoring, mourning, and acknowledging the dead in ritual form is a universal practice. We find death rituals throughout the history of humanity and everywhere on earth. The objects and symbols people use to mark a passing are many. A formal declaration of some kind is common. At Okjökull's funeral, this will include a reading of the death certificate by Oddur Sigurdsson, the glaciologist who first declared the Ok glacier deceased. With the thin paper form rattling in the wind, Sigurdsson points out that Okjökull's cause of death, as noted on the certificate itself, was "Death by heat. Death by humans." A handful of us say some words; we note that Ok may be the first of Iceland's glaciers to meet its end, but it will certainly not be the last. The crowd, huddled closely together against the wind, commits to finding ways to address the climate crisis. In times of rapid collapse, one cannot rest on ceremony alone. And so, any memorial to a fallen glacier is not only a moment of reckoning but also a response to fragility and a call to action.

If, in the past, icy places have been taken as natural configurations of a landscape, as mystical spaces of infinitude or as entities that can both provide life and bring death, that is now changing. In melting glaciers, we see heat absorbed: an atmosphere enacting a thermodynamic play upon bodies of ice. This is the heat of humans—as Sigurdsson put it—but, of course, this heat has not been produced equally by all humans. It is the industrialized world that has brought on the great melting at the top of the world (and the bottom as well).[5] As dramatic climatic impacts are increasingly visible and felt, and when our best science continues to pound out cataclysmic truths, cryohuman relations become experienced differently. People and ice now live together in more fragile circumstances. We are, therefore, called upon to respond in new ways and with new attentions to care. Circumstance that draws our collective attention to fragility, such as the "death" of a glacier, is also a disposition toward responding to the many fragilities that are surfaced: the loss of ice and the loss of life. These become surreal equations for cultivating compassion and care. Glaciers are not, according to the logics of Western science, living beings (cf. Cruikshank 2006). But in their expiration, and in memorializing their end, their fragility becomes a way to feel them "dying," like so many other beings at risk in the sixth great extinction now underway. Across these multiple scenes and senses of fragility, there is also opportunity to notice their entanglements, their shared causal roots, and coordinates, and to notice in the continuum of living and dying the mutual fate of both humans and nonhumans. Death is felt by the living, not the dead, and as one of my Icelandic friends put it, "funerals are rituals for the living."

WITHOUT A FUNERAL

Glaciers have become a key indicator of climatological breakdown, and their expiration is a signal for multiple forms of fragility that are felt differently, producing many forms of response. As receding glaciers and melting ice sheets have come to represent the perils of a cryosphere in collapse, another charismatic figure has also emerged as a signal species: the polar bear.

A farmer named Egill Bjarnason was the first to spot the bear in the northwestern Icelandic town of Sauðárkrókur in the summer of 2016. He was in no doubt that it needed to be killed immediately, as it was close to a farm where children had been playing. This was the first polar bear to have come ashore in Iceland since 2010. Polar bears are not native to the island but drift over on sea ice or swim from Greenland as their own cryospheres disintegrate. After the bear's carcass was dissected, it was clear that she had been both swimming

FIGURE 12.2
Polar bear shot by farmers in Northern Iceland, July 2016. Photo by Björn Jóhann Björnsson for *Morgunblaðið*.

for many miles as well as floating on drift ice. The shortest distance between Greenland and Iceland is 300 km. But the distance between Greenland and the shore where this polar bear was first seen is considerably longer—about 600 km. The bear was also a mother who was still lactating. So, it couldn't have been long since she was accompanied by her cubs.

There have only been a few hundred recorded sightings of polar bears in Iceland throughout the country's recorded history. The oldest of these was in 890 CE, sixteen years after the first settlers arrived on the island. During the Middle Ages, polar bears were sometimes tamed and used for entertainment, but since that time, no bear has been captured alive in Iceland. For several decades, it has been national policy in Iceland to kill polar bears on sight, as they are inevitably hungry after being afloat at sea. They are considered a grave danger to both residents and livestock.

On social media sites such as Facebook, the shooting of the mother bear produced a storm of controversy and emotional reckoning. Icelanders responded generally in two ways. One position held that people must protect themselves and their livestock. Given that the bears come ashore near-starving in remote parts of the island, it is up to local farmers or marksmen to ensure the safety of local residents. The alternate position was that Icelanders ought to revisit the shoot-on-sight policy and instead legislate more humane responses to bear landings, especially since they will likely increase as the neighboring island of Greenland steadily loses both land and sea ice. Jón Gnarr, the former mayor of Reykjavík, who had run (partly facetiously) on a platform that included hosting a polar bear at the Reykjavík Zoo, saw future bear migrations as a potential boon for the country. "Why not make a tourist attraction of a polar bear haven?" he asked. Jón Gunnar Ottósson, head of the Icelandic Institute of Natural History, along with many others, also decried the shooting of the bear, saying that it could have been tranquillized rather than killed. (Officials contended that it would have taken an hour by plane to get the tranquilizers to the site and that it would have been impossible to track and control the animal for that long.) A spokesman for PolarWorld, a German group dedicated to the preservation of the polar regions and the creatures that inhabit them, called the bear's death "an avoidable tragedy," adding, in full irony, "this is another great day for mankind."

The story of the polar bear circulated across the country via both conventional and social media, generating affective and discursive responses that spread quickly and with significant reach. Facebook, a platform that is extremely popular in Iceland (used by approximately three quarters of the population), allowed for a particularly public affective response. In its digitized retelling, and in the collective human warnings and mourning that the bear's story evoked, sentiment tilted in one or another political direction: indicating either the failure of humanity to maintain ecosystemic integrity or the bald prioritization of human lives over all others. Drawing together the plight of humans and nonhumans in this way, the loss of ice—arguably a banal phase change in water from solid to liquid—opened a political rift that surfaced distinct understandings of conservation, about what ought to be saved, how it ought to be saved, and why. The dead bear surfaced multiple fragilities: the loss of sea ice, the steady heating of the Arctic region, and the role of humans (if not all equally) in this process. Diverse fragilities, related but distinct, acknowledged and unacknowledged, illustrate the transversal quality of fragility and its felt responses. Dead bears become, both corporeally and symbolically, a locus for melt and a changing political landscape, as well as a response to a precarious cryohuman future.

FIGURE 12.3
Glacial lagoon. Jökulsárlón, Eastern Iceland, 2016. Photo by author.

Each year in the Arctic, sea ice forms and melts. In the past quarter century, sea ice has steadily declined—more than 30 percent from its previous average. Ice levels continue to hit record lows,[6] causing Artic climate experts to declare that "we are now in uncharted territory."[7] "The trend has been clear for years," explained one, "but the speed at which it is happening is faster than anyone thought."[8] Unlike on the Antarctic continent, melting sea ice in the Arctic exposes the dark, open ocean beneath, absorbing more sunlight and thus creating greater warming. Dark waters absorb heat, and the reflective "albedo" effect that bounces sunlight off the surface of white ice sheets and glaciers is also reduced with each phase of ensuing melt. The loss of the albedo effect in places across the Arctic is a graphic example of cryohuman relations between states of matter. Diminished albedo, weather patterning, and rising ocean and land temperatures are why the Arctic is heating up much faster than the rest of the planet.[9]

When she was a girl growing up in a little village in the northwest of Iceland, Helga Edmundsdóttir remembers the sound of sea ice. It terrified her at night. Ghostly moans were emitted as floating mountains of ice rubbed up against each other, aching out a frictional chorus. That is heard much, much less now. "Now," Helga explained, "I hardly ever hear that screeching sound of ice at sea. Or the sounds of it hitting up against the ships in the harbor. And while it scared me then, I do miss it now." The disappearing sound of sea ice strikes Helga as a memory of a sound more than an experience she can sense in the present. Silence becomes further confirmation of a melting world, a response without a call. Wider, darker seas and coastlines that have lost their ice reveal an erosion of a particular cryohuman encounter. And since sea ice also serves as bulwark and barrier to storm waves, the silencing of sea ice is also a signal of more disintegrations to come. Melting sea ice affects weather all over the world, especially as ocean currents are modified and their waters heated. In the constellation of ice and its reflective properties, solar radiation and absorbent seas, new configurations of fragility appear—their effects are different, but in their systemic interrelationship within a larger Earth system, they all share a common fragility requiring many kinds of expert and affective response.

RESPONDING LIKE A GLACIER

Sólheimajökull is a glacier about two hours southeast of Iceland's capital city of Reykjavík. There, every summer, Guðfinna Aðalgeirsdóttir teaches a glaciology class in addition to her regular research and teaching as a professor at the University of Iceland. Each year, she takes a group of students to Sólheim glacier, where they use a steam drill, which she likens to an odd little pressure cooker, to bore through the glacial ice "like a hot knife through butter." Once the drill tube is established, she and the students lower a long wire down into it, and it slowly snakes its way down into Sólheim's corpus. As the glacier's surface ice melts away over the course of the summer, the line will show more of itself, revealing the metrics of that season's ablation, or ice loss. It is a simple, low-impact technology of glacial reckoning.

For Guðfinna, glaciers are anything but static. In fact, she says, they are best understood as operating like a conveyor belt. They move, and they move material. Snow and ice accumulate at the higher altitudes of the glacier and are depleted in the lower reaches. There is a circulation of material from high to low and from solid to liquid. Glaciers can also be understood, Guðfinna says, in simple economic terms. They are, in many ways, like a bank account.

In the winter, positive accumulation fills up the bank. Deposits of snow and ice are made at higher elevations in the "accumulation zone." At the glacier's lower elevations, withdrawals occur in the form of "ablation"—the melting and calving of glacial ice. And just as you would your bank accounts, Guðfinna adds, you want to keep it in a healthy balance. We know, of course, that balance—what glaciologists call "mass balance"—is not being achieved of late and that deposits have not kept up with expenditures. Solheimjökull, like nearly all of Iceland's glaciers, is losing more each summer than it gains each winter.

Compared to many others, Icelandic glaciers are especially well documented. Since the Middle Ages, and arguably over the last twelve hundred years, Icelanders have been attuned to the glaciers that occupy their homeland. For Sólheim glacier, Guðfinna explains that they have excellent records going back to the 1930s. In the 1930s, temperatures had warmed, and glaciers retreated. In the 1960s and 1970s, it became cooler, and they grew. Since the mid-1990s, however, they have only gone in one direction, and that is toward "ablation."

The technical, glaciological term for ice loss is "ablation." In English, the word is defined in the first instance as "the surgical removal of body tissue." (Interestingly, the first person to thoroughly document Icelandic glaciers systematically was, by trade, a surgeon.) In the second definition, ablation denotes the melting or evaporation of snow and ice. About half of ablation events occur through calving (ice sheering) and the other half through melting. While there have always been advances and retreats of glaciers in Iceland, Guðfinna notes that the country's glaciers have now withdrawn further than they did in the relatively warm 1930s. She describes that in the Westfjords, on the northwestern peninsula, they are finding vegetation growth where glaciers once were. These surfaces, now exposed through melt, have been covered in ice for at least two to three thousand years. This is effectively "new land," newly naked because of melt.

As a scientist, Guðfinna is very interested in what glaciologists call "glacial response." She reminds me in our conversation that the Earth system has only accumulated about 150 years of intensive fossil fuel use. "The atmosphere and the glaciers," she says, "haven't managed to respond to it yet. Not fully. It is a slow system." And she goes on to say that it is a very "stochastic" system—having a random probability or pattern that may be analyzed statistically but that will not be predicted precisely. "If you push it that way, you can expect a dramatic effect." But Guðfinna explains:

> The climate models are not really managing to consider all the physics. We have weather forecast models that are similar, and they simulate the physics six or seven days into the future. This is a model that can tell you that about short-term weather, but not how the weather will be months and months away! And with climate models we are really asking them to tell us what the weather will be in a hundred years' time.

It is telling that Guðfinna turns to weather prediction as she describes glacial response. For her, and for several other glaciologists with whom I spoke, they felt their role as scientists was changing. Historically, glaciologists have been trained as geologists who might then specialize in cryoforms and their interactions. Glaciology, as the glaciologist Helgi Björnsson put it to me, "has always been closest to geology: observing what is happening, the forces and movements and cracks." Helgi himself began his studies and career in the "slow science" of geology. Both Helgi and Guðfinna are now convinced that glaciology has become an exercise in understanding how ice and melt are a response to larger systemic changes, including atmospheric conditions and weather. Glaciological expertise, like glaciers themselves, is also changing, being now more attuned to meteorology and the patterning of weather. If it began as a slow science, glaciology would now appear to be speeding up and adapting to new inputs of unprecedented weather events. Both Helgi's and Guðfinna's responses show how multiple fragilities manifest in different practices and temporalities of knowledge creation and the exercise of science. Compounding fragilities, their probable yet stochastic entanglements and outcomes, all shape how ice can now be thought of and known. Before we went our separate ways, Guðfinna wanted to share quite plainly her estimation of the present. "What we are doing now is pushing Earth systems into a regime that we have not been in, ever, naturally before. This is the largest uncontrolled experiment that we have ever done." Guðfinna's reflection portended a future as well, for, as she put it, "we shall see where it leads us."

WHEN GLACIERS ARE NEIGHBORS

Guðni Gunnarsson and his wife Hulda Magnúsdóttir have lived their entire lives near the village of Höfn in Southeast Iceland. They are sheep farmers, with a home at the foot of a glacial tongue at Fláajökull. They have an old dog and grown children, and Hulda is quick to bring cakes and coffee.

As we sit together around their neat wooden dining table, Guðni explains why he is not fond of glaciers. Like many of his friends and kin in this region,

FIGURE 12.4
Guðni Gunnarsson pointing to Fláajökull, a glacier that borders his farm, 2016. Photo by author.

he knows how monstrously destructive a glacier can be as it crawls over land, sometimes toppling barns and houses in its path. There is also the perpetual threat of a *jökulhlaup* (glacial outburst flood). The term was coined to describe the outburst floods of Iceland's Vatnajökull—the largest ice cap in Europe—but it has since become standard scientific terminology to indicate glacial floods caused by subglacial melting. Often brought on by volcanic eruptions beneath a glacier or ice sheet, a *jökulhlaup* can amass gigantic quantities of water that destabilize its icy vessel. For a time, an ice dam might hold water back, but it can just as easily burst without warning to unleash a flood of water thick with ice—with some pieces as large as cars—sweeping away everything in its path. That is why, Guðni explains, houses are placed higher up on the hillsides to avoid being washed away completely. *Jökulhlaups* in Iceland have been known to reach the size of the Amazon River during tropical flood stage. A critical difference between the tropical river and a *jökulhlaup* is that the latter is cold, fast, and unpredictable. Guðni knows all too well the stories of people and animals whisked far out to sea by glacial floods, lost to the frigid waters of the North Atlantic.

It was a challenge for Guðni to come up with anything positive to say about the glacier nested in the mountain near his home. Proximity is not easy. He conceded that in the 1930s and 1940s, his family used the glacier for ice. Prior to refrigeration, the glacier could provide adequate ice to keep freshly caught fish cold. Guðni also remembered teams of scientists coming to the glacier in the 1940s, but he was unclear what precisely they were looking for. What he returned to several times is that the glacier was, for him, a part of the mountain, not distinct from it. Speaking about the glacier as separate from the mountain where it lay was, for Guðni, an odd way to think of the glacier. It simply did not make sense to cleave them. As we finished off a final cup of hot coffee, Guðni did concede that, at times but only at times, he does see beauty in the glacier that lives in his backyard.

Glaciers are famous for their sublime beauty. But for those that know them well, they can also be menacing, threatening lives with their unstoppable mass and watery outbursts. For Guðni and Hulda, being proximate to the glacier is a place of fragility: a looming danger with a history of uneasy companionship for both human and animal neighbors. Their reflections on the glacier with which they live in icy intimacy illustrates how fragility always exists in the multiple and the experiential. However, the fragility that Hulda and Guðni express, given their history with and nearness to the glacier, is a sensibility that is itself receding into history. Where they were once to be avoided, glaciers (in Iceland and elsewhere) increasingly appear as objects of care and concern. Their mounting fragility inspires worries about the future and a time when there will be no ice remaining in the country called Iceland.

In media portrayals, the melting of polar ice is regularly used as a figure of apprehension and distress—a clear indicator of a climate transforming more rapidly than many had expected. But if our collective affective response to melting glaciers now tilts toward alarm (and rightly so), Icelanders remind us that this has not always been the case. Fragilities take many forms, producing different logics of response and distinct sensibilities about care and what ought to be preserved, saved, or relinquished. Recognizing this should not have us retreat from the omens that are embodied in melting ice. Rather, these multiple modes of response to fragilities, in the plural, can begin to show us the range of relations possible between cryospheres and human populations. Our response is due. But will we know if we have answered correctly?

THE FUTURE IS FRAGILE

In the pages of the IPCC reports, there is no ignoring the evidence of a growing number of fragilities that surround us. In sobering terms, the diagnostics of thousands of scientists illustrate that multiple environmental impacts caused by one source of destabilization—greenhouse gas emissions, past and present—"are irreversible for centuries to millennia." They likewise emphasize that these impacts are most stark in "changes [to] the ocean, ice sheets, and global sea level" (IPCC 2021, SPM 28), illustrating how the fragility of the atmosphere is directly tied to fragilities we can recognize and experience across cryoscapes and hydrospheres. Inscribed into the world's atmosphere, sea and land is an "unequivocal human influence."[10] As Marisol de la Cadena and Mario Blaser (2018, 3) rightly put it, "very few, if any, of the readers of Nature can currently deny that the planet is being driven down a perilous path."

With the growing awareness that we now inhabit an increasingly perilous world, new fragilities appear. But these vulnerabilities were always there. The Earth system may have seemed, in previous times and to some populations, to be impervious, ever regenerative, and immune to deep ruination. That was always a fallacy, but its lie (or ignorance) is now increasingly difficult to obscure with the usual claims demanding economic growth, expansion, extraction, and anthropocentric domination. With the exposure of multiple fragilities and the acknowledgment of their interrelatedness and origin stories in human conceits of control, there are also new opportunities for renewal and acknowledgment. Multiple, refracting, and contradictory fragilities call for a response that, because they must speak to unprecedented times, can be unprecedented in their depth and appeal: a mandate to create an ecosystem of mutual care. Placing headstones or monuments is one well-rehearsed human practice the world over that responds to the fragility of human life, but in an anthropogenic age of human disruption to ecosystemic balance, headstones can become a marker for the fragility of nonhumans as well, even those that were never technically "alive." As Beth Povinelli (2016) reminds us, the divide between life and death has long been of humanistic interest and inquiry. But in the Anthropocene, the divide between the living (species of the planet) and the nonliving (such as the cryosphere or lithosphere) has become a locus for ontological questions and existential debate: What is the distinction between living and nonliving when all biotic life appears imperiled by the nonliving world of water and ice, solar radiation, and atmospheric carbon? How does the fragility of life also, paradoxically, depend upon the nonliving world of water and ice, solar radiation, and atmospheric carbon for its very existence?

Scientific warnings will continue to swell and multiply. How environmental fragilities are deduced and conveyed by committed practitioners of science, such as Helgi and Guðfinna, will continue to morph and adapt to changing conditions. The condition of being mercurial. Greenhouse gases will also accumulate, as will dead bears. Each will point to divergent fragilities, one as cause and one as outcome, but in each is also embodied multiple potentials for response. To which fragilities do we give our attention, and what are the politics of care in a time of widespread imbalance across living and nonliving worlds? In these moments of recognition, our collective response continues to remain in question. People such as Guðni and Hulda will remember the ice, but one day, those who remember will be gone too. The past will be passed. Their reckonings with, and of, glaciers will become part of a genealogy of encounter that is fast disappearing as glacial threats evolve: not as ice destroying humans, but humans destroying ice. Taken together, we find the multiplication of fragilities, in the plural and in acceleration. These fragilities are not necessarily convergent, but they share a kinship, a root, a source of harm that signals a precarious future in the "blasted landscapes" (Tsing 2014) that we all now call home. For Icelanders, surviving as a human being on a remote northern island has always meant living with a profound recognition of nature's potency and destructive potential. It has meant an attention to precarity and fragility. There is a certain resignation and wisdom in the Icelandic expression *eftir veðri og vindum* (everything goes by weather and the winds). But in this abandonment to the elements is also a moment of reflection upon a world that is not made by humans alone and whose fragilities need not be the end of the story.

NOTES

1. "The Custodian" is a work of video art created by the photographer Judy Natal for her Future Perfect series. See https://everson.org/object-of-the-week/caring-for-the-land-the-custodian-by-judy-natal/. In five vignettes, acting as a metaphorical custodian of the land, The Custodian ceremoniously sweeps, tends, and mourns the Icelandic

landscape through acts of repetitious care that mirrors the domestic labor that women the world over typically perform.

2. See https://www.scientificamerican.com/article/what-is-iceland-without-ice/. *Scientific American* described the latter quantity as fifty of the world's largest trucks filled with snow every minute, all year long.

3. In the summer of 2019, Dominic Boyer and I organized the Okjökull memorial and the creation of the plaque that now sits atop Ok mountain. However, the idea to create the world's first memorial to a fallen glacier would not have come to us without the many conversations we had with Icelanders about loss, and about glacial loss in particular, as we were making the documentary film *Not Ok: A Little Movie about a Small Glacier at the End of the World* (2018). In the summer of 2018, we met with Icelandic authorities to acquire permission to place the marker on Ok mountain, which was granted after submitting a formal proposal. In August of that year, we hosted the world's first "un-glacier" tour to the summit of Ok mountain. Accompanied by about forty members of the Icelandic Hiking Society, we circumnavigated the Ok shield volcano, identified the site where the Ok glacier once existed, and located an appropriate stone on which to place the memorial marker the following summer. We invited the Icelandic author and environmentalist Andri Snær Magnason to write the words for the plaque. He felt it was important to include the carbon dioxide concentration in the atmosphere around the time of writing (415 parts per million); we agreed.

4. Haraway's "response-ability" also dovetails with the call from Max Liboiron and their colleagues to "intentionally move our scientific work" toward benefitting the communities with whom we work and toward a politics of engagement or "reconciliation science" (Liboiron, et al. 2021).

5. Currently, according to the IPCC, the majority of global sea level rise is caused by the melting of Arctic glaciers and the Greenlandic ice sheet. However, the disintegration of the Thwaites glacier in Antarctica, the largest glacier in the world, is accelerating, and scientists fear its collapse in the coming five to ten years. Sometimes called "the Doomsday Glacier," the calving and melting of Thwaites would produce a dramatic rise in sea level around the world, potentially raising it by more than two feet. See https://www.scientificamerican.com/article/antarcticas-doomsday-glacier-is-melting-even-faster-than-scientists-thought/#:~:text=Thwaites%20Glacier%2C%20often%20dubbed%20the,or%20just%20over%202%20feet.

6. See https://www.theguardian.com/environment/2016/dec/06/arctic-antarctic-ice-melt-november-record.

7. See https://www.theguardian.com/environment/2016/dec/19/arctic-ice-melt-already-affecting-weather-patterns-where-you-live-right-now.

8. The melting of Greenland's ice sheet is pouring about 250 billion tons of fresh water into the sea each year. Since fresh water is less dense than sea water, fresh water does not sink as rapidly, meaning that the current that brings warm water up from the depths of the Atlantic (the Atlantic meridional overturning circulation, AMOC) is

weakened. Scientists have already found that the current is at its weakest in a millennium. See https://www.nature.com/articles/nclimate2554.

9. See http://www.independent.co.uk/environment/arctic-warming-twice-rate-rest-of-planet-global-warming-snow-water-ice-permafrost-arctic-monitoring-a7710701.html#http://www.independent.co.uk/environment/arctic-warming-twice-rate-rest-of-planet-global-wa.

10. While the human impact is collective, its origins lie mainly in the resource exploitation of large, industrialized countries, and its outcomes will be felt most severely in those parts of the world least able to withstand catastrophic events such as drought, extreme storms, and infrastructural collapse.

REFERENCES

Alaimo, Stacy. 2008. "Trans-Corporeal Feminisms and the Ethical Space of Nature." In *Material Feminisms,* edited by Stacy Alaimo and Susan Hekman, 237–264. Bloomington: University of Indiana Press.

Barnes, Jessica, Michael Dove, Myanna Lahsen, Andrew Mathews, Pamela McElwee, Roderick McIntosh, Frances Moore, Jessica O'Reilly, Ben Orlove, Rajindra Puri, Harvey Weiss, and Karina Yager. 2013. "Contribution of Anthropology to the Study of Climate Change." *Nature Climate Change* 3 (June): 541–544.

Behar, Katherine, 2016. "An Introduction to Object Oriented Feminism." In *Object Oriented Feminism,* edited by Katherine Behar, 1–36. Minneapolis: University of Minnesota Press.

Boyer, Dominic. 2019. *Energopolitics: Wind and Power in the Anthropocene.* Durham, NC: Duke University Press.

Chakrabarty, Dipesh. 2009. "The Climate of History: Four Theses." *Critical Inquiry* 35 (Winter): 197–221.

Cruikshank, Julie. 2006. *Do Glaciers Listen? Local Knowledge, Colonial Encounters and Social Imagination.* Vancouver: UBC Press.

De la Cadena, Marisol, and Mario Blaser, eds. 2018. *A World of Many Worlds.* Durham, NC: Duke University Press.

Edwards, Paul N. 2010. *A Vast Machine: Computer Models, Climate Data, and the Politics of Global Warming.* Cambridge, MA: MIT Press.

Haraway, Donna J. 2015. "Anthropocene, Capitalocene, Plantationocene, Chthulucene: Making Kin." *Environmental Humanities* 6 (1): 159–165.

Heininen, Lassi, ed. 2015. *Future Security of the Global Arctic: State Policy, Economic Security and Climate.* London: Palgrave Pivot.

Howe, Cymene. 2018. "Melt as Sensory Labor." Theorizing the Contemporary, "The Naturalization of Work." https://culanth.org/fieldsights/melt-as-sensory-labor.

Howe, Cymene. 2019a. *Ecologics: Wind and Power in the Anthropocene.* Durham, NC: Duke University Press.

Howe, Cymene. 2019b. "Sensing Asymmetries in Other-than-Human Forms." *Science, Technology and Human Values* 44 (5): 900–910. https://doi/10.1177/0162243919852675.

Hulme, Mike. 2011. "Reducing the Future to Climate: A Story of Climate Determinism and Reductionism." *Osiris* 26 (1): 245–266.

IPCC. 2021. *Climate Change 2021: The Physical Science Basis. Contribution of Working Group I to the Sixth Assessment Report of the Intergovernmental Panel on Climate Change.* Edited by Valérie Masson-Delmotte, Panmeo Zhai, Anna Pirani, Sarah L. Connors, Clotilde Péan, Sophie Berger, Nada Caud, Yang Chen, Leah Goldfarb, Melissa I. Gomis, Mengtian Huang, Katherine Leitzell, Elisabeth Lonnoy, J. B. Robin Matthews, Thomas K. Maycock, Tim Waterfield, Ozge Yelekçi, Rong Yu, and Baiquan Zhou. Cambridge, UK: Cambridge University Press.

Liboiron, Max, Alex Zahara, Kaitlyn Hawkins, Christina Crespo, Bárbara de Moura Neves, Vonda Wareham-Hayes, Evan Edinger, Charlotte Muise, Mary Jane Walzak, Rebecca Sarazen, Jillian Chidley, Carley Mills, Lauren Watwood, Hridisha Arif, Elise Earles, Liz Pijogge, Jamal Shirley, Jesse Jacobs, Paul McCarney, and Louis Charron. 2021. "Abundance and Types of Plastic Pollution in Surface Waters in the Eastern Arctic (Inuit Nunangat) and the Case for Reconciliation Science." *Science of the Total Environment* 782: 146809. https://doi.org/10.1016/j.scitotenv.2021.146809.

Linnenluecke, Martina K., and Andrew Griffiths. 2015. *The Climate Resilient Organization: Adaptation and Resilience to Climate Change and Weather Extremes*. Cheltenham, UK: Edward Elgar.

Morton, Timothy. 2014. *Hyperobjects: Philosophy and Ecology after the End of the World*. Minneapolis: University of Minnesota Press.

Povinelli, Elizabeth. 2016. *Geontologies: A Requiem to Late Liberalism*. Durham, NC: Duke University Press.

Puig de la Bellacasa, María. 2012. "'Nothing Comes without its World': Thinking with Care." *Sociological Review* 60 (2): 197–216.

Puig de la Bellacasa, María. 2017. *Matters of Care: Speculative Ethics in More than Human Worlds*. Minneapolis: University of Minnesota Press.

Strauss, Sarah, and Ben Orlove, eds. 2003. *Weather, Climate, Culture*. Oxford: Berg.

Tsing, Anna. 2014. "Blasted Landscapes and the Gentle Art of Mushroom Picking." In *The Multispecies Salon*, edited by Eben Kirksey, 87–114. Durham, NC: Duke University Press. https://www.multispecies-salon.org/tsing/.

Watson, Donald, and Michele Adams. 2010. *Design for Flooding Architecture, Landscape, and Urban Design for Resilience to Flooding and Climate Change*. Hoboken, NJ: John Wiley.

Zolli, Andrew, and Ann Marie Healy. 2013. *Resilience: Why Things Bounce Back*. New York: Simon & Schuster.

13 CONVERSATION WITH STEVE JACKSON

FERNANDO DOMÍNGUEZ RUBIO (FDR): Both chapters talked about fragility processes, such as termination and reproduction, and different regimes of care and labor required to make them work. Can you tell us what you've learned from them and where you think the main points of connections or divergence are between the two.

STEVE JACKSON (SJ): One of the connections that I see between the chapters concerns their objects: glaciers and kings. These are both very powerful entities. And I think it's particularly interesting to think through the problem of fragility vis-à-vis entities that we very often take to be powerful. These are among the most powerful figures in their categorical realms. Glaciers move mountains. I live in a landscape in upstate New York that has been substantially carved by glaciers. And kings, especially this king, come pretty close to doing the same. That's true metaphorically in the social realm, including Louis's role in transforming European and subsequent world history through the advent of absolutism. But it's also true quite literally: kings *literally* move mountains, redirect rivers, and so on. So, when I think about these cases in relationship to problems of fragility, they're kind of like the "hard case" of fragility (even if actually I don't like the language of the "hard case" and I don't know why we should be so obsessed with them in science and technology studies [STS]). Anyway, if even things as powerful and irrefutable as glaciers and kings can be made amenable to an analysis grounded in fragility (and the forms of maintenance and care required to manage it), I think that's a pretty strong statement.

One way of putting this is to say that fragility is *also* for the strong, not just for the weak. And as the chapters show, this opens up recognition to forms of work that are typically occluded under the accomplished and reified form of things. So, the accomplished king—Louis XIV, in all his splendor—looks different from the king that we see *being accomplished* in Mukerji's text. And the glacier, in its classic textbook or Nature Channel form, looks quite different from the sort of the weak, sad, disappearing glacier that we see in Howe's chapter. I think this inversion can help to blow up some of our assumptions around how the world is organized, particularly in relation to a theory or understanding of power. A theory of power that includes fragility and care at its core is likely to be much more interesting than one that regards power only in its accomplished and (seemingly) irrefutable form or that defines power as the absence of fragility. We often assume that you are powerful when you're not vulnerable. But in fact, I think a more effective theory of power would include within itself moments of fragility and vulnerability.

Another commonality between these two texts is the presence of invisible or at least unlooked-for actors. I love the image of the glacial custodian that shows up in Howe's chapter. That's a wonderful image. And, of course, the artisanal shipbuilders that Mukerji describes, and how their presence in the production process is not only essential to the performance of kingly power but also threatening to that performance in a way. So, their presence is something that needs to be suppressed, so that the power of the king can come to seem self-sufficient or self-efficacious. For me, this presence of invisible or at least unlooked-for actors is one of the most powerful and compelling reasons to attend to the problems of fragility, care, and repair throughout the volume. Because there are acts and actors that such accounts can help call to light, who are often rendered invisible by the many other ways we have of imagining and theorizing the world.

In terms of divergences, and what the chapters do differently, first of all, I don't think divergences are contradictions, and the two texts are not fundamentally opposed or in tension in any deep way. But they each call out different elements and dimensions of the broader problem of fragility that we are tackling in this volume. I'm particularly struck and moved by the affective dimensions of Howe's chapter, and especially the sense of loss she tracks through a number of actors' relationship to the glacier. This idea that the fragility of the glacier is also deeply connected to *human* senses of connection to this particular entity and this particular kind of an environment.

We are used to seeing this in reactions when a polar bear shows up, but for the glacier itself, it's something else. The whole idea of a "glacial funeral" and the invocation of a deeply human sense of mourning in relationship to an object such as a glacier is really quite striking to me. Importantly, this sense is also present in the scientists she writes about: the mourning is "inside" the science, as it were. In STS, we're used to describing scientists as witnesses, but here we see the scientist as a kind of mourner, which strikes me as a very different kind of role. This is quite moving, and for me, it is one of the most distinctive elements of Howe's chapter. It's the part I keep thinking about after reading it.

In Mukerji's chapter, I was really struck by the notion of prophetic truth that she draws, in part from Foucault. It is an interesting thing to me in terms of extending how we think about the role of, and relationship to, material practice through the kinds of work that are being performed by the artisanal shipbuilders. A "first-level" version of that would be to say that the power of kings is produced by a variety of kinds of material transformations. You turn trees into masts and ships to build navies. And that constitutes a form of military power that we've long associated with kingship and the modern state. But the notion of prophetic truth adds another crucial layer to this materialist account. It highlights the idea not only that there is that kind of direct material transformation, but also that there is an ideal of care that is essential to the promissory dimension of state power. So, these artisans are not just building ships but also delivering a promissory note on the forms of organization that a modern state (Louis XIV's anyway) can produce. This is, for me, the most distinct thing coming out of Mukerji's chapter.

Then, when you think of these chapters together, another obvious take-away (which I think is true across other texts in the volume as well) is how they call out the sheer range and diversity of maintenance and care work vis-à-vis the "natural" and "social" worlds around us—of course, with all the scare quotes and red flags we've learned to attach to those terms. This demonstrates the value and utility of thinking these things together. Kingly power and the fate of glaciers are not things we usually put in the same room at the same time, and yet I think there's a lot to be learned by thinking about these cases together. This reminds me, in some ways, of the constant comparison principle or methodology from grounded theory: What are the things you can think together that wouldn't normally show up in a set? And how can the distinct features of each help illuminate or ask new questions about the other to break us out of our categorical thinking around any given entity or object?

FDR: Your own work is about maintenance and repair. How do you think these contributions relate to your work?

SJ: Thematically and conceptually, there are a lot of linkages. Empirically, though, it's quite different from the kinds of worlds, often computational, that I've tended to engage. But again, for me, that's an interesting opportunity. What Howe's chapter calls out nicely for me, what makes me think back toward my own kinds of sites, is the deep and extensive range of affective relations we can hold to entities or objects that we typically classify as things or natural entities—including forms of relations that we're more commonly used to in "human" relationships. The fact that you can mourn a glacier highlights a depth of connection and attachment that is useful in deepening our understanding of the interrelations between human and nonhuman worlds. Clearly, some of the people she talks about in her study have a relationship to glaciers that goes beyond an "object-like" or classically instrumental relation. They *matter* to them. When the glacier disappears, it matters to them enough that they mourn it. Of course, conducting a funeral for a glacier is also a political, maybe even a PR, move. It's a powerful kind of art piece in some ways. But the overall tone of the chapter shows that it goes beyond that function. People are legitimately mourning the loss of this thing in their life. And they are legitimately engaging, at least in the example of the custodian figure, in efforts to maintain, restore, or fight a rearguard action against its loss. That's more powerful than most of the sites I've encountered, although I've always agreed to this principle about the depth of affective relations that humans can hold with things and objects around them.

There is also something else, of course. Applying notions of maintenance, care, and, to some extent, repair to entities such as glaciers and incipient kings expands the range of entities to which the notion of repair, maintenance, and care can be applied. This is our own ongoing discussion over the years, and I've thought that maintenance and repair studies as a thing, or a field or whatever it is, has always gotten better and richer and deeper as new entities have been added into the space. This is a very computational way to say it, but a version of maintenance and repair studies that's trained on the corpus of a limited and particular set of things would be overfitted to those conditions, I think. When you expand maintenance and repair to a new and challenging set of objects, such as glaciers and kings, it causes you to think differently about some of those older or more traditional objects of study.

Again, this is an ongoing discussion that we've all been involved in. In both cases, they have this nice quality that I look for a lot of maintenance and repair work to do. The actions they study face both forward and backward in time. There is a narrower understanding of maintenance and repair work, which is about how we bring things back to what they were or how we keep things where they are right now. And, of course, there's some sense of that in the glacier work. But there is also a strong sense in which care and repair are practiced as a way of opening into, or onto, a new kind of world. So, it's not just how we go back or how we "freeze" (pun intended) an old world, but rather how we make maintenance and repair the fulcrum of change from which we transit, however we feel about that transit. We may not love it, we may not be excited about that transit, but the care work around glaciers is not *just* a mourning, and it's certainly not *only* an effort to stay in a world that has glaciers in these quantities in these locations. It is also about imagining and making a claim on a world that is coming in which the *absence* of glaciers, at least in this particular place, holds a particular valence and meaning.

FDR: One could say, using your own concerns, that in these chapters, these affective relations connect people to past, present, and future unfold at the hinge between fear and hope.

SJ: I think that's absolutely true. Fragility evokes both the sense of fear and threat to a past or current order. But it's also the condition of possibility for a different kind of order going forward. If the world wasn't fragile, if these *entities* weren't fragile but rather fixed, stable, and self-sufficient, that would imply a certain kind of stasis. The fact that they *are* fragile is both an invitation to and a requirement for ongoing action. The power of the king is always being buttressed and reproduced. It's always being cared for into the future. But that's also the possibility of change. And Iceland without glaciers may come to be a very different kind of place from the world that we see in Howe's chapter. I think that mix is somehow "baked" into the term. When we say fragile, it does have that sense of vulnerability, of loss and suffering, but I also think it's possible, even if this isn't the dominant reading, to mark fragility as the precondition for hope—for action and change into the future. In the case of the Icelandic glaciers, fragility is the precondition for a different kind of relationship that people might build in which different kinds of possibilities may exist, including different regimes of value and care. These may or may not halt the retreat of the glaciers, but they may perform other kinds of meaning and worth in the collective worlds of people and things.

JÉRÔME DENIS: And somehow these chapters also resonate with a paper you wrote with Lara Houston about the "poetics and politics" of repair, in which you show the importance of apprehending these two dimensions of care and repair work together. There is a lot of poetics in these two chapters that both foreground affective relations as you mentioned, but there is also politics, especially when they address the question of who is made visible and who is made invisible and when they describe the conditions in which people can work or act.

SJ: Yes. And I think that, among its other great virtues, Mukerji's chapter does an amazing job of reading history against the grain. It's quite challenging to call out the direct experience of the figures that she wants to call out, the ones that are working in these locations. And yet, the chapter manages to piece together enough to give us a sense of those lives from the map of the city to a description of the work. That effort, I think, is important. And, more generally, the question is: Whose experiences do we need to account for? This is really important and probably a question for the whole volume as well. In her chapter, Howe has this great question: To which fragilities do we give our attention? And what are the politics of care we want in a time of widespread imbalance across the living and nonliving worlds? I don't think care is a capacity that we distribute widely. So, the politics of attention, and which fragilities we attend to and which we don't, are quite important questions.

FDR: The two chapters bring forward questions of how power is related to a particular space or territory, revealing the tension between raising sovereignty and dealing with uncertainty. And these questions resonate with your work on the geopolitics of repair practices. Can you talk a little bit about these and how the question of fragility can help us to think about this tension?

SJ: Actually, I think I've learned this from Chandra herself over the years. I've always been fascinated by the embodied and territorial dimensions of power—the fact that states in particular are always about the inscription of power on a landscape, and that state power is also built and drawn out of landscape. So, obviously, principles of territory and territoriality are well established for entities that we identify as states. But they also apply broadly to other kinds of worlds. So, I am currently working on problems of computational sourcing and extraction: all the ways in which computational "things," everything from lithium extraction in South America to tin mining in Indonesia, are drawn from the earth, often in highly destructive but largely hidden or invisible ways—invisible at least to imaginations of computing centered on the Global North, and on moments of design, use, and the shiny form of the accomplished artifact. There's, of course, a complex and hugely problematic labor history involved in that story, and global networks of extraction (and abstraction) that really haven't budged much since colonial days, apart from the fact that the cast of extractors has broadened somewhat to include new economic centers such as China. So, the power of computing, too, comes out of territory, just like Louis XIV's power came from territory, including through things such as the global supply chains and infrastructures that knit these worlds together.

This is the kind of thing that I speculate on when I read Mukerji's chapter. What if we thought about the territoriality of computing in a way akin to the way she thinks about the territoriality of state power and the kinds of fragility that the work of the artisanal shipbuilders is designed to overcome? What if we rethought computing as a territorial practice, not unlike the way king making and glacial care are explored in the two chapters here? If we did, I think we might arrive at a very different conception and starting point for how we talk about and maybe even do computing.

FDR: Finally, what do you think about the overall intent or the volume to focus on fragility? And what do you think that we can gain from such a move? And also, what do you think the possible limitations or shortcomings or dangers of making such a move may be?

SJ: As I've already said, I'm very interested in fragility as a concept, both as a kind of sensitizing lens that helps to see and engage the world in specific ways and as a site or empirical topic, almost like a selection principle: What if we set out to study concretely fragile things? How would our understanding of the world change? So, the reason I like fragility as a frame, in these two chapters and across the volume as a whole, is that I think we have a tendency in the social sciences in particular to overstate the solidity and stability of the worlds around us. I think we've got stuck with some bad metaphors such as "structure." Why do we use a fixed and settled thing such as structure as a dominant metaphor to describe social life? I think fragility can help us overcome the tendency to regard the world as more fixed, stable, and orderly than it might be in practice. That's the first thing I really like about fragility.

Another danger of the critical social sciences in particular is that we sometimes have a tendency to overstate the efficacy (or at least the *self*-efficacy) of power. We tend to see power as this accomplished and overwhelming thing, which we do mostly for critical intent. But sometimes, I fear we buttress power in making those claims—we give power a little more credit than it deserves. We miss the ways in which power can be weak and glitchy and fragile and subject at very least to the constant work of replenishment, recuperation, and, yes, repair. As a question of political strategy, not understanding the fragilities of power prevents us from locating potential connections or maybe inflection points. It prevents us from identifying modes and places to engage power that might actually produce the effects that we would want. That tendency to overstate the efficacy of power comes out nicely in Mukerji's chapter, precisely because we see the king in his moments of fragility, and all the work that goes in to produce and to sustain what will only later come to seem an overwhelming and irrefutable picture and form of power (an absolutist model, in fact).

Finally, as mentioned earlier, attending to fragility in our own work, including how we make decisions about what and whose fragility to call attention to, is really a way of acknowledging and calling out our own practices of caring and not caring vis-à-vis the worlds around us. And since we don't have the resources or the headspace, or the heart space or whatever, to care for everything universally, it is always a matter of choices. We *choose* to care and not to care about things. And this choice, which is explicitly exposed in Howe's chapter, is directly connected to the question of the kind of world we want to live in and build.

There are dangers to fragility, of course. Some of them mirror dangers that also show up in the work that we've all been involved in together over the years around maintenance, repair, and care. One of these is the danger of romanticizing fragility, creating a kind of "heroic" notion of fragility that fails to fully account for the experiential pain and sting of that condition. And I guess fragility, if not well handled, might also imply a kind of backward-looking focus, a kind of gaze from the present looking back, with maybe not enough appreciation for how present churn and uncertainties are also a road into various kinds of futures. I don't think it has to be that way, but it could. And I guess, just to counter the earlier point I made about power, if there is a danger in overstating the (self-)efficacy of power, there is also a danger in overstating the fragility and therefore vulnerability of established powers or powerful actors. The point of Mukerji's chapter, for me, is to say that the forms of power attached to Louis XIV are and were not natural and inevitable; they were constructed and came, in part, out of specific moments and forms of fragility. But that's *not* to say that Louis XIV wasn't a powerful actor in the end, because he was. Fragility does not mean weakness. And maybe that's an important last elision to avoid. If something is fragile, it does not necessarily mean that it's weak. Fragility and the *artful response* to fragility, as I think comes out in Mukerji's text quite clearly, can be a very powerful mechanism, both of the operation of power in its established forms and for those seeking to contest, renegotiate, and reinvent its terms. We should therefore never mistake fragility for weakness.

14 CONCLUSION: WHAT FRAGILITY DOES

JÉRÔME DENIS AND DAVID PONTILLE

So, what have we provoked?

—Donna J. Haraway, *Staying with the Trouble: Making Kin in the Chthulucene*

From the diversity of their objects to the different inquiries their authors engage with and their own writing styles, the chapters of this volume offer many paths to navigate through it. In these concluding remarks, we would like to return to the book's title and to question the notion of fragility afresh. The journey through this collection, including the crosscutting conversation articulated in the four comments sections, indeed leaves us with a question: What have we learned about fragility and, most of all, what have we learned with it? Such interrogations lead to another one—more intimidating but also more urging if one wants to take the chapters' propositions seriously and really benefit from their differences instead of pretending to ignore them: What kind of concept is fragility?

One of the pitfalls this collection of texts definitely keeps us from falling into is the temptation to shape a sealed notion, which would gather a community of researchers who would be in charge of preserving its boundaries. As Lucy Suchman warns us in her comments, concepts are noxious when they are used as flags planted on an alleged new territory. This means that trying to identify the conceptual qualities of the term has nothing to do with defining what fragility *is* or *is not*. Thinking with specific notions and problems cannot be reduced to the creation of demarcation lines and the shaping of exclusionary categories. Concepts should help us to "acquire consistency without losing the infinite into which thought plunges" (Deleuze & Guattari, 1994, p. 42). Instead of trying to define what fragility is, then, we'd better try to explore what it *does*. What does fragility help us to understand, perceive, think? And maybe even more, what does fragility make us do? In what terms does it *oblige* us (Stengers, 2010)?

Not every chapter in this collection has raised these kinds of questions explicitly, obviously. Yet, neither does any of their authors "apply" fragility as a neutral well-defined term that would simply explain a set of phenomena or characterize the state of objects and living beings in a transparent manner. Because they all work with the notion, sometimes struggle against it, each text offers great insights into discovering, and experiencing, what fragility does and makes do. In the following pages, we propose to describe three main traits of this conceptual pragmatics. Fragility will first be depicted as an instrument that adjusts perceptual awareness. Highlighting its situated and relational properties, we then examine why fragility may also be conceived of, and carefully manipulated as, a provocative concept. Finally, we'll see that, provided that one learns to embrace its ambivalence, fragility can help to "Stay with the Trouble" (Haraway, 2016).

SENSITIZING

The first thing that the concept of fragility does concerns perception. Thinking with fragility subtly modifies our ability to see things and processes that remain overlooked in most cases. Fragility readjusts the gaze, bringing what is usually in the background to the fore. This is less a matter of perspective, though, than one of accuracy and "resolution." Thinking with fragility engages us with a refined reality, populated by new phenomena and new beings. This capacity to render certain things seeable, and to equip the perception of subtle texture changes on the surface of various beings, is what "sensitizing concepts" do, as Herbert Blumer calls them:

> The concepts of our discipline are fundamentally sensitizing instruments. Hence, I call them "sensitizing concepts" and put them in contrast with definitive concepts. . . . A definitive concept refers precisely to what is common to a class of objects, and by the aid of a clear definition in terms of attributes or fixed bench marks. . . . A sensitizing concept lacks such specification. . . . Instead, it gives the user a general sense of reference and guidance in approaching empirical instances.

> Whereas definitive concepts provide prescriptions of what to see, sensitizing concepts merely suggest directions along which to look. (Blumer, 1954, p. 7)

"Sensitizing concepts" do not have any analytical value in themselves. They are not analytical tools drawing on predefined classifications that would act as a filter for the thought. Rather, they intensify the presence of certain features and act as perceptive sharpeners that nurture open and provisional theorizations.

What does the use of fragility make us sensitive to throughout the chapters composing this volume? First, questioning fragility connects us with people who themselves are concerned with fragile entities, which they try to take care of in one way or another. The sensitizing operation at play here foregrounds *specific modes of attention*. The fragility of things and living beings engage certain people in largely overlooked perceptive and affective forms of action the chapters of this volume endeavor to describe in detail. This is particularly salient in Myriam Winance's account of the activities undertaken by the parents of multiply disabled children. These parents cultivate a continuous care as they interact with their children, which highlights the tension between "attention given to different forms taken by the child's fragility and as confrontation with different forms of resistance." Not only do they care about their children's daily learning and gradual development, with a growing autonomy in perspective, just like any other parents, but they also develop a focused attention on particular actions (e.g., feeding themselves, brushing their teeth alone), which provides situated indications on their children's fragilities and own resistance. This form of attention goes through a process of reciprocal adjustments, always uncertain and always to be redone, which requires the parents to continuously invent new practical solutions that specify their children's singularity as much as they instantiate it. In developing her analysis with fragility as a concept, Winance thus highlights the various ways in which people pay attention: from paying attention to children, to taking care of their singularities, to caring for the ambivalences that affect caregiving and care receiving. These modes of attention are not restricted to human beings though. As Cymene Howe shows in her chapter, the melting of ice that constitutes glaciers goes with various forms of response from their neighbors. People living, not only next to a glacier but with it, develop multiple ways of paying attention to its presence, composition, and retreat. For instance, glaciologists cultivate a careful expertise of ice and experience glaciers as a conveyor belt moving materials that go from solid to liquid according to the altitudes. Glaciers have thus become a key indicator of climatological breakdown. But melting ice also goes with the growing presence of polar bears close to farms that entails vigilant practices for the protection of residents and livestock. Living with ice also means, for some inhabitants, to be attentive to the sometimes-terrifying sounds generated by the sea ice as floating mountains of ice rub up against each other. Glaciers also go with the potential menace of destruction, as they may crawl over land and topple houses. They can also themselves disappear, and die, and people may then organize specific rituals, such as a proper funeral, to cultivate their memory. These multiple and ambivalent responses to fragility illustrate the diverse modes of attention it calls for.

These modes of attention themselves feed another sensitizing operation. Paying attention to fragility indeed amounts to acknowledging the *continuous transformation of matter*, and it reminds us that care, maintenance, and repair are not a matter of stability and closure (Jackson, 2014; Denis & Pontille, 2021). This is a crosscutting dimension in this volume: in every case that is described, every story that is narrated, fragility renders inter- and intra-actions (Barad, 2007) visible. Rather than assuming a preordered and quiet sociomaterial reality, it foregrounds the multiplicity of material flows at play in the existence of every entity. The power of the king, the children we breed, care communities, the bodies of workers, the production of scientific knowledge, the concern for healthy food, artificial reproduction processes, glaciers: everything is subject to more or less subtle transformations that are not external threats but rather the very conditions of continuity. Fragility makes us attentive to becoming rather than being.

The concept also sensitizes us to the importance of *minute practices and tiny gestures*. Such subtle and adjusted moves are depicted by Max Liboiron, who highlights the "contamination chores" at play at the Civic Laboratory for Environmental Action Research (CLEAR). In this laboratory, the size of the plastic pollution that is scrutinized amounts to one of dust. This means that any practitioner, hence any visitor, can potentially bring, through their shoes, clothes, hair, and belongings, other microplastics than the ones under scientific scrutiny at the workbench. To avoid such potential contamination, and the unexpected bias or inaccuracy of experiments, gestures need to be performed in an extremely controlled manner: from the ways in which certain things are touched, certain clothes are worn, certain movements are accomplished, to the way one breathes. Tiny gestures are also key in Marisol de la

Cadena and Santiago Martínez Medina's analysis of the artificial insemination of cattle. The broad bio-capitalist enterprise of genetically assisted reproduction of cows and bulls relies on the meticulousness of specific operations that are accomplished at extremely precise moments. For instance, identifying the static posture of a cow that indicates she is in heat is a matter of three seconds. While this delicate act requires continuous surveillance and thus a trained eye, it also calls for regular tactile and olfactive contact with the herd in order to acknowledge each individual's singularities, and more specifically each cow's "estrous cycle and her readiness for insemination." Similarly, the collection of semen from the most genetically prolific bulls involves a choreography of small gestures by the bull in full excitement and by three humans watching for the appropriate moment to introduce the electro-ejaculator, calibrate and activate the electric charge, and collect its reproductive substance. As Marisol de la Cadena and Santiago Martínez Medina demonstrate, other subtle practices are also performed to prevent the fragility related to insemination and embryo transfer. Combining focused attention with technical precision, associating exploratory phases with moments of diagnosis or confirmation, dealing with a plurality of entities—these small gestures, sometimes furtive, are largely unnoticed. However, if they emerge in most care and maintenance situations, it is because, beyond their insignificant appearance, they cultivate as they are repeated the routine fabric of the concern for the beings' fragility.

A third sensitizing operation makes *the collectives* involved in each configuration more salient. Although these groups of people (with their instruments, rules, skills, tricks of the trade, etc.) participate in the existence of fragile entities in various manners, they may be rendered invisible for diverse organizational or political purposes. As a sensitizing concept, fragility allows their presence and importance to be underlined. The driving forces of the restored, and then amplified, sovereignty of Louis XIV described in Chandra Mukerji's chapter is particularly telling in this respect. Mukerji indeed insists on the "mindful hands" of the royal fleet to underline how much, despite their geographical and social distances, they actively contributed to the influence of the Sun King. Located in Rochefort, outside the circles of power, the group of craftsmen recruited by Colbert was a combination of various expertise, which, through construction methods and craft techniques, progressively resulted in ships of unequaled stature. In order for the royal power to manifest itself publicly with all its magnitude, however, the mindful hands had to be kept invisible. In this way, unimpaired by the laborious work of the material, royal sovereignty could appear firmly established "as a product of impersonal forces."

The conceptual use of fragility also puts at the forefront the *working conditions* at play in numerous situations where fragilities need to be taken care of. The sensitizing operation here makes us pay attention to the very fragility of those who care for fragile entities. This is the main theme of Thomas Cousins's chapter studying the laboring bodies on the timber plantations in South Africa. If the exploitation of the plantations comes along with gestures directed toward the wood, it also demands a lot from the body of the women workers. These bodies, Cousins insists, are taken care of both by the private companies that have developed a specific nutrition program and by the people themselves through vernacular curative practices. In a postcolonial context, affected by poverty and the AIDS epidemic, the challenge is to "contend with a range of forces that splinter the effort to remain human." Although working conditions are exacerbated in such a context, their demanding and sometimes devastating nature is common to other maintenance and care situations, in which bodies struggle, wear out, and become damaged while dealing with material fragility (Gregson, 2011; Rifat et al., 2019). Put differently, the relational dimension of fragility is twofold: it concerns things and beings that are considered fragile by the ones who accompany them (or sometimes dismiss them), and it also reveals reciprocated fragilities, which are shared between these various entities and the people who care for them.

Following that path, we would like to emphasize a last sensitizing process, which refers to *the interdependencies* that are brought to the forefront by the concept of fragility. In her examination of the act of eating healthy food, Annemarie Mol gradually brings to light the different networks to which such food (e.g., sugar-free peanut butter) is connected (from the supermarket employees, the truck drivers carrying foods around, the workers in bakeries and peanut butter factories, to the farmers and farmhands who grow crops), the various entities and species involved (human beings, animals, plants, fruits, grains, food markets, agriculture systems, greenhouse gas emission, etc.), the multiplication of potential fragilities generated by these relationships, and the "kind of wholesomeness that's been lost through . . . commodification," as Lucy Suchman puts it in her comments. As already mentioned, by centering her study on the fragility of ice, Cymene Howe also highlights the variety of beings that make up the ecological environment of a glacier, whose manifestations are revealed in all their ambivalence. Similarly, the activities devoted to cultivating continuity between the fragments studied by Tomás Sánchez Criado and Vincent Duclos open up to the diversity of solidarities arranged between a multitude of actors. These different cases point, each in their own way, to what Marisol de la Cadena and Santiago Martínez Medina call "relations of mutuality" that are built up between beings involved in the same configuration, composing an *agencement* (Deleuze & Guattari, 1987).

As a sensitizing concept, fragility has thus at least two virtues. On the one hand, it makes us sensible to aspects of reality that remain in the background, generally because they are considered secondary and do not count in master narratives. Fragility participates in the densification of accounts by acknowledging the manifestation of unexpected beings and unnoticed relations. In this sense, fragility helps to enrich the "repopulated" descriptions of early actor–network theory (Latour, 1988) by taking into account not only the more successful and powerful actants but also the less heroic ones (Star, 1991). On the other hand, such a thickening operation paves the way for an ecological approach of care (Domínguez Rubio, 2016)—an "ecological thinking" (Puig de la Bellacasa, 2016) that refuses to reduce beings to supposedly substantial properties but rather invites us to grasp their qualities as relational effects. No object or living being is fragile in itself. What matters is when, why, and by whom it is considered and treated as fragile: through which mode of attention, by which gestures and instruments, according to which collectives, in which situation, and among which interdependencies.

PROVOCATIVE

To advocate the relevance of examining what concepts do and make do—rather than what they mean—amounts to questioning the performativity of language in scholarly practice. This has been an ongoing issue, notably in actor–network theory, since Michel Callon, among others, has investigated the performativity of concepts and formulas in economics (Callon, 1998; Callon et al., 2007). This has been an even more pressing concern in feminist technoscience studies, whose authors constantly sought to question not only the conditions of production of their own statements but also the types of realities that these statements contributed to performing (Haraway, 1996; Stengers, 1997). These feminist works remind us that "our" accounts in social sciences, as well as in science and technology studies (STS) obviously, cannot be transparent in any way. As performances, they are intrinsically "non-innocent" (Haraway, 1988). Trying to understand and be aware of what the concepts we use "do" is one of the means that can be used to question this non-innocence head on.

That said, the concept of fragility and the relationship the chapters in this volume bear to it invite us to unfold further the very idea of performativity. Too simple a version of it, indeed, tends to flatten the forms of textual agency, especially when it comes to questioning the power of academic accounts. Judith Butler's (1997) work provides a valuable resource to accomplish such unfolding and understand more deeply how concepts can *act*. Going back to John Austin's (1962) original reflections, Butler reminds us that the author of *How to Do Things with Words* made an important distinction between performative utterances. Austin, indeed, characterizes two different kinds of speech acts, or rather two ways for speech units to gain agency: an illocutionary dimension and a perlocutionary one. Illocution describes the fact that some speech acts are able to bring certain realities to existence at the very moment they are accomplished. This is the best-known aspect of Austin's analysis and what is generally discussed in STS when scholars evoke the performativity of language and, more generally, the world-making abilities of certain assemblages of words, practices, and technology. This is also more or less what we did in the previous section, when we insisted that the concept of fragility participates in bringing about dimensions of reality that were hitherto silent and remained unnoticed in the background of most situations. As a sensitizing concept, fragility helps us to make parts of the world that did not matter exist; it renders them both seeable and thinkable.

Butler invites STS scholars to expand their exploration of performativity in taking into account the other aspect of speech acts as detailed by Austin: perlocution. For Austin, certain speech acts are perlocutionary in the sense that they have consequences. The agency of language here is not observed through its capacity to perform certain realities as words are pronounced or written but rather through the effects they produce, which may occur far from the place and long after the moment when the concerned utterance was articulated. Reinscribed in the realm of social sciences, this aspect of performativity is quite difficult to address. Questioning the effects that the use of a concept may trigger is a particularly delicate matter. Regarding fragility especially, we think this is a crucial and necessary endeavor though.

And even if the possible repercussions of the concept are not systematically addressed throughout this volume, the question haunts most of its chapters. Actually, this is probably one of the main interests of the word "fragility" itself: it cannot be used for its sensitizing properties only. Fragility calls for being carefully manipulated as a *provocative* word—a word whose use has tremendous perlocutionary potentialities.

But what does it mean exactly to question the perlocutionary aspects of a concept, or even simply to call for being aware of them? What does it take to address this dimension of academic accounts agency? And why does fragility especially call for such questioning?

A way to give a provisional answer to these questions is to consider that the perlocutionary dimension implies situating the agency of concepts, and more generally scientific accounts, at ground level, which means that we should not only ask what a notion such as fragility does "in itself" but also pay attention and question what we, as scholars and citizens, do to it or, more exactly, what we do *with* it. Yet, several subtleties should be taken into consideration in this movement. First, paying attention to the perlocutionary dimension of speech acts expands the problem of agency beyond the realm of intentions and control. The problem is thus not only what we *intend* to do with fragility but also what we actually do with it—that is, what kind of consequences its use generates, whether we want it or not. This means—and this is the second subtlety—that such a question leads to another one, crucial in Butler's reading of Austin: while asking, "What do we do with fragility?" we should systematically add "to whom and/or to what?" This is the only way of taking the issue of consequences and repercussions seriously. Examining performativity in perlocutionary terms implies paying attention to the beings who may be, or concretely are, affected by our accounts. Finally, this also means that "we" here is anything but an indeterminate plural form aimed at erasing all traces of enunciators. The perlocutionary side of performativity raises difficult, but essential, questions regarding responsibility, both in the most straightforward definition of the term (Latour, 2004) and in its more "Harawayian" sense as response-ability (Haraway, 2008; Puig de la Bellacasa, 2017). The intrinsic relationality of the concept of fragility obliges everyone who uses it to be explicit about who they are and where they speak from.

These three points, these "subtleties," are addressed in more or less explicit terms in every chapter of this volume. Each author, indeed, proves to be precautionary, sometimes even worried, about what they end up doing *of* and *with* fragility. Their texts bear witness, in their own way, to the responsibilities that the use of the notion implies, way beyond the sole academic perimeter. This is also a prominent concern in the reactions of the discussants, who, as first readers of the chapters, have accepted to be affected by the concept and to share their thoughts and reactions. Such considerations are highlighted by the very diversity of uses of the notion encountered throughout this collection, which, far from simply illustrating various "interpretations," demonstrates different ways of working with the concept of fragility. Highlighting the fragile network of "mindful hands" that participates in performing Louis XIV's power (Mukerji) is obviously not the same as exploring the fragility of multiply disabled children (Winance). These are different descriptive and analytical gestures that not only bring certain realities into existence but also have effects on their objects and subjects: the multiplication of power sites, on one side, the re-qualification of children recalcitrance and resistance, on the other. Likewise, highlighting the unsettling fragility of a "powerful" glacier (Howe) differs greatly from exploring the connected, uneven, and situated affections through which "goods-in-tension" are accommodated (Mol).

Acknowledging that fragility is a provocative concept opens the way to a twofold concern. The first one consists in not clearing oneself of the possible harmful consequences of the provocation. The disruptive and negative effects of language are the starting point of Butler's reflection and of her invitation to take into consideration the perlocutionary dimension of speech acts. It is crucial to be aware that, in certain configurations, describing something or someone as "fragile" amounts for them "to be called a name" (Butler, 1997). In this volume, it is particularly explicit in Liboiron's chapter, in which they explain why fragility should not be used to describe the contamination chores in the CLEAR lab. It is to their standpoint a pejorative notion—a term that is uttered only from "outside" and which reflects a misunderstanding at best when not outright belittlement. To put it another way, no one can use the term "fragility" gratuitously and apply it as a universal framework for analysis. While being wary of potential destructive consequences, the second concern consists therefore in finding ways to cultivate the generative effects of the concept. If most authors of this volume, including us, are attached to the term, it is not because it can be used as a lens that mechanically and universally makes us sensible of unnoticed dimensions of sociomaterial reality but rather because we think it can contribute, for specific situations, to shaping forms of accurate, fair, and careful considerations or "qualifications," to use a term Winance borrows from Marielle Macé (2017).

Claiming the use of a possibly stigmatizing term such as fragility in academic texts is, of course, not really comparable to what Butler calls the counter-appropriation of insulting words. It is much less risky and therefore takes much less courage. Yet, there is a kind of "resignificance" (Butler, 1997) at play in the way fragility is used in this volume, in the sense that the chapters try to turn the pejorative bearing of the word into a new strength. This is, for instance, what Cousins does in articulating fragility with the idea of incompleteness, or what is at play in Duclos and Sánchez Criado's proposition to reconsider fragmentation processes. This is also what Winance proposes when she demonstrates how fragility and resistance are articulated in care relationships. As Butler explains, these attempts to reclaim a term and reinvent its use teaches us a lot about how performativity actually works: less in speech acts isolated from one another and encapsulated in a circumscribed moment than through the ongoing constitution of a weft of uses, "a ritual chain of resignifications whose origin and end remain unfixed and unfixable" (Butler, 1997, p. 14). The speech act is thus always embedded in a historical thickness and takes the form of "a certain nexus of temporal horizons" (Butler, 1997, p. 14). This means that the use of a concept such as fragility cannot be reduced to intrinsic or structural qualities. It is always situated, not only in space, as enunciated from a certain standpoint, but also in time, as responding to previous uses and meant to renew both description and critique. In this sense, it would be vain to pretend that this volume and the analyses it carries will have the same scope and will produce the same effects in a few years' time. Fragility is a word for these times—a tenuous counterproposal to the obsessions for robustness, dramatic disruption or apocalyptic catastrophe, and a companion to repair, maintenance, and care.

"Whereas illocutionary performatives produce ontological effects (bringing something into 'being'), perlocutionary performatives alter an ongoing situation" (Butler, 2010, p. 151). To fully embrace the situatedness of a concept such as fragility and to acknowledge its perlocutionary dimension, it is important to identify the situation we're starting from when using it: What exactly do we want to alter? What "technoscience agendas" do the accounts and stories we shape with fragility seek to "erode"? (Law & Singleton, 2000,

p. 767). Beyond sensitizing concerns, what kind of difference do we attempt to make with fragility? Among the situations that are altered in the chapters of this volume, we can highlight at least two major ones. The first one points to what Steve Jackson describes as "overstating the (self-)efficacy of power" in his comments. The concept of fragility indeed offers a way to de-essentialize descriptions of power, emphasizing the uncertainty, heterogeneity, and instability of processes that lead to asymmetries and generate inequities. What is altered here, though, is not so much the situations of power themselves than the premises of their critique. As Jackson explains, acknowledging the fragilities of power decenters the accounts assuming that power is inherently stable and monolithic and opens up new horizons for critics by identifying "inflection points" that may be more effective, actionable, and pertinent in terms of political strategy.

The second "situation" that is altered by the different uses of the concept of fragility in this volume may be found in every account that puts forward disruption and even catastrophe. Fragility is a shared, mundane, and relational condition. Its recognition liberates the eye from the exciting and intoxicating attire of the apocalypse. It helps to turn away from the fascination for clearly identified events and marked rupture so as to explore the generative subtle oscillations of the ordinary (Denis & Pontille, 2023). In this sense, fragility contrasts greatly with the apparently closely related—and rather hegemonic—notion of resilience. The latter, which populates uncountable narratives from the media to academic literature, describes the capacity to withstand shocks, the ability to "bounce back" after a disruption. Resilience emphasizes the adverse event and the (too often individual) response to it. Discontinuity is at its core. Rather than dramatic crisis and heroic resistance, fragility points toward the "modest possibilities of partial recuperation and getting on together" (Haraway, 2016, p. 10). Fragility is thus a matter of continuity—unsteady continuity, wobbly, restless, multiple, and constantly in motion, but continuity nevertheless.

TROUBLING

Fragility does anything therefore but simplify our understandings of things or clarify our perception of phenomena. It is not one of these terms that functions as a box, or a suitcase, in which one could place pieces of reality in order to carry them easily from one reasoning space to another. It's the very opposite. As a sensitizing concept, fragility is an instrument of irreduction (Latour, 1988), an operator for thickening descriptions. As a provocative concept, it generates an imbalance, a tension even. As Puig de la Bellacasa evokes in her comments, "engaging with fragility should never be easy."

Resisting reductionism and cultivating discomfort are two crucial perceptual, affective, and conceptual operations that thinking with fragility helps to carry out. Thus, as a situated, relational, and ambiguous concept, fragility allows us to "stay with the trouble" (Haraway, 2016). It is as much sensitizing and provocative as it is *troubling*. This dimension of what fragility does is particularly important when the concept is associated with repair, maintenance, and care, as it is in this collection. There is, indeed, a serious risk of romanticizing these practices as if they were intrinsically good and fair. As Murphy highlighted, care needs to be unsettled in order to escape reification and conservatism and to avoid the erasing of "its entanglements in histories of persistent racism, class privilege, [and] colonialism" (2015, p. 719). This is a pressing issue nowadays, as care, while gaining incredible popularity, tends to be promoted as a universal solution to problems that it participates in oversimplifying and depoliticizing. By contrast, to trouble and unsettle care is a way to resist the "lure of restorative fantasies" (Duclos & Criado, 2020, p. 154). The chapters in this collection demonstrate how thinking with fragility can help to carry out "the hard and imperfect work" (Murphy, 2015, p. 732) of such unsettling.

Fragility also troubles the anthropocentrism that a too narrow idea of care may convey. As a shared and situated condition, fragility shapes precious connections not only through species but also between living beings and things, acknowledging the liveliness of matter beyond the scope of agency (Ingold, 2013). In that sense, it also draws paths to "make oddkin" (Haraway, 2016) and assembles sociomaterial *agencements* on account of their instabilities and transformations rather than their alleged sturdiness and inertia. This is especially striking in Howe's chapter in which fragility connects people and ice, and its reckoning more generally invites us to notice, "in the continuum of living and dying, the shared fate of both humans and nonhumans." This is also crucial in Cousin's text, which navigates the ambiguity of the responses to fragility from the hot cooked meals in the plantations to the popular curative substances used by workers. The troubling operation of both chapters lies in their ability, while following fragilities, to circulate from things to people and other living beings without falling into a mere indifferentiation.

Such an invitation to trouble comes with a catch though. As our detour through Butler's reflections on performativity reminded us, the troubling qualities of fragility cannot be separated from its call for response-ability, the way it *obliges* the ones who use it (Stengers, 2010). This is what Puig de la Bellacasa insists on in her concluding remarks: "an argument for fragility is generating an involvement." The most important obligation transpiring from the texts in this collection is to be found in the generative properties of fragility. As troubling as it may be, thinking with fragility does not lead to paralysis or infinite oscillations. On the contrary, it unfolds the present and its openness and allows us to connect aspects of the past with possible futures that call for action. Thinking with fragility obliges us to acknowledge such openness—more, to nurture it. It is through such engagement that we may address Butler's (2010) concerns and warnings, creating *from* and *with* fragility generative forms of name calling that diffract and reverse the situations in which people are simply called a name.

To put a provisional end to this discussion, let's turn to Antoine Hennion, with whom we both organized a seminar called "Maintaining/sustaining: Fragility as a mode of existence" a few years ago. In his notes, published afterward in the journal *Pragmata*, he summarizes:

> A pragmatics of fragilities, of these places, these entities, these moments, these present situations calling for a response . . . , will only make sense if it is at once an ethic of the situation, a technique of attention, and a capacity to act (or not to act). (Hennion, 2019, p. 495, *our translation*)

So, what does fragility do? Fragility is a matter of ambivalence, of uneasiness, including that of academic accounts. As a concept, it thus calls for *response-ability* (Haraway, 2008). But fragility is also a matter of becoming. As Geof Bowker highlights in his comments, fragility helps us to turn words into verbs and fully recognize the incompleteness of all things. It invites us to acknowledge the openness and unknown resonances of life. Instead of the artificial comfort of clarity, univocity, and reductions, fragility embraces, and even feeds, the trouble. Fragility obliges us to reshape collectives and to constantly question what/who is rendered visible, what/who is made absent, in order to reveal what is considered normal, what is deemed strong, stable, and immobile. But rather than being paralyzed by these questions and hindered by these concerns, fragility obliges us to turn them into *matters of care* (Puig de la Bellacasa, 2017) and carefully go on and on.

REFERENCES

Austin, J. L. (1962). *How to do things with words*. Oxford University Press.

Barad, K. (2007). *Meeting the universe halfway: Quantum physics and the entanglement of matter and meaning*. Duke University Press.

Blumer, H. (1954). What is wrong with social theory? *American Sociological Review, 19*(1), 3–10.

Butler, J. (1997). *Excitable speech: A politics of the performative*. Routledge.

Butler, J. (2010). Performative agency. *Journal of Cultural Economy, 3*(2), 147–161.

Callon, M. (Ed.). (1998). *The laws of the markets*. Blackwell.

Callon, M., Millo, Y., & Muniesa, F. (Eds.). (2007). *Market devices*. Blackwell.

Deleuze, G., & Guattari, F. (1987). *A thousand plateaus: Capitalism and schizophrenia* (2nd ed.). University of Minnesota Press.

Deleuze, G., & Guattari, F. (1994). *What is philosophy?* Columbia University Press.

Denis, J., & Pontille, D. (2021). Maintenance epistemology and public order: Removing graffiti in Paris. *Social Studies of Science, 51*(2), 233–258.

Denis, J., & Pontille, D. (2023). Before breakdown, after repair: The art of maintenance. In A. Mica, M. Pawlak, A. Horolets, & P. Kubicki (Eds.), *Routledge international handbook of failure* (pp. 209–222). Routledge.

Domínguez Rubio, F. (2016). On the discrepancy between objects and things: An ecological approach. *Journal of Material Culture, 21*(1), 59–86.

Duclos, V., & Criado, T. S. (2020). Care in trouble: Ecologies of support from below and beyond. *Medical Anthropology Quarterly, 34*(2), 153–173.

Gregson, N. (2011). Performativity, corporeality and the politics of ship disposal. *Journal of Cultural Economy, 4*(2), 137–156.

Haraway, D. J. (1988). Situated knowledges: The science question in feminism and the privilege of partial perspective. *Feminist studies, 14*(3), 575–599.

Haraway, D. J. (1996). Modest witness: Feminist diffractions in science studies. In P. Galison & D. J. Stump (Eds.), *The disunity of science: Boundaries, contexts, and power* (pp. 428–441). Stanford University Press.

Haraway, D. J. (2008). *When species meet*. University of Minnesota Press.

Haraway, D. J. (2016). *Staying with the trouble: Making kin in the Chthulucene*. Duke University Press.

Hennion, A. (2019). "Maintenir/soutenir: De la fragilité comme mode d'existence," Séminaire de recherche du Centre de sociologie de l'innovation (CSI), 2017–2019. *Pragmata, 2*, 484–500.

Ingold, T. (2013). *Making: Anthropology, archaeology, art and architecture*. Routledge.

Jackson, S. J. (2014). Rethinking repair. In T. Gillespie, P. Boczkowski, & K. Foot (Eds.), *Media technologies: Essays on communication, materiality and society* (pp. 221–240). MIT Press.

Latour, B. (1988). *The pasteurization of France*. Harvard University Press.

Latour, B. (2004). Why has critique run out of steam? From matters of fact to matters of concern. *Critical Inquiry, 30*(2), 225–248.

Law, J., & Singleton, V. (2000). Performing technology's stories: On social constructivism, performance, and performativity. *Technology and Culture, 41*(4), 765–775.

Macé, M. (2017). *Sidérer, considérer: Migrants en France*. Verdier.

Murphy, M. (2015). Unsettling care: Troubling transnational itineraries of care in feminist health practices. *Social Studies of Science, 45*(5), 717–737.

Puig de la Bellacasa, M. (2016). Ecological thinking, material spirituality, and the poetics of infrastructure. In G. C. Bowker, S. Timmermans, A. E. Clarke, & E. Balka (Eds.), *Boundary objects and beyond: Working with Leigh Star* (pp. 47–68). MIT Press.

Puig de la Bellacasa, M. (2017). *Matters of care: Speculative ethics in more than human worlds*. University of Minnesota Press.

Rifat, M. R., Prottoy, H. M., & Ahmed, S. I. (2019). The breaking hand: Skills, care, and sufferings of the hands of an electronic waste worker in Bangladesh. In *Proceedings of the 2019 CHI Conference on Human Factors in Computing Systems—CHI '19* (pp. 1–14). ACM.

Star, S. L. (1991). Power, technology and the phenomenology of conventions: On being allergic to onions. In J. Law (Ed.), *A sociology of monsters? Essays on power, technology and domination* (pp. 26–56). Routledge.

Stengers, I. (1997). *Power and invention: Situating science*. University of Minnesota Press.

Stengers, I. (2010). *Cosmopolitics* (Vol. 1). University of Minnesota Press.

CONTRIBUTORS

Geoffrey C. Bowker is Emeritus Donald Bren Chair at the School of Information and Computer Sciences, University of California at Irvine. Together with Leigh Star he wrote *Sorting Things Out: Classification and its Consequences* (MIT Press, 1999); his most recent books are Memory Practices in the Sciences (MIT Press, 2005) and (with Stefan Timmermans, Adele Clarke and Ellen Balka) the edited collection: *Boundary Objects and Beyond: Working with Leigh Star* (MIT Press, 2015). He is currently working on time and computing under the rubric 'life at the femtosecond'.

Thomas Cousins is Clarendon-Lienhardt associate professor in the Social Anthropology of Africa at the University of Oxford and Fellow of St. Hugh's College. Having grown up in three southern African countries, he studied at the University of Cape Town, completed a PhD at Johns Hopkins University in 2012, taught in the Department of Sociology and Social Anthropology at Stellenbosch University until 2017, and now teaches in the School of Anthropology and Museum Ethnography, Oxford. His research attends to the everyday and how health and illness are configured, mediated, and absorbed in postcolonial Africa. He has written on HIV, hunger, global health, information technology, zoonosis, kinship, and sexuality. He continues to examine the entanglements of biography and biology in postcolonial South Africa, where questions of repair concatenate across many domains of life.

Tomás Sánchez Criado is Ramón y Cajal Senior Research Fellow at the Open University of Catalonia's CareNet-IN3 group. His ethnographic and public engagement work focuses on different instances of relational knowledge and material politics in a wide variety of settings where care is invoked as a mode of intervention, be it as a practice of articulating more or less enduring ecologies of support or as a particular mode of technoscientific activism democratizing knowledges, design practice and infrastructures. info: www.tscriado.org, @tscriado.

Marisol de la Cadena, became an anthropologist in Peru, England, France and USA. She is a professor in the STS and Anthropology departments at UC Davis. Her most recent book is *Earth Beings. Ecologies of Practice Across Andean Worlds* (Duke University Press, 2015) for which she co-labored with Mariano and Nazario Turpo, Andean *runakuna* from Cuzco. She co-edited (with Mario Blaser) *A World of Many Worlds* (Duke University Press, 2018.) Currently she works on what she calls 'labscaped cows, cow-formed landscapes" in Colombia.

Jérôme Denis is a professor of science and technology studies at Mines Paris and director of the Center for Sociology of Innovation. He studies invisible data work in various organizations and explores the variety of maintenance practices and policies, mainly in urban settings.

Fernando Domínguez Rubio is an associate professor, Department of Communication, UCSD. His work is located around the outer rims of sociology, science and technology studies, anthropology, art, design, and architecture. His book, *Still Life: Ecologies of the Modern Imagination at the Art Museum* (University of Chicago Press, 2020), develops an ecological approach to the work of care and repair required to keep artworks alive. He was the 2021 winner of Mary the Douglas Prize and the 2021 winner of the Annual Book Award of the Association for the Study of the Arts of the Present (ASAP), and he also received an honorary mention for the 2021 Robert K. Merton Award of the American Sociological Association.

Vincent Duclos is associate professor in the Département de Communication Sociale et Publique at the Université du Québec à Montréal. His ethnographic work focuses on global capitalism, digital technology, and medicine—and the many ways that they are increasingly entangled. He is preparing a book about the Pan-African e-Network, and he also works on global health modeling and standardization during and beyond the SARS-CoV-2 pandemic.

Cymene Howe is professor of anthropology and the founding co-director of the Science and Technology Studies Program at Rice University. Her books include *Intimate Activism* (Duke University Press, 2013); *Ecologics: Wind and Power in the Anthropocene* (Duke University Press, 2019); and the co-edited collections *Anthropocene Unseen: A Lexicon* (Punctum, 2020), *Solarities: Elemental Encounters and Refractions* (Punctum, 2023), and *The Johns Hopkins Guide to Critical and Cultural Theory* (John Hopkins University, Press, 2022). Her research has been funded by the National Science Foundation, the Fulbright Commission, and the Andrew W. Mellon Foundation, and she was awarded the Berlin Prize for transatlantic dialogue in the arts, humanities, and public policy. Her current research examines the changing dynamics between people and bodies of ice in the Arctic region and sea level adaptation in coastal cities around the world. From her research in the Arctic region, she created the documentary film *Not Ok: A Little Movie about a Small Glacier at the End of the World* (2019) and initiated the memorial for Okjökull, the world's first funeral for a glacier fallen to climate change.

Steve Jackson is a professor of information science and science and technology studies (STS) at Cornell University. His work combines ethnographic and theoretical traditions from pragmatism, critical theory, and STS to study how people build and maintain order, value, and meaning in and with the worlds around them. He is especially interested in places where new computing practices meet social and material worlds, with implications for sustainability, collaboration, and inequality. He has written extensively on problems of infrastructure, maintenance, repair, and hope. His most recent venture is the Computing On Earth Lab, an experimental collaboration that brings together social scientists, humanists, artists, and engineers to rethink the material and planetary foundations of computing.

Max Liboiron is a professor in geography at Memorial University, where they direct the Civic Laboratory for Environmental Action Research (CLEAR). CLEAR develops feminist and anticolonial methodologies to study marine plastic pollution. Liboiron is author of *Pollution is Colonialism* (Duke University Press, 2021) and co-author of *Discard Studies: Systems, Wasting, and Power* (MIT Press, 2022).

Santiago Martínez Medina is a physician from the Universidad Nacional de Colombia and has a PhD in anthropology from the Universidad de los Andes, Bogotá. His current field of inquiry is at the interface between anthropology, science and technology studies, environmental humanities, and multispecies studies. His ethnographic work articulates diverse empirical scenarios based on the relationships between practices, knowledge, and bodies. In *Anatomización. Una disección etnográfica de los cuerpos*, his last book, he develops an ethnographic analysis of how the anatomical body is made in the medical school and its ontological, epistemic, and political implications in the face of other possible presences within the bodies.

Annemarie Mol is professor of anthropology of the body at the Amsterdam Institute for Social Science Research. She is the author of *The Body Multiple: Ontology in Medical Practice* (Duke University, 2013); *The Logic of Care* (Routledge 2008); *Eating in Theory* (Duke University Press, 2021) and *Eating is an English Word* (Duke University Press, 2024). She is also a co-editor of *Complexities: Social Studies of Knowledge Practices* Duke University Press, 2002); *Care in Practice: Tinkering in Clinics, Homes and Farms* (Columbia University Press, 2010) and *On Other Terms: Interfering in Social Science English* (Sage, 2020). After having worked on health care, bodies, topologies, translation, and what it is to eat, she currently studies, with a spirited team, valuing practices related to the complex good of "clean" in urban spaces, households, wastewater treatment plants, and the sciences.

Chandra Mukerji is distinguished professor emerita of communication and science studies at the University of California, San Diego, and Chercheuse Correspondante, Institut Marcel Mauss, Paris. She has written extensively on landscapes and the social mobilization of inarticulate, material forms of culture, and she has written on war as a material communication. She is currently studying artisanal conceptions of the sovereign under Louis XIV, looking at the Sun King figure in the gardens of Versailles as organizing a vision of sovereign possibility. She was co-recipient in 2012 of the Distinguished Book Award for *Impossible Engineering* (Princeton University Press, 2015), the highest award given a book by the American Sociological Association. She also received the Mary Douglas Prize in 1998 for *Territorial Ambitions and the Gardens of Versailles* (Cambridge University Press, 1997) and the Robert K. Merton Award in 1991 for *A Fragile Power* (Princeton University Press, 2016).

David Pontille is senior research at the French National Center for Scientific Research and member of the Center for the Sociology of Innovation, Paris, France. His work is organized around three themes: writing practices, technologies for evaluating scientific research, and maintenance activities in different professional environments.

María Puig de la Bellacasa works at the History of Consciousness Department, UCSC. Her book *Matters of Care. Speculative Ethics in More than Human Worlds* (Minnesota University Press, 2017) connects debates on more than human ontologies and ecological practices to a feminist materialist tradition of critical thinking on care, participating to the contemporary reframings of the ethics and politics of care across disciplines. She is also a co-editor of the volume *Ecological Reparation: Repair, Remediation and Resurgence in Social and Environmental Conflict* (Bristol University Press, 2023), which engages with ways of dealing with social and environmental degradation while creating and maintaining livable and just worlds, and of *Reactivating Elements. Chemistry, Ecology, Practice* (Duke University Press, 2021). She is currently working on a book on human–soil relations, *When the Name for World Is Soil*, which explores ongoing transformations in ecological cultures and connects practices and narratives in scientific knowing, social and community movements, and art interventions through the ways they may advance transformative ethics, politics, and justice in troubled naturecultural worlds.

Lucy Suchman is professor emerita of the anthropology of science and technology at Lancaster University, UK. Before taking up that post, she was a principal scientist at Xerox's Palo Alto Research Center (PARC), where she spent twenty years as a researcher. Her current research extends her long-standing critical engagement with the fields of artificial intelligence and human–computer interaction to the domain of contemporary militarism. She is concerned with the question of whose bodies are incorporated into military systems, how, and with what consequences for social justice and the possibility for a less violent world. Lucy is the author of *Human–Machine Reconfigurations* (Cambridge University Press, 2007). Recent publications include "The Uncontroversial 'Thingness' of AI," *Big Data & Society*, 10(2) (2023); "Imaginaries of omniscience: Automating intelligence in the US Department of Defense," *Social Studies of Science*, 53(5) (2023), 761–786; and "Algorithmic Warfare and the Reinvention of Accuracy," *Critical Studies on Security*, 8(2) (2020), 175–187.

Myriam Winance is a sociologist at CERMES3, INSERM. Her research focuses on the issue of disability. Her objective is to analyze the way this notion is defined in our society through policies and institutional facilities, on the one hand, and through the practices and experiences of people, on the other. Her research combines a socio-history of disability policy, the sociology of health and the sciences, and technology studies. They examine notions of care, of the person, of the body, and of disability. Initially, she was interested in the question of "prostheses" and the evolution of disability policies. Her recent research has been on the history and daily life of people living with several impairments in two studies: (1) the emergence of new categories in French policies to name those people; (2) the making of ordinary life by families, one of whose members has multiple disabilities. In relation to these research activities, she is developing methodological thinking concerning qualitative research in the field of health. She is interested in the question of interdisciplinarity and that of participative research. She explores the different forms of research by examining the political and scientific pertinence of each one.

INDEX

Page numbers followed by an *f* denote a figure.

Infrastructures Series

Edited by Paul N. Edwards and Janet Vertesi

Paul N. Edwards, *A Vast Machine: Computer Models, Climate Data, and the Politics of Global Warming*

Lawrence M. Busch, *Standards: Recipes for Reality*

Lisa Gitelman, ed., *"Raw Data" Is an Oxymoron*

Finn Brunton, *Spam: A Shadow History of the Internet*

Nil Disco and Eda Kranakis, eds., *Cosmopolitan Commons: Sharing Resources and Risks across Borders*

Casper Bruun Jensen and Brit Ross Winthereik, *Monitoring Movements in Development Aid: Recursive Partnerships and Infrastructures*

James Leach and Lee Wilson, eds., *Subversion, Conversion, Development: Cross-Cultural Knowledge Exchange and the Politics of Design*

Olga Kuchinskaya, *The Politics of Invisibility: Public Knowledge about Radiation Health Effects after Chernobyl*

Ashley Carse, *Beyond the Big Ditch: Politics, Ecology, and Infrastructure at the Panama Canal*

Alexander Klose, translated by Charles Marcrum II, *The Container Principle: How a Box Changes the Way We Think*

Eric T. Meyer and Ralph Schroeder, *Knowledge Machines: Digital Transformations of the Sciences and Humanities*

Geoffrey C. Bowker, Stefan Timmermans, Adele E. Clarke, and Ellen Balka, eds., *Boundary Objects and Beyond: Working with Leigh Star*

Clifford Siskin, *System: The Shaping of Modern Knowledge*

Lawrence Busch, *Knowledge for Sale: The Neoliberal Takeover of Higher Education*

Bill Maurer and Lana Swartz, *Paid: Tales of Dongles, Checks, and Other Money Stuff*

Katayoun Shafiee, *Machineries of Oil: An Infrastructural History of BP in Iran*

Megan Finn, *Documenting Aftermath: Information Infrastructures in the Wake of Disasters*

Ann M. Pendleton-Jullian and John Seely Brown, *Design Unbound: Designing for Emergence in a White Water World*, Volume 1: *Designing for Emergence*

Ann M. Pendleton-Jullian and John Seely Brown, *Design Unbound: Designing for Emergence in a White Water World*, Volume 2: *Ecologies of Change*

Jordan Frith, *A Billion Little Pieces: RFID and Infrastructures of Identification*

Morgan G. Ames, *The Charisma Machine: The Life, Death, and Legacy of One Laptop per Child*

Ryan Ellis, *Letters, Power Lines, and Other Dangerous Things: The Politics of Infrastructure Security*

Mario Biagioli and Alexandra Lippman, eds., *Gaming the Metrics: Misconduct and Manipulation in Academic Research*

Malcolm McCullough, *Downtime on the Microgrid: Architecture, Electricity, and Smart City Islands*

Emmanuel Didier, translated by Priya Vari Sen, *America by the Numbers: Quantification, Democracy, and the Birth of National Statistics*

Andrés Luque-Ayala and Simon Marvin, *Urban Operating Systems; Producing the Computational City*

Michael Truscello, *Infrastructural Brutalism: Art and the Necropolitics of Infrastructure*

Christopher R. Henke and Benjamin Sims, *Repairing Infrastructures: The Maintenance of Materiality and Power*

Stefan Höhne, *New York City Subway: The Invention of the Urban Passenger*

Timothy Moss, *Conduits of Berlin: Remaking the City through Infrastructure, 1920–2020*

Claude Rosental, translated by Catherine Porter, *The Demonstration Society*

Blake Atwood, *Underground: The Secret Life of Videocassettes in Iran*

Huub Dijstelbloem, *Borders as Infrastructure: The Technopolitics of Border Control*

Dylan Mulvin, *Proxies: Standards and their Media*

Eric Monteiro, *Digital Oil: Machineries of Knowing*

Klaus Hoeyer, *Data Paradoxes: The Politics of Intensified Data Sourcing in Healthcare*

Dirk van Laak, *Lifelines of Our Society: A Global History of Infrastructure*

Jonathan Silver, *The Infrastructural South: Techno-Environments of the Third Wave of Urbanization*

Christine E. Evans and Lars Lundgren, *No Heavenly Bodies: A History of Satellite Communications Infrastructure*

Fernando Domínguez Rubio, Jérôme Denis, and David Pontille, eds., *Fragilities: Essays on the Politics, Ethics, and Aesthetics of Maintenance and Repair*